Choosing to Co-operate

Choosing to Co-operate
How States Avoid Loss

EDITED BY JANICE GROSS STEIN
AND LOUIS W. PAULY

The Johns Hopkins University Press
Baltimore and London

To Michael and Caryl, for choosing to co-operate even when they faced no prospect of loss

Reprinted from *International Journal* 46, no. 2,
© Canadian Institute of International Affairs 1992
Johns Hopkins edition © 1993 The Johns Hopkins University Press
Printed in the United States of America on acid-free paper

The Johns Hopkins University Press
2715 North Charles Street
Baltimore, Maryland 21218-4319
The Johns Hopkins Press Ltd., London

Library of Congress Cataloging-in-Publication Data

Choosing to co-operate : how states avoid loss / edited by Janice Gross
    Stein and Louis W. Pauly.
        p.   cm.
"Reprinted from International journal 46, no. 2"—CIP info. sheet.
    Includes bibliographical references and index.
    ISBN 0-8018-4610-2 (alk. paper : bound).—ISBN 0-8018-4611-0 (alk.
paper : pbk.)
    1. International relations—Psychological aspects. 2. International
cooperation—Psychological aspects. I. Stein, Janice Gross. II. Pauly,
Louis W.
JX1395.C5225   1993
327.1'7'019—dc20   92-36269

A catalog record for this book is available from the British Library

CONTENTS

Preface

At a departmental seminar at the University of Toronto in the autumn of 1990, two very talented graduate students presented papers on co-operation in international political economy and security. The ensuing discussion revolved around the differences between the pursuit of absolute and relative gain in the two domains. In the comparatively benign world of the international economy, states could seek absolute gains through co-operation. On the far more dangerous issues of security, states had no choice but to seek relative advantage. This was the conventional wisdom in the room. In the lively discussion that followed in the corridor, several of us were struck by the common focus of leaders on avoiding loss when they chose co-operate. From that discussion the idea for this volume was born.

The contributors to this project, who first came together in March 1991, were agreed on three broad tasks. We were all interested in pushing analysis to the level of decision-makers themselves and in exploring the dynamics of policy choice. Second, even though decisions to co-operate are often risky decisions, there was a scarcity of analysis informed by propositions from cognitive psychology about the importance of loss as a motivator for risk-seeking behaviour and we wanted to expand that literature. Finally, we were interested in examining decisions to co-operate across the 'two solitudes' of the academic study of international relations – security studies and international political economy.

With these tasks as our common focus, our first meeting then proceeded to dissolve into the confusing thicket of debate on paradigms, theories, and levels of analysis that has come to typify the field. We did agree, however, to examine several fundamental propositions drawn from prospect theory, developed by cognitive psychologists, and to compare these propositions with those of neo-realism and neo-liberalism. We agreed, in short, to bring some comparative evidence from case-studies back to the conference table.

At a second meeting a few months later, we examined the relevance of the three sets of propositions to five cases in which leaders considered whether or not to co-operate. Out of that discussion came two central conclusions: namely, that the way decisions are framed can have an important effect on policy outcomes and that the desire to avoid perceived loss can serve as a powerful motivator for leaders to choose to co-operate in both arenas of international politics. These themes are explored in greater detail throughout the volume.

Janice Gross Stein develops the theoretical context and policy consequences of our collective project in the introductory chapter. The case-studies by Michael Mastanduno, Debora L. Spar, Louis W. Pauly, David A. Welch, and Louise Richardson examine these two central ideas in detail. Finally, Timothy J. McKeown synthesizes the results of the case-studies and sketches their implications both for policy and for future research in this area.

We are grateful to a number of people and institutions that made our collaborative effort possible. We would especially like to thank Andrew Moravcsik for playing the role of discussant – and gadfly – at both of our meetings. His comments always made us think again. Michael Donnelly and James Busumtwi-Sam also provided constructive commentary. None of our meetings would have taken place without the assistance of David A.T. Stafford and Nancy Snelgrove of the Canadian Institute of International Affairs, Sylvia Ostry, Leonard Waverman, and Mary Lynn Bratti of the Centre for International Studies at the University of Toronto, and Ron Daniels and Pia Bruni of the International

Business and Trade Law Program at the University of Toronto. Ilone Eurchuk kept our budget in order and Hyla Levy and Marian Reed typed repeated versions of illegibly edited manuscripts. We are grateful to the Department of Political Science at the University of Toronto for lending us their services. The editors of *International Journal*, Robert O. Matthews and Charles Pentland, encouraged the original publication of this collection, and Marion Magee, the associate editor, worked her superb editorial magic on the final manuscript. Christopher Blackburn provided an index for the subsequent publication from the Johns Hopkins University Press.

Much appreciated financial support for this project came from a grant by the John D. and Catherine T. MacArthur Foundation to the Canadian Institute of International Affairs, a conference grant (#643-91-0021) from the Social Sciences and Humanities Research Council of Canada, and grants from the International Business and Trade Law Program, the Centre for International Studies, and the Department of Political Science – all of the University of Toronto. Louis Pauly would especially like to thank the Social Sciences and Humanities Research Council of Canada for research grant #410-91-1308. Janice Gross Stein would like to express special appreciation to the United States Institute of Peace, to the Canadian Institute for International Peace and Security, and to the Connaught Committee at the University of Toronto for providing release time for her to think about this project.

Choosing to Co-operate

One

International co-operation and loss avoidance: framing the problem

JANICE GROSS STEIN

CO-OPERATION AS LOSS AVOIDANCE

Individuals, organizations, and states routinely co-operate across a broad range of activities. Much of this co-operation is the product of harmonious interests and does not require explanation. More puzzling is co-operation that occurs despite divergent interests, or when convergent interests have to be identified and co-ordinated before the parties can achieve jointly what they could not accomplish individually.[1] This kind of co-operation is the focus of this volume. In this collection, we explore how political leaders think about international co-operation. We then examine three explanations of how, when, and why leaders decide to co-operate. Advocates of liberal, realist, and cognitive explanations all concur that assessments of gains and losses are central

Professor of Political Science, University of Toronto, Toronto, Canada; recently editor of *Getting to the Table: Processes of International Prenegotiation* (1989) and co-author (with Richard Ned Lebow) of *We All Lost the Cold War* (forthcoming).

I would like to acknowledge the helpful comments of Barbara Farnham, Alexander L. George, Robert Jervis, Robert O. Keohane, Edward A. Kolodziej, Richard Ned Lebow, Jack Levy, Michael Mastanduno, Timothy J. McKeown, Andrew Moravcsik, Louis W. Pauly, Louise Richardson, Debora L. Spar, and David A. Welch. I am grateful to the United States Institute of Peace, the Canadian Institute for International Peace and Security, the Connaught Committee of the University of Toronto, and the Centre for International Studies at the University of Toronto for their generous support for research and writing. Any errors in argument and inference are mine alone.

1 For a similar definition of international co-operation, see Robert O. Keohane, 'Multilateralism: an agenda for research,' *International Journal* 45(autumn 1990), 731-64. Keohane defines co-operation as 'the extent to which governments' policies are effectively co-ordinated in such a way as to become consistent with one another.'

to decisions to co-operate, but each treats leaders' assessments of their gains and losses in a distinct way.[2]

Central to the debate among different explanations of international co-operation is the criterion that leaders use in making a choice to co-operate.[3] Scholars who begin with neo-liberal assumptions typically conceive of co-operation as the maximization of subjective expected utility among 'egoists' who are interested primarily in absolute gain.[4] Realists, however, argue that states generally behave as 'defensive positionalists' and compare their expected gains with those of others. Despite this emphasis on relative gains, realists concede that states can still co-operate under certain conditions.[5] Although they differ on fundamentally important issues, both these traditions build on models of rational choice and generally discuss co-operation in the language of 'gain.'[6] Whether states seek 'absolute' or 'relative' gain, it is the pursuit of gain that typically motivates states to co-operate with one another when they cannot independently achieve the benefits that they seek.[7]

2 Realists and neo-liberal institutionalists analyse 'state' behaviour, where states are treated as unitary rational actors, while cognitive explanations refer to individuals. In this collection, we use 'states' and 'leaders' as appropriate to the explanation under discussion.

3 Arthur Stein argues that a 'metadecision' precedes the actual decision to co-operate. States first choose the decision criterion they think appropriate to a particular relationship or problem and then assess pay-offs and make concrete decisions given that earlier choice. The metadecision is critical to the prospects of co-operation or conflict: *Why Nations Cooperate: Circumstance and Choice in International Relations* (Ithaca NY: Cornell University Press 1990), 193.

4 For the classic statement of neo-liberal arguments, see Robert O. Keohane, *After Hegemony: Cooperation and Discord in the World Political Economy* (Princeton NJ: Princeton University Press 1984).

5 Joseph Grieco, *Cooperation among Nations: Europe, America, and Non-Tariff Barriers to Trade* (Ithaca NY: Cornell University Press 1990).

6 Models of rational choice do not always specify the maximization of subjective expected utility. When preferences for risk are built into rational models, the minimization of maximum losses may be specified as the appropriate decision criterion. This is especially the case when cardinal utilities are difficult to calculate.

7 Formally, of course, models of subjective expected utility aggregate gains and losses, or costs and benefits, in a single utility function. Neo-liberal as well as realist arguments, which build on models of strategic interaction, encompass these aggregated estimates of utility. The maximization of subjective expected

This volume looks at the problem of co-operation somewhat differently. Drawing on psychological rather than rational models of choice, we suggest that the way leaders frame the problem for decision is critically important to their assessment of gains and losses. We examine the proposition that leaders often make co-operative choices not to make gains but to avoid losses. At times, they choose to co-operate not because co-operation promises substantial gains that could not be realized independently, but because they anticipate that the failure to co-operate will bring losses. The decision of President Sadat of Egypt in 1977 to go to Jerusalem, for example, may be plausibly explained as an attempt to avoid the immediate and certain losses that he thought would ensue at home if the condition of 'no war, no peace' continued much longer.[8]

When leaders choose to co-operate to avoid loss, they may do so under two quite different sets of conditions. Subjective expected utility models of rational choice appear to provide a straightforward analysis of these kinds of decisions. They anticipate that when people identify options that promise no benefits, only costs, they choose the option that minimizes their expected losses. When leaders confront difficult problems with no 'good' choice, if they are rational, they choose to co-operate if that option promises the lowest expected costs.

---

utility can occur in the domain of gains, where expected gains are maximized, or in the domain of losses, where expected losses are minimized. Similarly, although realists write of 'relative gains,' defensive positionalists can minimize relative losses when they choose to co-operate. The discourse of both traditions, however, rather than their formal models, speaks primarily of 'gain.'

One important exception is Arthur Stein's discussion of dilemmas of common aversions, where the parties agree on what they want to avoid, but not on the preferred outcome. Although states have a common interest in avoiding a particular outcome, they will arrive at the outcome of mutual aversion individually unless they co-ordinate their strategies. Beyond their shared desire to avoid their mutual aversion, they disagree about which of several equilibria they prefer. See *Why Nations Cooperate*, 36, note 25.

8 See Janice Gross Stein, 'The political economy of strategic agreements: the linked costs of failure at Camp David,' in Peter Evans, Harold Jacobson, and Robert Putnam, eds, *Double-Edged Diplomacy: International Bargaining and Domestic Politics* (Berkeley: University of California Press, in press).

While parsimonious and intuitively appealing, a rational explanation of this kind of decision to co-operate begs some fundamentally important questions. Most importantly, the losses a leader identifies could at times be as convincingly conceived as gains. Although Sadat focused on the losses of continued international conflict, he could well have framed the freeing of resources from the military sector as a gain. From the perspective of the outside observer, distinguishing between gains and losses is often arbitrary. Especially when there are no clear objective measures of losses and gains, models of rational choice cannot explain why a leader frames a problem in terms of losses rather than of gains. Cognitive models, however, can help to explain why leaders frequently focus on loss.

Research in the laboratory has discovered that people generally pay far more attention to losses than to gains.[9] They do so in large part because pain is more compelling than pleasure. It is far more painful, for example, to lose $1,000 in the street than it is pleasurable to win $1,000 in a lottery. Consequently, in framing their choices, people weigh losses more heavily than they do gains. Decisions to co-operate, like all decisions, should reflect this generalized tendency to loss aversion.[10]

Explanations of international co-operation will at times yield different predictions and policy prescriptions depending on whether they are informed by rational choice models based on utility maximization or by behavioural decision theory premised on loss aversion. This introductory chapter looks briefly at neo-liberal explanations of co-operation, which assume rational calculation of subjectively expected utility, and then at the realist

9 Loss aversion implies that the same difference between two options will be given much greater weight if it is viewed as a difference between two disadvantages, relative to a reference point, than if it is viewed as a difference between two advantages.

10 While decisions to co-operate internationally should reflect this tendency to loss aversion, estimates of expected losses are far more difficult to analyse systematically outside the confines of the laboratory. It is often very difficult to measure differences in estimated losses when formal measures of equivalence do not exist.

critique of neo-liberalism which focuses on a rational assessment of relative gain. It goes on to review 'prospect theory,' which was developed by cognitive psychologists to explain anomalies in choice which rational models cannot accommodate. Prospect theory offers different explanations of both the framing of problems and the choices leaders make.

In the rest of this volume, we examine decisions on whether or not to co-operate, using all three analytical perspectives. Michael Mastanduno explores the American decision to co-operate in the negotiations with Japan over structural impediments in mutual trade, Louis Pauly examines the decisions by the industrialized economies to co-operate on multilateral economic surveillance through the International Monetary Fund (IMF), Debora Spar analyses the Japanese and American decisions to co-operate in the co-development of the FSX fighter aircraft, David Welch examines Israel's decision to co-operate with the United States during the Gulf War by refraining from retaliation, and Louise Richardson explores the failure of Britain and the United States to co-operate during the Suez crisis of 1956.

In explaining these decisions, we pay particular attention to the way leaders framed their choices. Explaining decisions to co-operate forms one subset of the larger problem of explaining political choice. In the conclusion to this volume, Timothy McKeown reviews the capacity of rational and psychological models to explain these choices, considers how well psychological explanations address anomalies left untouched or unresolved by rational models, and explores the implications of these five cases for a broader theory of social choice.

ABSOLUTE GAINS: NEO-LIBERAL INSTITUTIONALISM

Analysts of the international political economy have led the way in proposing explanations of international co-operation. Beginning from neo-liberal premises, some draw an implicit analogy between the international system and an imperfectly competitive market, and between the state and the firm. Neo-liberal institutionalists treat states as self-interested independent actors that seek to maximize subjective expected utility. States are generally, although not always, represented as 'egoists' interested primarily in maximizing their absolute gains.

In the context of an anarchic international system, neo-liberal institutionalists have defined the conditions that inhibit self-interested states from achieving co-operative outcomes even when it is in their joint interest to do so. Among the most prominent of these conditions are the uncertainties associated with estimating the intentions of others, high and unequal information and transaction costs, and the short time horizons of political leaders and officials. International institutions, it is argued, can address all three of these central obstacles to the choice of collaborative strategies. By defining norms and rules and by stabilizing expectations, institutions make intentions more transparent. By reducing information and transaction costs, they reduce uncertainty. And, by lengthening the 'shadow of the future,' they make it possible for self-interested members to consider a single choice within the context of a longer term relationship, thereby securing jointly preferable outcomes that each could not achieve individually.[11] Neo-liberal institutionalists insist that state behaviour is not only a function of the defining condition of the international system – its anarchy – but also of international institutions which can constrain states and make their actions intelligible to others.[12]

Neo-liberal institutionalists explain variations in co-operative behaviour by variations in patterns of capabilities and interests, in the scope of interdependence, and in the complementarity of domestic political structures. They pay particular attention,

11 When relationships are modelled as a prisoner's dilemma, experiments have established that play in an iterated game allows the players to achieve the jointly preferable outcome which they are unable to reach in a single game. See Robert Axelrod and Robert Keohane, 'Achieving cooperation under anarchy: strategies and institutions,' and Kenneth Oye, 'Explaining cooperation under anarchy: hypotheses and strategies,' *World Politics* 38(October 1985), 226-54 and 1-24, respectively.

12 Robert O. Keohane, 'Neoliberal institutionalism: a perspective on world politics,' in Keohane, ed, *International Institutions and State Power: Essays on International Relations Theory* (Boulder CO: Westview 1989), 1-20.

however, to contractual problems in an anarchic environment. Even when states can maximize absolute gains through collaboration, even when there are strong convergent interests and complementary domestic structures, they may be unable to reach agreement. The possibility of co-operation can be thwarted by externalities, uncertainties, asymmetries in the availability and cost of information, and the fear that others will exploit the opportunity to cheat. Consequently, neo-liberal institutionalists emphasize problems of compliance and monitoring. Institutions that succeed in establishing agreed norms and rules (regimes) provide standards for acceptable behaviour and encourage expectations to converge. In so far as they build in procedures to monitor behaviour, they reduce uncertainties, information costs, and, over time, transaction costs. There is some evidence that even on issues of security, where the consequences of error are usually greater than in the arena of economic exchange, regimes have proven indispensable in facilitating co-ordination between adversaries who share a common aversion to war. They have done so by providing facilities for detection and warning against cheating and defection.[13]

Institutions, however, can ease contractual obstacles to co-operation only among states that seek independently to maximize their absolute gains. Neo-liberal institutionalists do not argue that states always seek to do so. Robert Keohane, for example, acknowledges explicitly that under some conditions states do seek relative gains. He emphasizes, however, that such behaviour is conditional on the nature of prevailing rules and expectations rather than on essential or defining characteristics of the international system.[14] On this issue, neo-liberal institutionalists differ significantly from neo-realists, who see the search for relative gains not as conditioned by international norms and rules but as endemic and pervasive.

---

13 Joseph S. Nye Jr, 'Nuclear learning and U.S.-Soviet security regimes,' *International Organization* 41(summer 1987), 371-402, and Janice Gross Stein, 'Detection and defection: security "regimes" and the management of international conflict,' *International Journal* 45(autumn 1985), 599-627.
14 Keohane, 'Neoliberal institutionalism,' 11.

RELATIVE GAINS: NEO-REALISM

Neo-realists begin by characterizing anarchy as the defining characteristic of the international system. Kenneth Waltz, the leading neo-realist theorist, treats states as unitary rational actors and claims that states choose among strategies on the basis of calculations of relative gains.[15] They do so, he reasons, because states constantly fear for their survival in an anarchic world. They fear that other states might use their relative advantage either immediately or in the longer term to threaten their fundamental security and survival. They accordingly pay attention not to what they gain absolutely, but to the differences between their gains and those of others. The realist model of rational choice is not the independent maximization of expected utility, but the maximization of relative advantage, even at the cost of individual utility.

In a provocative recent study, Joseph Grieco extends the model of relative gains seeking beyond traditional security issues to issues of international political economy.[16] Examining the negotiation of rules regarding non-tariff barriers between the United States and Europe in the 1970s, Grieco contends that states behaved as 'defensive positionalists'; they compared their anticipated gains to those of others and used relative gain as their decision criterion. To the extent that states use relative advantage as their decision criterion regarding a good that is not fixed, and in an arena where mutual benefits are generally depicted as large, his analysis suggests that states approach a broad range of international issues as relative gains maximizers.[17] Grieco concludes that the neo-realist model of relative gains provides a better explanation of the presence or absence of international co-

---

15 Kenneth Waltz, *Man, the State and War* (New York: Columbia University Press 1959), 198, and *Theory of International Politics* (Reading MA: Addison-Wesley 1979).

16 Grieco, *Cooperation among Nations.*

17 Realist analysis traditionally focused heavily on disputes over territory in the Westphalian system of sovereign states. Territory is a fixed good and, consequently, territorial conflicts are necessarily constant sum; the gain of one is the loss of the other. When a game is constant sum, the distinction between maximizing relative gains and absolute gains collapses.

operation than the neo-liberal institutionalist model does. Grieco suggests further that co-operation is most likely when the distribution of gains maintains the previous distribution of capabilities. The use of relative gain as the criterion of decision may not impede collaboration when it does not disturb the underlying power balance. By implication, should an agreement redistribute resources sufficiently to disturb an underlying balance, co-operation is unlikely. By extension, Grieco suggests that a state's sensitivity to relative differences is positively correlated with a decline – and negatively related to an increase – in its relative capabilities. He speculates that the very weak and the very strong are least sensitive to considerations of relative gains; it is those states in the middle, which simultaneously fear the strong and worry about a decline in status, which are most sensitive to considerations of relative gains.

Grieco's analysis has policy implications that are substantially different from those of neo-liberal institutionalists. This is particularly so for the design of co-operative strategies in institutional frameworks. To the extent that states worry about gaps in gains, realists argue that it is important to build in low exit costs from institutional commitments. Although high exit costs reduce uncertainty, they simultaneously sharpen concern about the future impact of current shifts in relative position. If the decision criterion states use in choosing whether or not to co-operate is the maximization of relative gains, then lower exit costs and periodic reviews of commitments appear likely to facilitate rather than impede co-operation. From this perspective, institutions can indeed promote co-operation in so far as they are useful in setting outer boundaries to the generation of gaps in relative gains.

DEFINING THE DECISION PROBLEM

The dispute about relative and absolute gains may be more apparent than real. A relative gain can be considered a re-specification of a time-related concept of absolute gain.[18] It is the

18 Duncan Snidal argues persuasively that the hypothesis of relative gains seeking is

fear of absolute loss – extinction – that drives the emphasis on relative gain. The critical issue is the length of the time horizon self-interested states use when calculating their interests. In direct contradiction to neo-liberal institutionalists, realists implicitly hold that it is the long shadow of the future that inhibits co-operation as self-interested rational actors trade off the immediate or short-term absolute gains of co-operation against long-term absolute costs. Realists sometimes draw the analogy to firms forgoing immediate benefits in order to capture market share; when they do so, their objective is to increase their long-term and absolute (monopoly) rents. The competition for market share is a struggle for relative advantage only in the short term. By extension, absolute gain can be converted into relative gain by lengthening the time horizon even further. Even co-operative agreements that offer equal absolute gains cannot be part of a stable solution if deviation from the agreement will bring large relative gains in the future.[19] This proposition can again be re-specified in terms of absolute gains on an even longer time horizon.[20]

When a decision problem is re-specified as a problem of absolute gain over increasingly longer periods of time, important theoretical and interpretive questions of the impact of uncertainty and the weighting of long-term versus short-term gains arise

---

a mis-specification of the maximization of absolute gains, with differing time horizons. See 'Relative gains and the pattern of international cooperation,' *American Political Science Review* 85(September 1991), 701-26, and 'International cooperation among relative gains maximizers,' *International Studies Quarterly* 35(December 1991), 387-402.

19 Robert Powell, 'Absolute and relative gains in international relations,' *American Political Science Review* 85(December 1991), 1303-20, argues persuasively that whether states seek relative gains depends on the consequences of action at the present for future values.

20 Even when the decision problem is modelled in terms of relative gains, it has been argued that they matter only in the very special case of two-state interaction and when absolute gains are totally excluded from the decisional calculus. A small increase in the number of actors dramatically decreases the impact of relative gains considerations in impeding co-operation. Snidal ('Relative gains and the pattern of international cooperation') models the impact of relative gains with larger numbers of actors and finds that their impact virtually disappears. Consequently, relative gains seeking should matter significantly less in a multipolar world than in a bipolar one.

immediately. Behavioural decision research suggests that people generally overweight immediate and certain gains at the expense of long-term and less certain benefits; they also tend to convert high probabilities into certainties. Even more important, a relative gains criterion may matter in predicting behaviour in so far as leaders think in terms of, and choose to maximize, relative gains. There is some empirical evidence that, under certain conditions, leaders have used relative gains as a decision criterion.[21]

The interesting puzzle is why and when states or, more precisely, their leaders use different criteria to make their choices.[22] The answer rarely lies in the inherent nature of the issue – or good – at stake. With the exception of territorial issues, almost every issue can be framed in either absolute or relative terms. Trade issues can be – and are – framed in broadly mercantilist or liberal terms and most security issues can be – and are – framed as issues of 'national' (that is, relative) or 'common' security.

Disagreements among policy-makers responding within the same state to the same issue at the same time are also common. In 1978, most of the Egyptian delegation at Camp David, behaving as 'defensive positionalists,' took Israel's position as their reference point, framed the security issue in terms of relative gains,

21 They appear to have done so not as an exclusive criterion but as one in a sequence. A careful reading of Grieco's empirical evidence suggests that negotiators may have maximized relative gains within a broader context of absolute gains. The analysis does not distinguish clearly between relative gains as an exclusive decisional criterion and the attempt to maximize relative gains once absolute gains on central issues were assured. The problem is then redefined as a disagreement about how to divide the surplus from trade and exchange. For a more elaborate discussion, see Arthur Stein, *Why Nations Cooperate*, 137n50. The interesting and difficult theoretical question is how and why states use the two decision criteria to make choices.

22 Jonathan Tucker examines collaboration between firms by looking not only at their interest in absolute welfare benefits but also at their concern about loss of utility from unfavourable shifts in relative position. He argues that rational actors do not use a fixed strategy of maximizing either welfare or positional payoffs but rather 'satisfice' by optimizing a trade-off between these two objectives. This trade-off is not constant, but varies depending on the relative positions of the two players. See 'Partners and rivals: a model of international collaboration in advanced technology,' *International Organization* 45(winter 1991), 83-120.

and argued that Israel would gain far more than Egypt from the proposed agreement. Consequently, they opposed the terms of the agreement at Camp David. President Sadat, however, using as his reference point the return of the Sinai Peninsula occupied during the war in 1967, emphasized the absolute losses from the failure to agree, and chose to co-operate.[23]

Disagreements of this kind among leaders suggest that the same decision problem can be framed very differently, with very different implications for choice. If it is the framing of the decision problem that shapes the choices leaders make, the debate between neo-liberals and neo-realists has taken place largely out of context. What is critical is how leaders think about co-operation, what gains and losses they identify, and what overriding criterion they use to make their choice. Prospect theory provides helpful answers to some of these questions.

PROSPECT THEORY:
FRAMING THE PROBLEM AND LOSS AVERSION
Behavioural decision theory treats choice differently than does liberal or realist theory. Although liberals specify absolute gain and realists relative gain as the criterion of decision, both typically use rational models of choice that do not look at the process of choosing. Behavioural decision theory investigates how people make their decisions and the impact of this process on the choices they make.

Prospect theory, which was developed by cognitive psychologists working within this tradition, asserts that the way people frame a decision determines in part how they see the consequences of choice. People first choose a reference point and then assess the gains or losses of options from that point.[24] Outcomes

---

23 Stein, 'The political economy of strategic agreements: the linked costs of failure at Camp David.'
24 Unlike subjective expected utility models, prospect theory assumes that changes in value rather than final assets are critical to peoples' calculations. Daniel Kahneman and Amos Tversky, 'Prospect theory: an analysis of decision under risk,' *Econometrica* 47(March 1979), 263-91.

that are above the reference point are treated as gains and those that fall below are considered as losses. Because people are generally averse to loss, whether an outcome is treated as a gain or a loss has a significant impact on the choice they make. Indeed, when an identical outcome is re-framed as a loss rather than as a gain, people reverse their preference and make a different choice.[25]

A personal example nicely illustrates the impact of a reference point on the assessment of gains and losses. If I had expected to write ten pages of this chapter today but wrote only five, what matters is the 'loss' of the five pages rather than the 'gain' of five pages in the total length of the manuscript to be completed. My reference point was my expectation. Rather than consider how much I had accomplished, or my net gain, I estimated loss from the reference point I had chosen. I did not consider my total assets but rather the deviation from my reference point. Investors similarly will consider the attractiveness of different financial options in relation to a reference point they choose rather than evaluate the impact of alternatives on their net assets, as orthodox utility maximization expects. The selection of a reference point is therefore central to the subsequent assessment of options and to the choices people make.

There is no formal theory of framing which identifies the reference points leaders are likely to choose under different conditions.[26] The status quo is an obvious point of salience, and psychologists and economists have established some processes that systematically bias people in favour of the status quo. The endowment effect suggests that people frequently demand much more to give up an object than they would be willing to pay to

25 Amos Tversky and Daniel Kahneman, 'The framing of decisions and the psychology of choice,' *Science* 211(30 January 1981), 453-8. Tversky and Kahneman obtained systematic reversal of preferences by varying the description of the reference point. Preference orderings depend on frames.

26 Tversky and Kahneman ('Prospect theory,' 275) acknowledge that they have not yet developed a theory of framing and consequently restrict their experiments to decision problems 'where it is reasonable to assume either that the original formulation of the prospects leaves no room for further editing, or that the edited prospects can be specified without ambiguity.' These conditions almost never apply to problems of choice in international politics.

acquire the same object.[27] The principal effect of endowment is to enhance not the attractiveness of what one owns but the pain of giving it up; forgone gains are less painful than perceived losses. It is often easier, for example, to accept a three-year freeze in salary than a one-time cut, even when the one-time cut would be less costly over the long term. In addition, people normalize or adjust more quickly for gains than they do for losses – in part because of the endowment effect.[28] Individuals therefore have a strong tendency to remain at the status quo because the disadvantages of movement loom larger than the advantages.

Although the status quo is often the obvious reference point, at times people use others such as their aspirations or expectations. This is especially likely when they are dissatisfied because the current status quo represents a loss from a previous reference point – a loss which they have not yet accepted. In international relations, reference points may be influenced by leaders' subjective perceptions of legitimacy and entitlements.[29] Throughout a decade of negotiations between Egypt and Israel, for example, President Sadat used as his reference point the return of the Sinai; he never normalized for a loss he considered illegitimate. Israel's leaders used the status quo as their reference point as they quickly normalized for gain, but their commitment to the status quo was less intense than Sadat's expectation that he would recover territory that was properly Egyptian. The different framing of the same problem by the two parties made negotiations

27 Daniel Kahneman, Jack L. Knetsch, and Richard H. Thaler, 'Anomalies: the endowment effect, loss aversion, and the status quo bias,' *Journal of Economic Perspectives* 5(winter 1991), 193-206; Richard Thaler, 'Toward a positive theory of consumer choice,' *Journal of Economic Behavior and Organization* 1(1980), 39-60; Jack L. Knetsch and J.A. Sinden, 'Willingness to pay and compensation demanded: experimental evidence of an unexpected disparity in measures of value,' *Quarterly Journal of Economics* 99(August 1984), 507-21; and Jack L. Knetsch, 'The endowment effect and evidence of nonreversible indifference curves,' *American Economic Review* 79(December 1989), 1277-84.

28 Robert Jervis discusses the difference in the way people generally normalize for gain and for loss. People normalize for gains more quickly than they do for losses in part because of the endowment effect: 'Political implications of loss aversion,' *Political Psychology* 13(June 1992).

29 Janice Gross Stein and David A. Welch, 'Entitlement and legitimacy in decision making, unpublished paper, October 1991.

very difficult. Before agreement could be reached, Israel's leaders had to re-frame the problem. They did so by moving their reference point to a different dimension of the problem.[30] Earlier, they had concentrated primarily on their relationship with Egypt, but as the negotiations progressed, they focused on their relationship with the United States. The losses from the failure to co-operate then became visible and salient, and agreement followed.

Although prospect theory has not yet specified a formal theory of framing, cognitive psychologists have identified a number of biases and heuristics which can affect the stability of a reference point as well as the generation and editing of estimates of gains and losses from that point. The original reference point may serve as a perceptual 'anchor'; new information is then adjusted in relationship to the anchor.[31] In assessing the likelihood of losses and gains from different outcomes, probabilities may be evaluated by the ease with which similar instances come to mind or by how representative an event is. These heuristics of 'anchoring,' 'availability,' and 'representativeness' make people insufficiently sensitive to new evidence.[32] Behavioural decision research suggests that reference points and estimates of the probability of gains and losses are likely to be more stable than they should be in the face of new information.[33]

30 In the unstructured decision problems characteristic of 'real world' international politics, re-framing can occur both by shifting the dimension which provides the reference point and by moving the reference point. I am indebted to Robert Jervis for this distinction.

31 Glen Whyte and Ariel S. Levi analyse the American decision to blockade during the Cuban missile crisis and argue that the reference point served as the anchor against which new information was interpreted: 'Reference level formation, framing effects, and the Cuban missile crisis,' unpublished paper, nd.

32 For a critical analysis of the relevance of the heuristic of representativeness to foreign policy decisions, see Robert Jervis, 'Representativeness in foreign policy judgments,' *Political Psychology* 7(September 1986), 483-505.

33 Salancik suggests as well that four characteristics of acts leading to the formation of the initial reference level will determine its rigidity: the explicitness of the reference point, its revocability, the volition with which it is adopted, and public commitment to that point: 'Commitment and control of organizational behavior and belief,' in B.M. Staw and G.R. Salancik, eds, *New Directions in Organizational Behavior* (Chicago IL: St Clair Press 1977), 1-54.

The framing of a problem is among the most important components of decision-making, yet we know all too little about why people frame problems the way they do. Models of rational choice do not consider the origin of decision frames; they work within a frame that they take as given.[34] They do not treat choice as reference-driven behaviour, especially under conditions of incomplete information, 'dirty' and 'noisy' information environments, or inexperience. Yet these are precisely the conditions leaders usually encounter, especially when they confront choices in foreign policy.

Although prospect theory does not provide a model of how decision problems are framed, it does suggest that framing is influenced by the norms, habits, and expectancies of decision-makers, by the sequence of editing operations, and by the kinds of problems people face.[35] In international politics there is almost always more than one obvious reference point for leaders facing a problem. Consequently, a given decision problem can often be framed in more than one way.[36] When prospect theory is applied to foreign policy decisions, it cannot predict the refer-

---

34 Realist theory similarly provides inadequate guidance on the construction of state preferences in an anarchic international system.

35 Tversky and Kahneman, 'Rational choice and the framing of decisions,' s257. They list several components of the process of editing. People *code* when they identify a reference point and frame outcomes as deviations (losses or gains) from that reference point. They *simplify* by rounding off probabilities: they treat highly likely outcomes as certain and discard very unlikely outcomes. They eliminate *dominated* alternatives. They *combine* the probabilities of identical outcomes. They also *separate* a riskless component of a prospect from a risky component and the latter is then evaluated in terms of its deviation from the reference point; this leads to inconsistent preferences when the same choice is presented in different forms. They also *cancel* components common to all prospects, which can lead to similar distortions. See also Kahneman and Tversky, 'Prospect theory,' 284-5.

36 Amos Tversky and Daniel Kahneman, 'Rational choice and the framing of decisions,' *Journal of Business* 59(October 1986, part 2), s251-78. In laboratory experiments, significant changes in preference occurred simply by changing the labelling of the outcomes from positive to negative. The framing of decisions depends on the language of presentation, on the context of choice, and on the reference point that is selected. See also Paul Slovic and Sarah Lichtenstein, 'Preference reversals: a broader perspective,' *American Economic Review* 73(September 1983), 596-605.

ence point that leaders are likely to select. Unlike models of rational choice, however, prospect theory is both historical and contextual in its emphasis on reference points that grow out of leaders' experiences and expectations as well as the type of problem they face.[37]

Prospect theory does provide an explanation of how people choose among competing options once a problem is framed. This process of evaluation differs from rational models in several important respects. First, attitude towards risk is not only a function of the personal characteristics of leaders but also of the characteristics of the situation. Leaders choose a reference point related in part to the situation they face. Once a problem has been framed, people are generally risk averse with respect to gains and risk acceptant with respect to losses they identify from the reference point they have chosen.[38] They are more willing to take risks to avoid losses than to make gains, in large part because losses loom far larger than gains.[39] Framing is critical because of loss aversion; whether an outcome is framed as a gain or as a loss changes the choices people are likely to make.[40]

Finally, people generally tend to overweigh outcomes that are certain in comparison with those that are merely probable.[41]

---

37 Kahneman and Tversky, 'Prospect theory,' 275. Kahneman and Tversky argue that 'choice is a constructive and contingent process. When faced with a complex decision problem, people employ a variety of heuristic procedures in order to simplify the representation and evaluation of prospects. The heuristics of choice do not really lend themselves to formal analysis, because their application is contingent on the method of elicitation, the formulation of the problem, and the context of choice.': Amos Tversky and Daniel Kahneman, 'Advances in prospect theory: cumulative representations of uncertainty,' *Journal of Risk and Uncertainty*, 1992.

38 This proposition is reversed when people estimate the probability of an outcome as low. For small probabilities, the prediction is for risk seeking for gains and risk aversion for losses.

39 The value function is steeper for loss than for gain. Jack S. Levy cites tennis player Jimmy Connors's comment: 'I hate to lose more than I like to win.': 'An introduction to prospect theory,' *Political Psychology* 13(June 1992), 175.

40 Further, sensitivity to changes in gains and losses decreases as people move away from the reference point. Losses close to the reference point are weighted more heavily than subsequent losses in evaluating options.

41 All the experiments which tested prospect theory were done under conditions of

Very likely but uncertain outcomes also are often treated as if they were certain.[42] The certainty effect magnifies the impact of risk aversion with respect to gains and risk seeking with respect to losses. Prospect theory predicts that people will choose a sure gain rather than take a chance on a larger gain that is probable, even if the latter promises higher expected utility.[43] They will also choose to take a chance on a larger loss that is merely probable rather than face a smaller loss that is certain, even when the certain option would minimize expected loss.[44] Both these predictions contradict the expectations of standard models of rational choice.[45] With these predictions in mind, we turn now to the implications of prospect theory for choices to co-operate.

----

risk, where the probability distribution is known. In international relations, the probability distribution for the outcomes leaders have to estimate is itself unknown. Formally, the former is described as decision-making under risk while the latter is decision-making under uncertainty. Some experimental evidence suggests that differences between the two do not seriously affect the process of choice since people make subjective estimates of likelihood even when the distribution is unknown.

42 Kahneman and Tversky describe the former as the 'certainty effect' and the latter as the 'pseudocertainty effect': 'Prospect theory,' 282-3, and 'Rational choice and the framing of decisions,' s268. See also George A. Quattrone and Amos Tversky, 'Contrasting rational and psychological analyses of political choice,' *American Political Science Review* 82(September 1988), 719-36, 730. People also tend to overweigh small probabilities and underweigh moderate and high probabilities.

43 In experiments in the laboratory, people repeatedly chose a sure gain of $3,000 over an 80-per-cent chance to win $4,000 (or $3,200) and a 20-per-cent chance of nothing. If faced with the same two negative prospects, however, people prefer to risk an 80-per-cent chance of losing $4,000 and a 20-per-cent chance of no loss to a certain loss of $3,000. These results are contrary to the expectations of a model of a subjective expected utility. The experiments that have been done, however, generally work with very small differences in magnitudes of gain and loss. These small magnitudes may well make these results much less robust, given diminishing marginal utility.

44 This pattern of choice is consistent with the weight that the certainty effect gives to an alternative.

45 The strongest evidence for violation of the expectations of models of subjective expected utility comes from experiments where identical choices are framed first in terms of gains and then in terms of losses and people reverse their preferences. See Tversky and Kahneman, 'Rational choice and the framing of decisions,' s251-78, and 'The framing of decisions and the psychology of choice,' 453-8.

PROSPECT THEORY AND
INTERNATIONAL CO-OPERATION

Very few scholars have applied prospect theory to decisions on international issues, in part because the controlled environment of the laboratory and the international environment are so different.[46] In the laboratory, probabilities are given and measures of equivalence are clear; this is never the case in the messy world of foreign policy decision-making. Until it is tested against cases of international decision-making, it is not clear how well prospect theory will travel outside the laboratory. Those who have considered the relevance of prospect theory generally expect loss aversion to contribute to international conflict.[47] It can contribute to crisis instability and the escalation of conflict, limit the effectiveness of deterrence, and inhibit agreements that would otherwise seem rational.[48]

46 For an application to political choice, see Quattrone and Tversky, 'Contrasting rational and psychological analyses of political choice,' 719-36.

47 Jervis ('Political implications of loss aversion') and Jack S. Levy ('Prospect theory and international relations: theoretical applications and analytical problems') consider the implications of prospect theory for international decisions. Prospect theory has thus far only been applied to cases of international conflict. Whyte and Levi ('Reference level formation, framing effects, and the Cuban missile crisis') find the American decision to impose the blockade consistent with the expectations of prospect theory. Audrey McInerney suggests that the Soviet Union faced a choice between two alternatives that were each unattractive relative to the status quo in the Middle East in 1966-7 and was willing to take high risks to stem its losses: 'Prospect theory and Soviet policy toward Syria 1966-67,' *Political Psychology* 13(June 1992). Rose McDermott finds that President Carter, when he was considering an attempt to rescue the hostages, faced unattractive choices in the context of a deteriorating international and domestic context. He chose the risky rescue mission to avoid these losses but also anticipated gains if the risky attempt succeeded: 'Prospect theory in international relations: the Iranian hostage rescue mission,' *Political Psychology* 13(June 1992). Barbara Farnham finds that President Roosevelt reframed the decision to intervene to resolve the Munich crisis in response to motivational factors: 'Roosevelt and the Munich crisis: insights from prospect theory,' *Political Psychology* 13(June 1992).

48 Risk aversion with respect to gains and the endowment effect, on the other hand, together work to enhance international stability. In so far as states value what they have more than what others have, they are even less likely to take risks to make gains that are only probable. See Jervis, 'Political implications of loss aversion.' International stability is distinct from international co-operation, the focus of this volume. Stability, unlike co-operation, requires no co-ordination of convergent or divergent interests.

When two adversaries each consider that they face no 'good' choices, loss aversion can contribute to crisis instability and to war. At the extreme, an adversary who considers that the status quo is deteriorating may choose to pre-empt if its leaders are certain that the other side will strike first. Leaders may also choose preventive war if they are convinced that war is inevitable and their position is deteriorating. The wars between Germany and France in 1870 and the United States and Japan in 1941 have been interpreted as a consequence of loss aversion.[49] When two adversaries each consider themselves to be defending the status quo and find themselves in the domain of losses, escalation is especially likely. Even more alarming, the magnitude of the loss need not be great; initial deviations from the reference point, even if they are small, can loom disproportionately large and can induce risky behaviour.[50]

Loss aversion helps to explain as well why a state fighting a limited war escalates. If its leadership fears certain and immediate losses from a continuation of the status quo, then the larger risks of escalation which are probable rather than certain may be preferable. Prospect theory captures some of the dynamics of American decisions in Vietnam and Israel's decision to launch deep penetration raids against Egypt in 1970.[51] Loss aversion and the certainty effect also predict limiting conditions to a strategy of deterrence. Deterrence may work against an

49 Jack S. Levy, 'Declining power and the preventive motivation for war,' *World Politics* 40(October 1987), 82-107.
50 Robert Jervis, *The Meaning of the Nuclear Revolution* (Ithaca NY: Cornell University Press 1989) and 'Political implications of loss aversion.' Levy makes a similar argument in 'Prospect theory and international relations.' On the other hand, during the Cuban missile crisis, Premier Khrushchev of the Soviet Union anticipated certain political losses from the withdrawal of the missiles but even greater losses if the conflict escalated to war. This latter estimate provided a powerful brake on escalation. It is not clear, however, whether Khrushchev had normalized for the gain and considered the deployed missiles the new status quo.
51 Jervis, 'Political implications of loss aversion.' Jervis notes that bureaucratic politics in the United States also explains American incremental escalation in Vietnam. Bureaucratic politics was not a factor, however, in Israel's decision to escalate the war of attrition against Egypt in January 1970.

adversary who identifies gains, but it is far less likely to work against an opponent who sees certain losses from a deteriorating status quo.[52]

Scholars who have examined loss aversion and the endowment and certainty effects suggest that each alone and the three together can impede international co-operation. If both sides in a bargaining situation treat their own concessions as losses and those of the other side as gains, then each side will overvalue its own concessions relative to those of its negotiating partner. This is especially likely to occur when each side uses the status quo as its reference point. Each side feels that the cost of making a concession is greater than the gain the other's concession provides. The bargaining space is thereby reduced, and trades that are 'rational' are missed.[53]

We derive a somewhat different proposition from prospect theory applied to decisions on whether or not to co-operate. We suggest first that *leaders are likely to choose to co-operate when they identify immediate and certain losses from the failure to co-operate*. This proposition is consistent with the expectations of both rational and cognitive explanations. We suggest further that *leaders may still choose to co-operate when they identify smaller but certain losses from defection and larger but uncertain losses from co-operation*. Under these conditions, co-operation is not the rational choice.[54]

---

52 Robert Jervis, Richard Ned Lebow, and Janice Gross Stein, *Psychology and Deterrence* (Baltimore MD: Johns Hopkins University Press 1985), Richard Ned Lebow and Janice Gross Stein, *When Does Deterrence Succeed and How Do We Know?* (Ottawa: Canadian Institute for International Peace and Security 1990), and Richard Ned Lebow and Janice Gross Stein, 'Beyond deterrence,' *Journal of Social Issues* 43(1987), 5-71.

53 See Knetsch and Sinden, 'Willingness to pay and compensation demanded,' 507-21, and Knetsch, 'The endowment effect and evidence of nonreversible indifference curves,' 1277-84. Jervis ('Political implications of loss aversion') applies these arguments to the prospects of peace.

54 Prospect theory has been tested largely in the laboratory, under experimental conditions. The experiments have generally tested for only a limited range of differences among pay-offs. In applying the theory outside the laboratory to political decisions, we cannot specify with any confidence how 'risky' political leaders are likely to be in different kinds of situations. Anecdotal evidence

Michael Mastanduno argues in this volume, for example, that the American agreement with Japan over structural impediments can be understood as a risky choice. The administration identified certain losses from the failure to agree but at the same time acknowledged that the Structural Impediments Initiative was a gamble with larger but only probable losses. It could fail and Congress could adopt even harsher anti-liberal trade policies than it would have when the agreement was reached.

Israel's agreement to attend the regional peace conference proposed by the United States and the Soviet Union in October 1991 also fits nicely with these expectations. Israel's leaders found themselves in the domain of losses. Using the status quo as their reference point, they identified the functionally certain loss of badly needed loan guarantees and a severe strain in their relationship with the United States if they failed to agree. They also identified large and probable losses, measured as deviations from the territorial status quo, were the conference to succeed.[55] As predicted by prospect theory, they chose to avoid the immediate certain losses from the failure to agree. Prospect theory therefore suggests that agreements will be made that would not be considered 'rational' in standard models of subjective expected utility. It can explain co-operation as a risky choice when leaders find themselves in the domain of losses.

---

suggests that certain propositions of prospect theory may not hold in international politics when an outcome is perceived as a disaster. In the Cuban missile crisis, for example, Khrushchev chose a certain and immediate loss over an uncertain disaster when he agreed to withdraw Soviet missiles from Cuba rather than run a further risk of nuclear war. President Kennedy too was willing to suffer a certain political loss by agreeing publicly to withdraw the Jupiter missiles from Turkey rather than run a further risk of nuclear war. Tversky and Kahneman suggest that loss aversion may reflect the importance or prominence of the dimensions of choice. Loss aversion appears to be more pronounced for safety than for money and more pronounced for income than for leisure: see 'Loss aversion in riskless choice: a reference dependent model,' *Quarterly Journal of Economics*, 1992.

55 Author's interview of senior Israeli official, August 1991. Israel's choice could conform to the expectations of rational models if its leaders had thought that the conference was likely to fail because of Arab unwillingness to participate. The senior official voiced no such expectation.

THE RESEARCH AGENDA

Contributors to this collection of essays set themselves several tasks. In the first instance, we examine whether leaders decide to co-operate when they are in the domain of losses as well as when they seek to maximize gain. Many studies of decisions to co-operate do not consider this distinction important because they analyse expected utility, which aggregates expected gains and losses in one estimate. To explore decision-making in the domain of losses, we examine cases where states failed to co-operate as well as cases of co-operation and search for the gains as well as the losses leaders expected.

Our selection of cases was deliberately broad in the hope of capturing distinctive patterns. We include cases of international co-operation among allies where consideration of relative gains should be absent. Spar, Pauly, and Welch all search for relative gains seeking as well as for expected utility maximization and loss aversion in their examination of the Japanese-American decision to co-develop the FSX fighter, the evolution of IMF surveillance, and Israel's decision to co-operate with the United States, respectively. Considerations of relative gains among allies across a range of cases would be anomalous for realist theories and would require explanation.

We also include cases drawn from both international political economy and international security to examine variations across the fields. Mastanduno's examination of the negotiations between the United States and Japan over structural impediments and Pauly's exploration of multilateral economic surveillance fall within the field of international political economy. Spar's analysis of the American-Japanese agreement to co-develop the FSX aircraft cuts across international political economy and security, while Welch's and Richardson's analyses are in the domain of security. Much of the literature suggests that it is far easier to co-operate on issues of international political economy than it is on issues of international security because of the greater consequences of error in decisions affecting security.[56] We

56 See Robert Jervis, 'Security regimes,' *International Organization* 36(winter

suspect that this is not a central divide and deliberately chose cases from both policy arenas to analyse similarities and differences.

In those cases where leaders chose to co-operate to avoid loss, their decisions can be explained in several ways. Leaders may have chosen to co-operate to minimize expected losses; loss avoidance would then be the rational choice. Alternatively, the decision to co-operate may have been the risky choice, which did not minimize the highest expected losses. Explanations of decisions to co-operate are subject to 'equifinality,' in that similar choices can be produced by different causal patterns. Our interest is to identify the sequence in which leaders choose to co-operate to avoid certain losses, even at the risk of larger but less certain losses in the future. We do not suggest that this is the only or even the most important explanation of choices to co-operate. We do seek to establish that leaders make these kinds of choices and speculate on the conditions under which they do so.

The most stringent test of rational and psychological models would require that we reconstruct the utility calculus of leaders to determine whether the choice to co-operate departed from rational norms. Since leaders rarely provide explicit estimates of likelihood and value, it is extraordinarily difficult to test the predictions of the two models directly against the evidence. We approximate this kind of test by focusing not only on the decisions leaders made but also on the process of choosing as political leaders considered whether or not to co-operate.

Rational models of choice say nothing formally about the process of choice. They take preferences as given and deduce the rational decision.[57] Despite this silence, analysts of decision-mak-

---

1982), 357-78, and Charles Lipson, 'International cooperation in economic and security affairs,' *World Politics* 37(October 1984), 1-23. For an extensive analysis of the conditions which promote co-operation on security issues, see Alexander L. George, Philip J. Farley, and Alexander Dallin, eds, *U.S.-Soviet Security Cooperation: Achievements, Failures, Lessons* (New York: Oxford University Press 1988). Axelrod and Keohane suggest that the divide between political economy and military security is not as significant as it is generally considered to be: 'Achieving cooperation under anarchy: strategies and institutions,' 227.

57 There is a voluminous literature on models of rational choice. For a critical summary of the debate about processes of choosing and their impact on

ing have elaborated a set of norms which guide a 'rational' process of choice.[58] These norms dictate an active search for information and options, estimates of the likelihood and value of the consequences of these options, revision of estimates in response to new information, and choice of the option that promises the highest expected utility. In a rational process of choice, people are expected to think about outcomes in terms of their final welfare or total assets.

Prospect theory, part of the broader tradition of behavioural decision theory, argues strongly that the process of choosing shapes choice. The process it depicts differs substantially from the rational norms associated with utility maximization. Leaders begin with a reference point and frame their estimates of gains and losses as deviations from that reference point. They may choose the status quo or an aspiration level.[59] They use the language of 'loss' and 'gain' from that point, rather than consider their total assets or final position. They should also pay more attention to losses than to gains. Moreover, because losses loom larger than gains, they may at times exaggerate losses in comparison with the calculations of rational choosers. Although prospect theory does not specify a formal theory of the process of choosing, it recognizes the importance of the process on the decisions that are made.

Behavioural decision theory generally pays a great deal of attention to the search for and processing of information. In their estimates, people tend to treat very likely occurrences as certain and discard very unlikely consequences. The use of heuristics like anchoring, availability, and representativeness reduces their sensitivity to new or discrepant information. These kinds of processes of search and estimation look very different from that

---

preference formation, see Richard Ned Lebow and Janice Gross Stein, 'Rational deterrence theory: I think, therefore I deter,' *World Politics* 41(January 1989), 208-24.

58 For a detailed discussion of a rational process of choice, see Janice Gross Stein and Raymond Tanter, *Rational Decision-Making: Israel's Security Choices, 1967* (Columbus: Ohio State University Press 1980).

59 If leaders choose the position of another state as their reference point, relative gains considerations – or relative losses – enter through the framing process.

implicit in models of rational choice and should leave distinct traces that can be identified.

In our case-studies, we look carefully at the process of choice, using a detailed set of indicators.[60] Richardson examines how British leaders anticipated likely American reaction to the use of force against President Nasser; Welch analyses the kind of information Israel's leaders sought from the United States as they debated whether or not to accede to the American request to refrain from the use of force against Iraq. Mastanduno looks at how American officials calculated trade-offs as they negotiated with Japan over structural impediments to trade and Spar examines the estimates American and Japanese officials developed of the consequences of co-production and independent production by Japan. Pauly explores how American officials estimated the consequences of a failure to co-operate on multilateral economic surveillance.

To the extent that these processes approximate rational norms, it is more convincing to argue that leaders made choices that maximized their utility. If they sought to avoid loss, they did so as rational decision-makers who tried to choose the option which promised the lowest expected cost. If decision processes violated rational norms in important ways, then behavioural decision theory will be much more illuminating. Evidence of this kind of decision process then suggests that leaders chose to avoid loss, even if this was a 'sub-optimal' decision. Where direct evidence does not permit us to establish whether decisions to co-operate to avoid expected loss were rational, we evaluate the choice in part by the processes leaders used to make their decisions.

This test is appropriate in so far as behavioural decision research suggests that the framing of the problem shapes choice. To establish the importance of framing, our case-studies investigate whether other frames that would give rise to different

60 See appendix A for the set of questions which guided the investigation of the decision processes. Using these questions, each investigator searched for evidence of a rational process and utility maximization, rational process and relative gains maximization, and cognitive processes which violate rational norms of search and evaluation.

choices were possible and whether decision-makers disagreed amongst themselves about the appropriate frame. Spar documents this kind of disagreement in her analysis of American agreement to co-develop the FSX fighter with Japan, as does Welch in his discussion of Israel's decision to co-operate with the United States. If other frames that would lead to different choices were possible or if the frame was contested, then the importance of framing is clear.[61]

After analysing how decisions to co-operate were made, we speculated about why they were framed the way they were. Framing takes place in an international context against a background of domestic politics. We asked why leaders chose the reference point they did, especially if they did not choose the status quo. When do leaders choose as a reference point the position of others?[62] When are their aspirations or expectations the point of reference? Under what conditions can a decision frame shift over time?

In choosing to co-operate, leaders can identify personal and political as well as international gains and losses. These gains or losses can cut different ways and leaders may weigh them differently under different conditions.[63] Our case-studies are too few

---

61 The importance of framing can be assessed through a more stringent criterion. It could be argued that framing makes a difference only if preferences deviate from what would be expected by external incentives, the dictates of domestic politics, optimal strategies, bounded rationality, and risk propensities. This argument suggests that structures dictate pay-off and preferences. As we have seen, however, changes in verbal descriptions of the same problem can reverse preferences. We therefore treat framing as a critical *intervening* variable between structure and choice.

62 Timothy J. McKeown suggests that relative gains consideration – or the selection of another's position as the reference point – by agents is a product of tournament-like expectations on the part of a controlling set of principals. If relative performance is the criterion principals use with reference to their agents, then domestic political losses will ensue from the failure to do 'relatively' well internationally rather than from the failure to provide anticipated benefits, irrespective of how comparable groups in other states fare. See 'What is the basis for relative gains seeking,' unpublished paper, 1991.

63 Arthur Stein suggests that the context in which decisions are made – whether a state's position has been deteriorating and the kinds of future leaders can look forward to – also matters: *Why Nations Cooperate*, 110.

to permit more than preliminary speculation about the impact of the structure of the international environment, the distribution of capabilities, and domestic political competition on the decision frames political leaders use. They do provide evidence, however, of considerable variation in the possible sources of frames. Spar suggests, for example, that the different frames used by different American officials can be traced to their political constituencies. The historical and ideological context, cognitive and motivational processes, and the personal idiosyncrasies of leaders can also be important. Richardson argues that the frame Prime Minister Eden used can be explained in part by his personal experiences and in part by the historical analogies he drew. We see these five case-studies as a 'plausibility probe,' as a first attempt to explore why leaders frame problems of international co-operation the way they do. In so far as the decision frames leaders use shape their subsequent choices, it is important that we learn more about why political leaders frame international problems the way they do.

FRAMING THE PROBLEM OF CO-OPERATION
Four of our five cases establish that leaders chose to co-operate after they framed the problem as the avoidance of loss. American and Japanese officials twice chose to co-operate to avoid loss, the industrialized economies co-operated on multilateral economic surveillance to avoid loss, and Israel acceded to the American request to refrain from military retaliation against Iraq to avoid losses in its relationship with Washington.

Loss aversion, however, also, led to conflict. Richardson demonstrates that in 1956 when British leaders considered that abstention from the use of force, in accordance with American wishes, involved certain loss, they discounted the larger but probable losses of a use of force against President Nasser. In 1973, President Sadat chose to go to war to avoid the immediate and certain losses of the status quo; five years later, he signed an agreement with Israel to avoid the certain losses of the status quo. In large part because loss aversion appears to be a powerful explanation of decision, it is also indeterminate as an explanation of choices to co-operate.

Explaining decisions to co-operate is part of the larger problem of explaining political choice in the international arena. As these cases clearly demonstrate, choice is contextual, embedded in a specific historical and political setting, and shaped by what leaders have learned as well as by the constituencies they represent. Whether or not leaders choose to co-operate does not depend principally on whether the problem is one of absolute or relative gains, since the one can almost always can be translated into the other, but on the prior question of how leaders frame the problem.

Even though the impact of loss aversion on political decisions to co-operate in foreign policy remains indeterminate, important policy implications flow from evidence that framing matters. It should be useful for policy-makers to pay attention to the frames of other parties to a negotiation. Controlling the ways in which complex problems are broken down and simplified at the negotiating table will have important consequences for the choices other parties make. Knowing another's reference level should make it much easier to estimate which sanctions, incentives, or concessions will help to bring about an agreement. Offering concessions, for example, that do not make up a deficiency between assets and a reference level will generally not work. Because re-framing a problem changes risk propensities, if policy-makers can re-frame international problems to identify and emphasize the almost certain losses from the failure to agree, co-operation should become more likely.[64]

Anecdotal evidence supports some of these implications of prospect theory. In preparing for the Middle East peace conference in Madrid in October 1991, the American secretary of state warned the Palestinian leadership that they had the 'most to lose'

---

64 I am grateful to David Welch for these suggestions. See also James K. Sebenius, 'Challenging conventional explanations of international cooperation: negotiation analysis and the case of epistemic communities,' *International Organization* 46(winter 1992), 323-66.

if they did not participate in the negotiations.[65] Mr Baker provided almost no assurances of the gains they would make at the table, but highlighted the losses they would experience if they stayed away. He thus tried both to make relative position at the current status quo the salient reference point for Palestinian leaders and to highlight the certain losses of the failure to agree. This strategy by a third party was designed to manipulate the framing of the problem to enhance the prospects of a choice to co-operate. Similarly, successful international institutions may frame issues in such a way that the failure to co-operate creates certain short-term losses. Public diplomacy may be especially valuable in its capacity to make these certain losses visible and salient to leaders and thereby to induce co-operation that would otherwise not occur.[66]

We noted earlier that behavioural decision theory suggests that some agreements that would be rational are perhaps not made because of the impact of loss aversion, the certainty effect, and the endowment effect.[67] Opportunities to co-operate are therefore missed. Mastanduno's analysis of American negotiations with Japan, Spar's examination of the American and Japanese decisions to co-produce the FSX aircraft, Pauly's discussion of multilateral economic surveillance, and Welch's account of Israel's decision to co-operate with the United States during the Gulf War all suggest that when a decision problem was re-framed to highlight the certain costs of non-co-operation, leaders decided to co-operate. When problems were re-framed, opportunities to co-operate were created.

These are encouraging if only preliminary results. Our evidence suggests that political leaders in five different cases dem-

65 *New York Times*, 2 August 1991.

66 Personal communication from Robert O. Keohane, 3 January 1992.

67 Max Bazerman has documented the impact of framing in experimental studies of bargaining. He compared the performances of experimental subjects when the outcomes of bargaining were formulated as gains or losses. Subjects who bargained over the allocation of losses more often failed to reach agreement and find the optimal solution. See M.H. Bazerman, 'Negotiator judgment,' *American Behavioral Scientist* 27(November-December 1983), 211-28.

onstrated a pervasive bias towards loss and that this bias influenced the choices they made. We need to do a great deal more to establish leaders' estimates of loss with confidence and to specify their impact on political choice under different political and international conditions. Examination of these cases expands and amplifies the analysis of the sources of international co-operation and suggests that the impact of loss aversion on political choice merits further attention.

APPENDIX A: GUIDELINES FOR
THE INVESTIGATION OF DECISION PROCESSES

Expected utility models
How can we do 'best' or 'least badly'?
1 Did leaders search extensively for options? Did they identify at least the obvious options and their obvious consequences?
2 Did decision-makers search for information about all the consequences of the options they identified?
3 Did they make probabilistic judgments about the consequences of these options?
4 Did they assign estimates of cost and benefit – gain and loss – to the consequences of these outcomes?
5 Did decision-makers have a set of consistent and transitive preferences?
6 Did decision-makers compare across the expected values of the options they identified?

If *all* these criteria are present, expected utility maximization is an appropriate and powerful model of the decision process and its outcome. For our purposes in this project, we are interested in establishing if, when decision-makers chose this way to co-operate, the expected utility of the option to co-operate was the highest positive value or the lowest negative value.

Relative gains models
How can we do 'better' or 'less badly' than they do?

1 Did decision-makers search for and identify the obvious options and their consequences for themselves and their partner-adversary?

2 Did decision-makers have a set of consistent and transitive preferences?

3 Did they estimate a set of consistent and transitive preferences for their partner-adversary in the relationship?

4 Did they rank order or assign cardinal utilities to their own and their partner-adversary's preferences?

5 Did they compare the *differences* between their preference set and that of their partner-adversary?

6 Did they choose the option which maximized these differences, however calculated?

If *all* these criteria are present, a model of relative gains is an appropriate and powerful model of the decision process and its outcome. If decision-makers violated some of these norms but nevertheless attempted to maximize relative difference, however formulated, we want to know. We are also interested in knowing whether leaders tried to maximize relative gains or minimize relative losses.

Prospect theory
How can we best avoid loss?

1 Did decision-makers seem to have a clear reference level – a sense of an 'aspiration level' or 'target' which defined minimally acceptable pay-offs? Is there evidence that they viewed the status quo at or above the reference level? Below that reference level? Has the status quo recently shifted in their favour? Against them? If it shifted in their favour, have they normalized (adjusted for) the gain? If it shifted against them, have they normalized (adjusted for) the loss? We would expect decision-makers to normalize much more quickly for gain than for loss.

2 Do you find evidence that preferences were not stable, consistent, and invariant across decision-makers? If they were

not, do preferences emerge or mutate as the decision-makers participate in the decision process? How (if at all) does the nature of the process shape the evolution of their preferences?

3 Do you find any evidence of the use of heuristics in the generation of options and/or in the estimation of the likelihood of their consequences, if likelihoods were considered at all? Was there obviously truncated search in which options inconsistent with prevailing beliefs and ideological constructs were eliminated a priori? Did decision-makers think in probabilistic terms at all? If they did, how did they make these probabilistic judgments: by 'anchoring' against the status quo, by availability, by representativeness?

4 Did decision-makers weight loss more heavily than gain? How heavily was their attention weighted towards consideration of losses versus consideration of gains? What did they talk preponderantly about? Loss aversion is one of the most robust principles of behavioural decision theory. If the status quo has recently shifted against them, did decision-makers place a good deal of weight on restoring it? If the status quo has recently shifted in their favour, did they give preponderant attention to avoiding a reversal? Or, if it shifted in their favour, were they tolerant of losses that would still leave them at or above the old status quo? Finally, what configuration of estimates did decision-makers generate? Did they become more or less concerned about losses that are extremely large? Did they pay more attention to losses that they considered highly probable (or certain) or to losses that they considered unlikely but serious? Did they worry about certain large losses, uncertain large losses, certain small losses, and/or certain small losses?

5 What sort of method ('rule') did decision-makers use to arrive at their final choice?

Two

Framing the Japan problem: the Bush administration and the Structural Impediments Initiative

MICHAEL MASTANDUNO

Imagine two families, living on opposite sides of a wide boulevard. They agree to visit each other's homes and make a critical assessment of the wallpaper, the furniture, the family budget, and the eating habits of the children. Each recommends changes for the other: rearranging the furniture, eating less meat (and more rice), visiting the grandparents more often. Each agrees to adopt its neighbour's recommendations, to implement them on a specified timetable, and to monitor the results. The neighbours expect to become better friends as a result.

The Structural Impediments Initiative (SII) was a novel and ambitious attempt to rectify the trade and payments imbalance between the United States and Japan. It was launched as a joint initiative by President Bush and Prime Minister Uno in June 1989, and, following a year of concentrated formal negotiations and informal meetings, a final agreement was signed in June 1990. The SII required each side to scrutinize and seek to alter policies and practices in the other which are normally considered the preserve of domestic politics. For example, the United States emphasized the manner in which Japan utilized its land, the

Associate Professor of Government, Dartmouth College, Hanover, New Hampshire; author of *Economic Containment: Cocom and the Politics of East-West Trade* (1992).

I am grateful to the other contributors to this volume, and to Joseph Massey, Michael Donnelly, and Nelson Kasfir for thoughtful comments and suggestions. I also thank the Council on Foreign Relations for the International Affairs Fellowship that enabled me to work at the Office of the United States Trade Representative and participate in the SII negotiations as a member of the United States delegation.

work and leisure habits of Japanese citizens, and the exclusionary purchasing habits of and long-term relationships among Japanese firms. Among the issues stressed by Japan were the lack of patience and planning by American firms, the inadequate efforts of the United States government in the fields of education and labour training, and the excessive reliance of individuals, firms, and the government on instruments of debt. In the agreement, each side pledged to eliminate or modify many of the structural barriers identified by the other. The Japanese government agreed to bolster the administration and enforcement of its anti-monopoly laws, to increase spending by specified amounts on public infrastructure, to improve the efficiency of its distribution system, and to relax restrictions on the operation of large retail stores. The Bush administration promised to promote saving by the public and the private sector, to encourage firms to adopt long-term strategies, to reduce the federal budget deficit, and to improve the quality of education. The two governments agreed to meet periodically over the following three years to assess the implementation of the agreement and to resolve problem areas.

That the United States and Japan agreed to engage in the sɪɪ, much less to reach detailed agreements, might be considered puzzling. The two sides had co-operated in the past on specific compartmentalized issues such as the adjustment of exchange rates, the removal of sectoral trade barriers, or the co-ordination of macro-economic policies. Yet they had never before attempted any negotiations as comprehensive, and as intrusive domestically, as the sɪɪ.

The general tendency of governments is to guard their domestic political and economic autonomy. For one government to allow another, in the context of a trade negotiation, to criticize and expect changes in long-standing practices and institutions unambiguously considered the preserve of domestic politics is highly unusual. For governments to make a formal commitment to alter such structures and practices is all the more extraordinary. Thus, it is not surprising that the sɪɪ was greeted with scepticism and a prediction of failure by many informed observers.[1] That the initiative succeeded requires explanation.

The central premise of this volume is that how government officials frame decisions affects significantly both the decisions reached and the prospects for international co-operation. Are decision-makers motivated by the opportunity to gain – in relative or absolute terms – or by the prospect of loss?[2] How decisions are framed, in turn, can be influenced by an array of international, domestic, and individual factors. The act of framing may be viewed as an intervening variable between the dependent variable of co-operation and the independent variables normally identified to account for its absence or persistence. The purpose of this chapter is to assess the extent to which framing mattered in the initiation and completion of the sii. I focus on the American policy process during 1989 and 1990, the first two years of the administration of President George Bush. How did United States officials frame the decision to engage in the sii? Why did they frame it that way? What impact, if any, did the manner in which they framed it have on the ultimate outcome of bilateral co-operation?

American policy-makers framed the decisions both to engage in the sii and to conclude it successfully primarily in terms of loss avoidance. They conceived of the sii as a means to avoid short-term tactical and long-term structural losses. In the short term, the sii enabled officials of the executive branch of the United States government to deflect what they perceived as a challenge from the legislative arm to their control over the formulation and substance of trade policy. Executive officials believed that without the sii, Congress was likely to adopt meas-

---

1 See, for example, the statement of Rudiger Dornbusch in United States, Congress, Senate, Committee on Finance, Subcommittee on International Trade, *United States-Japan Structural Impediments Initiative (SII)*, part 2, hearings, 101st Cong, 1st sess, 6-7 November 1989, 49, 56.

2 A detailed discussion on framing and on the logic of the pursuit of absolute gain, relative gain, and loss avoidance is provided by Janice Gross Stein's introduction to this volume.

ures which would jeopardize the successful completion of the Uruguay Round of multilateral trade negotiations under the General Agreement on Tariffs and Trade (GATT) – the administration's top priority in trade policy – and drive American policy in the illiberal direction of managed trade. The SII was also viewed as a means to preserve the multilateral trading system over the long run. Bush administration officials believed that Japan was a potential system wrecker, that its domestic political and economic structures and practices were fundamentally incompatible with those of other advanced industrial states. The considerable trade and payments imbalance between the United States and Japan was a symptom, and a politically explosive one, of that incompatibility. The failure to transform Japan would lead ultimately to the demise of the multilateral system.

Framing in terms of loss avoidance led American officials to take risks they otherwise might have avoided.[3] The SII was a major gamble and created expectations of profound change in relations between the United States and Japan. At the same time administration officials appear to have exaggerated – at least to some extent – the detrimental consequences of not engaging in the SII. By initiating the SII, the administration may actually have increased the likelihood, at least in the short run, of the detrimental consequences it sought to avoid.

The decision to frame in terms of loss avoidance can be traced to the domestic structure of the United States. In trade policy, the executive arm of government is caught between the constitutional authority and domestic demands of Congress on the one hand and the country's international obligations on the other.[4] While Congress has delegated considerable authority to

3 According to prospect theory, an emphasis on loss avoidance will lead policy-makers to deviate from the expectations of a rational actor framework. For example, decision-makers can be expected to take greater risks than they ordinarily would and to exaggerate the consequences of those options they identify as likely to produce loss. See Amos Tversky and Daniel Kahneman, 'The framing of decisions and the psychology of choice,' *Science* 211(30 January 1981), 453-8, and Daniel Kahneman and Amos Tversky, 'Prospect theory: an analysis of decision under risk,' *Econometrica* 47(March 1979), 263-91.

4 See G. John Ikenberry et al, *The State and American Foreign Economic Policy* (Ithaca NY: Cornell University Press 1988).

the executive since the 1930s, by the 1980s officials feared a loss of control and an effort by Congress to regain the initiative and use it at cross-purposes with the executive's continuing efforts to maintain and extend the multilateral liberal trading order.[5] The passage by Congress of the Omnibus Trade and Competitiveness Act of 1988 with its Super 301 provision raised the spectre of a second 'Smoot-Hawley' – an image as powerful in the foreign economic sphere as that of Munich in the political-military sphere.[6]

More broadly, the structure of the political system in the United States tends to create incentives for policy-makers to frame issues in terms of loss avoidance. The fragmented and decentralized nature of the system, the numerous points of access enjoyed by interest groups, and the important role of public opinion pose, from the perspective of the executive, a continuing fear of policy incoherence. The threat is especially pronounced in trade policy, an issue-area in which the state is particularly exposed to societal pressures.[7]

The fact that American officials framed in terms of loss avoidance significantly influenced the prospects for co-operation. It prompted officials to adopt a (risky) co-operative strategy in the first place and to ensure that negotiations were completed successfully. If the issue of trade and payments imbalances had been framed in terms of relative gains, it is unlikely that officials would have pursued the SII. If they had pursued it, they would have emphasized different priorities in the negotiations, and it would have been more difficult to extract Japanese concessions. Either the United States, or Japan, might have walked away dissatisfied and unwilling to complete the agreement. If the deci-

5 I.M. Destler, *American Trade Politics: System under Stress* (Washington: Institute for International Economics 1986), and Robert Z. Lawrence and Charles L. Schultze, eds, *An American Trade Strategy: Options for the 1990s* (Washington: Brookings 1990).

6 Public Law 100-418, Omnibus Trade and Competitiveness Act of 1988, 23 August 1988. Section 1301 of the act contains the highly controversial Super 301 provision.

7 Stephen D. Krasner, 'United States commercial policy: unravelling the paradox of internal weakness and external strength,' in Peter Katzenstein, ed, *Between Power and Plenty* (Madison: University of Wisconsin Press 1978), 51-88.

sion had been framed in terms of absolute gains, officials might still have proposed the sii but would have negotiated it differently. The final outcome might have been greater co-operation than was actually achieved.

The next section analyses the decision to initiate the Structural Impediments Initiative. Subsequent sections examine, respectively, the bargaining strategy of the United States as the negotiations progressed and the endgame which resulted in a successful agreement. A concluding section explores some implications of this case-study for the study of international relations and foreign policy decision-making.

WHY THE SII?

A persistent and sizable bilateral trade deficit with Japan was among the most important foreign policy problems faced by the incoming Bush administration in 1989 (see figure 1). Sectoral negotiations with Japan during the 1980s in telecommunications, medical equipment, tobacco, beef, citrus products, and semiconductors had led to agreements to open Japan's markets but had done little to alleviate the deficit. The same was true of exchange rate adjustment – the so-called Plaza strategy initiated in 1985 – even though it had succeeded in significantly depreciating the dollar and appreciating the yen.

Bush administration officials recognized, along with most economists, that the United States trade and payments deficits had less to do with trade policy and more with macro-economic policy, in particular the gap between savings and investment in the United States. Nevertheless, as the trade deficit mounted so did pressure from Congress for a more aggressive trade policy, with Japan as the most prominent target. Congressional frustration was reflected in the decision to sanction Japan in 1987 for violating a bilateral semiconductor agreement and in 1988 for the sale of sensitive technology to the Soviet Union by a subsidiary of Toshiba. In 1989 the first major foreign policy crisis of the Bush administration involved whether to abide by a previous agreement with Japan to co-develop the FSX aircraft. Pressure from Congress and some agencies in the administration led to

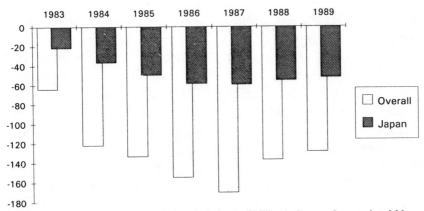

FIGURE I   United States merchandise trade balance ($billions). Source: International Monetary Fund, *Direction of Trade Statistics Yearbook 1990*, 402.

reconsideration of that agreement. As that crisis was resolved, the administration faced another – whether to employ the Super 301 provision of the 1988 Trade Act as a weapon against Japan.

The Super 301 decision placed the administration in a quandary. The provision, which directed executive officials to identify priority trading partners and negotiate the elimination of objectionable trading practices under strict time limits and the threat of retaliation, was widely perceived in the international community as a unilateral exercise of power that was incompatible with the spirit of multilateralism and the GATT.[8] Administration officials feared that to use it would create diplomatic friction and, more importantly, might compromise the willingness of other states to co-operate in bringing the Uruguay Round to a successful completion by the end of 1990 – a top priority for the administration.[9]

Not to use Super 301, however, would provoke a confrontation with Congress. The provision was the centrepiece of the 1988 Trade Act and the prime instrument of an attempt by Congress to force the executive to 'get tough' with the trading partners of

8 Jagdish Bhagwati, ed, *Aggressive Unilateralism* (Ann Arbor: University of Michigan Press 1990).
9 'Super 301 Trade Liberalization Priorities,' fact sheet distributed by the Office of the United States Trade Representative, 25 May 1989.

the United States. Architects of the provision, in particular Senators John Danforth and Max Baucus, made it clear that they expected Super 301 to be used and Japan to be named a priority country. Super 301, Danforth frequently asserted,' was drafted with Japan in mind.[10] Administration officials feared that to evade Super 301 would damage their credibility on trade policy with Congress and, even worse, might embolden congressional hardliners to enact protectionist legislation.

The problem was compounded by the manner in which priority practices were to be designated. Each year the Office of the United States Trade Representative (USTR) compiles a report that catalogues, by country, trade barriers which impede American exports. In the 1988 Trade Act, Congress directed the executive to use the 1989 report as a basis for designating priority countries and practices. For Japan alone, that report documented thirty-four barriers, ranging from the very specific (for example, prohibitions on the purchase of foreign satellites) to the very general (for example, the distribution system).[11] As the executive interpreted Super 301, each priority practice would require a set of negotiations to eliminate the objectionable barrier. Both diplomatically and administratively, it would be impossible to negotiate across the entire range of Japanese barriers.

The Bush administration was profoundly divided over whether to employ Super 301. Some, including the chairman of the Council of Economic Advisers, Michael Boskin, and the director of the Office of Management and Budget, Richard Darman, advised the president against doing so, on the grounds that to use the provision would likely spark a trade war. The State Department warned that Super 301 would trigger an emotional outburst in Japan against the United States. Others, such as the United States trade representative, Carla Hills, and the secretary of commerce, Robert Mosbacher, supported at least the modest

10 See Richard Lawrence, 'Policy dispute over Japan may develop,' *Journal of Commerce*, 21 March 1989, 1.
11 *1989 National Trade Estimates Report on Foreign Trade Barriers* (Washington: Office of the United States Trade Representative 1989), 97-114.

use of Super 301 to maintain the administration's credibility with Congress and as a signal to trading partners of the United States that the administration was resolved to open markets by whatever means necessary.

On the eve of his decision, President Bush was lobbied personally by Senate hardliners. Eventually he decided to identify Japan as a priority country, but to soften the blow in two ways. Brazil and India were also named, to avoid the complete isolation of Japan, and only three Japanese priority practices were cited – import restrictions on satellites, supercomputers, and forest products. The administration thereby attempted to walk a fine line between its international obligations and domestic pressures. It feared, however, that its softer line would not be sufficient to placate Congress. Administration officials thus sought a complement to Super 301 which would address trade problems with Japan more fully.

The idea for the SII had originated in the Treasury Department late in 1988. Officials conceived of it as a natural follow-on to the structural dialogue of 1985-6, the yen-dollar talks, and other discussions in the Organization for Economic Co-operation and Development and the Group of Seven on structural rigidities and trade and payments imbalances.[12] At about the same time, officials in the USTR concluded that structural impediments were largely responsible for the slow pace of American exports to Japan since neither the steady appreciation of the yen nor the removal of formal trade barriers had led to bilateral trade adjustment. A 'structural' initiative, combining macro-economic and trade policy measures, was one of five (not mutually exclusive) options for dealing with Japan presented by the USTR to the incoming administration in 1989.[13]

12 See the statement of the Treasury under secretary, David C. Mulford, in *U.S.-Japan Structural Impediments Initiative*, part 1, 20 July 1989, 3-5.
13 The other four were to eliminate sector-specific barriers using Super 301 and other tools, to use non-trade leverage to eliminate trade barriers, to co-operate with the private sector and target export promotion in areas where trade agreements had previously been reached, and to 'pluralize' American policy by seeking support from other countries for market opening efforts in Japan. Interviews, Office of the United States Trade Representative, July 1990.

With this interest on the part of two key agencies, some type of structural initiative with Japan might have been adopted by the Bush administration under any circumstances. Clearly, however, in the absence of the administration's decision on Super 301, the sii would not have achieved the prominence and priority it was granted. The sii appeared to be a perfect complement to Super 301. It enabled the administration to demonstrate to Congress that it was addressing virtually the entire range of Japanese trade barriers, even if not under the terms of Super 301. And it allowed the administration to request negotiations with Japan without the legislatively mandated threat of retaliation that Japanese officials found so offensive.

The link between the Super 301 decision and the sii was unambiguous. Both were announced on 25 May 1989; the former by the trade representative and the latter by the president. Hills referred to the sii in her statement as a 'separate administration initiative' that would be pursued 'outside of Section 301.'[14] It would, however, run concurrently with the Super 301 negotiations with Japan on satellites, supercomputers, and forest products. Japan subsequently agreed to the American proposal, provided that the sii was conceived as a 'two-way street,' with American as well as Japanese impediments as subjects for discussion. In a joint statement, President Bush and Prime Minister Uno later announced that the purpose of the sii would be 'to identify and solve structural problems in both countries that stand as impediments to trade and balance-of-payments adjustment with the goal of contributing to the reduction of payments imbalances.'[15] The two sides also agreed to produce an interim sii report by the spring of 1990 – about the time that the three Super 301 negotiations would be completed, and just before the administration would have to determine whether to employ this controversial trade weapon for another year.

This outline of developments suggests that United States officials framed the decision to engage in the sii primarily in

14 'Super 301 Trade Liberalization Priorities.
15 'Joint Statement of President Bush and Prime Minister Uno on Economic Issues, 14 July 1989, reprinted in *Department of State Bulletin* 89(September 1989), 78.

terms of loss avoidance. Their reference point was the status quo, including executive control over trade policy and the preservation of the multilateral trading system over the long run. Thus, their principal concern was to do 'something' to demonstrate to Congress that the administration was attacking Japanese trade barriers, even if not by the method Congress preferred. Although the idea of a structural initiative had been floating around the bureaucracy, the administration appears to have proposed the SII without a prior systematic assessment of its costs and benefits relative to alternative means to reduce the trade and payments deficit. The proposal for a non-Super 301 negotiation with Japan came first; the specific details – such as the inclusion of American impediments as well as Japanese ones – came later.

Framing in terms of loss avoidance increased the propensity of the administration to take risks. In its first year, the Bush administration earned a reputation as being excessively cautious in foreign policy matters. At a time of dramatic change and opportunity in East-West relations, the administration's approach to the Soviet Union and Eastern Europe was characterized and criticized as little more than a defence of the status quo. The SII, however, was clearly a risky venture. Unlike past structural 'dialogues' with Japan (the industrial policy dialogue of 1983-4, for example), the SII created the expectation of significant results. It was, after all, a substitute for Super 301, itself a 'results-oriented' strategy. Yet the results promised by the SII were not simply the removal of specific trade barriers but profound changes in the very nature of Japan's political and economic system which would trigger a sizable reduction in the United States trade deficit. Such changes were difficult for any government to accept and implement, especially when imposed by foreigners, in a compressed time-frame, under the threat of retaliation. Critics depicted the SII as the 'second coming of General Douglas Macarthur [*sic*],' as a not-so-subtle attempt by the United States to impose a second occupation of Japan.[16] Not surprisingly, administration officials quickly sought to dampen

16 Dornbusch statement, 98.

expectations; Hills stressed that the most that should be expected of Japan in a year was a 'blueprint and downpayment' on structural change which would not immediately affect the trade balance.[17] Senator Baucus and others countered by emphasizing that Congress viewed the SII as part of the 301 process, and as such expected 'concrete results, not endless talks.'[18]

Bush administration officials seem to have exaggerated the negative consequences of not engaging in the SII. They feared that without the SII to supplement their modest application of Super 301, Congress would either resort to protectionist legislation or otherwise compromise their ability to conduct trade policy with an emphasis on multilateral liberalization. An alternative to GATT-based multilateralism − 'managed' or 'results-oriented' trade − was gathering support at the time within Congress, the American business community, and among others frustrated by Japan's persistent trade surpluses.[19] Administration officials, seeking to stem this tide, explicitly cast the SII − the idea of fundamentally reforming Japan − as an alternative to managed trade.[20]

Nevertheless, it is arguable that the administration overestimated the potential wrath of Congress. When frustration with Japan peaked in the mid-1980s, Congress had turned primarily not to protectionism − although fire-breathing threats of it were routine − but to aggressive market-opening measures. Super 301 was the pinnacle of congressional frustration and response. In accordance with its wishes, the administration did use Super 301 and duly named Japan as the primary target. Moreover, the law did grant executive officials wide discretion in choosing priority practices for negotiation. While some in Congress might quibble with the administration's choices, even ardent supporters of

17 Noted by Senator Lloyd Bentsen, *U.S.-Japan Structural Impediments Initiative*, part 2, 6-7 November 1989, 2.
18 *Ibid*, part 1, 20 July 1989, 1-2.
19 See *Analysis of the U.S.-Japan Trade Problem*, Report of the Advisory Committee for Trade Policy and Negotiations (Washington, February 1989).
20 Statement of John Taylor, Council of Economic Advisers, in *U.S.-Japan Structural Impediments Initiative*, part 3, 5 March 1990, 16.

Super 301 conceded that to use it against the whole range of Japanese practices would be impractical, in that it would force the administration either to retaliate massively against Japan or to concede by its failure to retaliate that Super 301 was a bluff.[21] The executive could have plausibly argued, without proposing the SII, that it had complied with the intent of the legislation and should now be given a chance to show results.

The principal concern of Congress was the trade deficit and here time was on the administration's side. While remaining very high, the bilateral deficit had peaked in 1987 and begun a descent in 1988 which continued in 1989 (see figure 1). The trend should not have been unexpected, given the major exchange rate adjustment of 1985-7. American exports to Japan increased from $28 billion in 1987 to $38 billion in 1988, and to almost $45 billion in 1989.[22] In at least some sectors in which the United States government had pressed Japan to open markets, exports had achieved especially rapid growth.[23] Between 1985 and 1989, the overall volume of manufactured goods imported by Japan doubled.[24] To be sure, and as the administration continually noted, the adjustment in trade with Japan was taking place more slowly than that with other industrial and even some developing states. The point is not that the Japan 'problem' had been solved or that structural barriers did not exist, but that the administration could plausibly have argued that progress was being made and that even the modest application of Super 301 was sufficient in itself to keep the pressure on Japan to increase imports.

Similarly, the administration may have overplayed the potential for Congress to disrupt its GATT strategy. The authority to conduct the Uruguay Round had already been delegated and

21 Statement of R.K. Morris, National Association of Manufacturers, in *ibid*, part 2, 6-7 November 1989, 12.
22 International Monetary Fund, *Direction of Trade Statistics Yearbook 1990*, 402.
23 *Analysis of the U.S.-Japan Trade Problem*, chap 6.
24 Statement of Robert Lawrence in *U.S.-Japan Structural Impediments Initiative*, part 2, 6-7 November 1989, 58, and, more generally, Edward Lincoln, *Japan's Unequal Trade* (Washington: Brookings Institution 1990).

those negotiations were not to conclude until the end of 1990, with most of the important bargaining expected to take place at that time. In this regard, the decision on the application of Super 301 in 1989 was not nearly as important as that of 1990 would be, when it would be fresh in the minds of eleventh-hour negotiators. If anything, by initiating the ambitious sii, the administration may have inadvertently increased its own burden. Shortly after the sii announcement, Senator Baucus, one of the staunchest supporters of Super 301, asserted that in the long run the sii was more important than Super 301 and that 'only sii holds out the prospect of significantly improving the overall bilateral trade deficit.'[25] Baucus later characterized the sii as 'the most important trade negotiation that the u.s. has ever entered into' and, in the event the sii did not 'succeed' on schedule, threatened to propose legislation that would require the administration to initiate Super 301 investigations into the major structural barriers to trade with Japan.[26]

NEGOTIATING THE SII: THE IMPORTANCE OF UNITY
The manner in which the sii was launched left considerable room for officials to devise a negotiating strategy. The Bush-Uno announcement provided little guidance, referring only generally to a need to identify and resolve structural problems in both countries. The initial statement of Hills mentioned only that the negotiations would focus on 'anticompetitive practices' such as bid-rigging and group boycotts and 'major structural barriers' such as Japan's distribution system and pricing mechanisms.[27]

The negotiating strategy eventually adopted by the Bush administration was noteworthy in two respects. First, American officials decided explicitly not to set specific negotiating priorities. They divided Japanese structural impediments into six major areas: savings and investment, land use, pricing mechanisms, the distribution system, keiretsu relationships, and exclu-

---

25 U.S.-Japan Structural Impediments Initiative, part 1, 20 July 1989, 1-2.
26 Ibid, part 2, 6-7 November 1989, 1.
27 'Super 301 Trade Liberalization Priorities.'

sionary business practices. Each area was subdivided further, barriers were identified, and changes recommended. Overall, officials identified literally hundreds of impediments and proposed remedies. However they made no effort to emphasize in negotiation those barriers whose elimination would have the greatest impact on the trade imbalance. In fact, they did not even attempt to calculate the trade impact of any particular barrier or category of barriers.

The second interesting aspect of the negotiating strategy was that officials made no effort to link the remedies they proposed with those the Japanese suggested. While American officials were identifying Japanese impediments, their Japanese counterparts were identifying America's own impediments to its ability to balance its trade and payments. Japan's list of such impediments included savings and investment patterns, anti-trust and environmental regulations, leveraged buyouts, offshore production by United States firms, labour training, and even the failure of the United States to adopt the metric system. In the negotiations, however, the United States and Japanese agendas proceeded on separate tracks. In a typical negotiating session, one day was devoted to American 'points of interest' and the next day to Japanese ones. No effort was made to relate the two agendas to one another or to make trade-offs across them (for example, 'we'll reduce our budget deficit if you increase your spending'). The SII was, in effect, two negotiations rather than one.

The negotiating approach of the United States is a puzzling one from the perspective of relative gains theory, which would expect the American team to set negotiating priorities based on a comparison of the benefits likely to accrue to the United States and Japan from the adoption of any particular proposal.[28] The United States would likely emphasize those barriers whose

28 Relative gains calculations in trade policy are discussed in Joseph M. Grieco, *Cooperation among Nations: Europe, America, and Non-Tariff Barriers to Trade* (Ithaca NY: Cornell University Press 1990), and Michael Mastanduno, 'Do relative gains matter? America's response to Japanese industrial policy,' *International Security* 16(summer 1991), 73-113.

removal would benefit American producers at the expense of Japanese ones or which would minimize advantages currently enjoyed by Japanese.

In practice, however, the United States team made no such calculations, either explicitly or implicitly. To be sure, certain American proposals were framed with relative gains in mind. The USTR emphasized the Japanese government's exclusionary procurement practices and toleration of anti-competitive behaviour not only because they were market-distorting but because they were perceived to grant Japanese firms important advantages in international competition. Similarly, breaking Japanese firms of the habit of purchasing intermediate goods and components through long-term relationships from Japanese suppliers (for example, auto parts) was deemed likely to enhance in particular the competitive position of American firms which were perceived to hold a comparative advantage in such products based on their performance in third markets. Such proposals, however, were assigned no more weight by the United States negotiators than others which might actually strengthen Japan competitively (spending to improve Japan's transportation infrastructure, for example) or which might benefit East Asian or European producers more than those based in the United States (for example, proposals to move more consumer goods through the Japanese distribution system).[29] The United States team neither set priorities based on relative gains nor made the kind of calculations necessary to do so.

An emphasis on absolute gains would have required United States officials to make a different calculation and to focus not on 'who would gain more' but on the combination of proposals likely to enable the United States to gain the most, independent of the gains of Japan. Again, such calculations were absent. Top American officials were unclear about what they hoped to gain; some stressed reduction in the trade imbalance, others empha-

29 David Russell, 'America's hollow victory,' *Business Tokyo* 4(June 1990), 32-5.

sized market access regardless of the trade imbalance.[30] More importantly, there was no systematic effort to sort through the hundreds of American (and Japanese) proposals and estimate their probable impact according to either criterion. Clearly, some proposals were likely to have a greater impact on the bilateral imbalance than others; compare, for example, the Japanese proposal that the United States reduce its federal deficit with the American proposal that the Japanese work fewer weekends. The failure of the executive to set priorities or to quantify the impact of particular proposals clearly frustrated members of Congress who wondered aloud how the negotiating team would know whether it had succeeded in the SII.[31]

A sensitivity to absolute gains would have led American officials to emphasize bargaining and trade-offs *across* the American and Japanese agendas. Japan and the United States were not working at cross-purposes; both were seeking measures to rectify bilateral trade and payments imbalances. If the United States team had sought to maximize absolute gains, it would have focused on both American and Japanese practices that impeded adjustment. Instead, the United States team emphasized Japanese barriers and devoted relatively little time and effort to an analysis of Japan's proposals. The United States frequently acknowledged Japan's criticisms, but in response it typically emphasized either that the administration had already adopted remedies stressed by Japan (for example, budget deficit reduction, relaxation of export controls) or that proposed remedies were unnecessary (for example, there was no need to eliminate 'buy American' regulations because United States regulations were more transparent than those of other governments, and in

---

30 The State and Treasury Departments stressed bilateral deficit reduction, while the USTR focused on market access. The deputy United States trade representative, Lynn Williams, stated that the United States should pursue the SII even if it had a trade surplus with Japan. See *U.S.-Japan Structural Impediments Initiative*, part 1, 20 July 1989, 6-7.
31 Comments of Senators Baucus and John Heinz, *ibid*, 10, 13-15.

any case the United States was pushing for the comprehensive reform of government procurement practices in the GATT). Critics of the SII in the United States often argued that if the Bush administration really wanted to eliminate the trade and payments imbalance, it should simply embrace Japan's proposals; American proposals, ironically, were 'unlikely to make a dent.'[32]

The negotiating strategy of the United States was consistent with the Bush administration's overriding emphasis on loss avoidance. First, by not setting priorities, the United States minimized bureaucratic conflict. As was evident in the FSX and Super 301 debates, the Bush administration was profoundly divided on how to deal with Japan. The Department of Commerce and the USTR were often pitted against the Department of State, the Council of Economic Advisers, and the Office of Management and Budget on trade issues, and Treasury clashed with other agencies on macro-economic issues. A commitment to set priorities would have forced the administration to confront these divisions and possibly to determine which agency's approach and which issues were most important. By not setting priorities, each agency could bring to the SII table its particular concerns and preferred solutions to the Japan problem. Thus, Treasury could stress savings and investment issues and Japan's inflated land values; the USTR, business-government collusion and exclusionary practices by Japanese firms; State, the inefficiency of Japan's distribution system; Commerce, the pricing mechanisms that render American exports less attractive in Japan. Other agencies – Justice, Agriculture, the Council of Economic Advisers, Labor – were brought into the process to offer institutional expertise and to advance their own concerns and remedies vis-à-vis Japan. The proposals put forward by the United States represented the sum of the concerns of the various executive agencies, from the significant to the trivial, and, not surprisingly, there were numerous areas of overlap.

It was critical for the executive to minimize bureaucratic con-

32 Dornbusch statement, 98.

flict because it feared the loss of control over trade policy to Congress. The sii was conceived to demonstrate control, to show Congress that the executive could handle and resolve the Japan problem without the need for drastic congressional initiatives. Bureaucratic conflict, especially out in the open, would suggest that the executive could not handle the problem and would increase the incentives for members of Congress to seize the initiative. In public hearings, senators dissected the statements of officials for signs of discord, noting with concern that Japan would easily exploit inter-agency divisions and render the sii impotent.[33] There was also concern over which agency was truly in charge. Hardliners preferred the USTR, and Senator Danforth expressed his dismay at the prominent role of the State Department, suggesting that State was a pushover in negotiations because it was afraid to offend Japan.[34] Senators and private sector officials voiced the additional concern that American negotiators typically were 'laughed at' or not taken seriously by Japan, because they tended to be divided and unprepared.[35]

Executive officials obviously needed to shed these images. They deemed unity, consensus, and exhaustive preparation to be as important, if not more so, as the substance of the sii. Officials took great satisfaction, for example, from the reports in the press after the first round of talks that Japanese negotiators expressed surprise at how well prepared their American counterparts had been. The leaders of the United States negotiating team were also quick to point out to Congress that after several rounds, their team had held together cohesively while that of Japan had shown some fissures.[36] The under secretary of commerce stated before Congress: 'I, frankly, having been involved in trade issues since 1983 in the executive branch, think the u.s. Government has already gotten something out of the structural impediments initiative, in that you have five Government officials sitting here

33 *U.S.-Japan Structural Impediments Initiative*, part 1, 20 July 1989, 19.
34 *Ibid*, 11.
35 Comment by T. Boone Pickens, *ibid*, part 2, 6-7 November 1989, 32.
36 Comment of Lynn Williams in *ibid*, part 3, 5 March 1990, 20.

who are representing agencies that are the focal point of u.s.
trade concerns in absolute agreement on what the nature of the
problem is.'[37]

A second piece of evidence that the Bush administration's
emphasis was on loss avoidance is the relative lack of interest of
the United States team in Japan's agenda or in trade-offs across
the two agendas. To be sure, American negotiators were uncom-
fortable at the thought of changing domestic practices on the
advice of Japan, even though they obviously had no qualms
about demanding similar types of large-scale changes from
Japan. American – and Japanese – officials were used to trade
negotiations as a one-way street. Moreover, to embrace Japan's
agenda would be to acknowledge that the administration was not
doing all it could to maximize American competitiveness –
clearly a message it did not want to send to the Congress.

Thus, even though executive officials readily acknowledged
the macro-economic causes of the bilateral imbalance, for them
the real issue of the sii had to be Japanese impediments. In the
short run, progress in attacking those barriers, not in reducing
the federal budget deficit, was needed to hold off the feared
congressional assault on trade policy. Importantly, officials
believed the same to hold true for the long run. They viewed the
unique institutional structure of Japan, and the enormous economic success it spawned, as possessing the potential to destroy
the GATT-based trading system. In the early rounds of the sii,
United States officials went to great lengths to establish the international 'uniqueness' of Japan – its exceptionally high prices, its
low propensity to import manufactured goods, its remarkably lax
anti-trust enforcement. The United States team made much of
academic studies, and Japanese sources, which established these
points.[38] They believed it was critical to demonstrate that Japan
was not only different from the United States but also out of step

37 Comment of Michael Farren in *ibid*, 22.
38 See, for example, Mordechai E. Kreinin, 'How closed is Japan's market? Additional
   evidence,' *World Economy* (December 1988), 529-41, and Robert Z. Lawrence, 'Does
   Japan import too little? Closed minds or markets,' in *Brookings Papers on Economic
   Activity*, no 2 (Washington: Brookings Institution 1987).

with the advanced industrial world more generally. This approach greatly irritated Japanese officials (a Ministry of Finance official pounded the table in round one, shouting 'we are not unique!'), in part because it was associated with the 'revisionist' attack on Japan gaining popularity at the time in the United States.[39] American officials assured their Japanese counterparts that both the critique and the medicine of the SII were for their own good. It was necessary to integrate Japan, and its massive economy, more fully into the world trading game, so that other players did not eventually opt out in frustration.

Put differently, United States officials believed that they and the world economy had reached a critical juncture. One rather rocky road led to the SII and the other to managed trade. For the Bush administration the choice was simple, because to take the latter path meant the ultimate demise of the GATT. The Brookings economist, Robert Lawrence, in rejecting managed trade and defending the SII, captured nicely the administration's sentiment: 'If you believe, as I do, that at some point in the future, twenty years down the road, what we want is not simply a single European economy, but a single world economy, then we have to learn how to adjust the structural friction points that occur across economies.'[40] The perceived danger, of course, was that the SII gamble might fail and that Congress would turn to managed trade – supported by a frustrated business community, an integrated European Community, and even a 'revisionist' academic community, all convinced that the Japanese system was incapable of fundamental change and simply must be contained.[41]

ENDGAME: 'HOW COULD WE WALK AWAY?'

The first several rounds of talks ended in stalemate. United States officials brandished their detailed lists of the structural

39 See Clyde Prestowitz, *Trading Places: How We Are Giving our Future to Japan and How to Reclaim It* (rev ed; New York: Basic Books 1990), and Karel van Wolferen, *The Enigma of Japanese Power* (New York: Knopf 1989).
40 *U.S.-Japan Structural Impediments Initiative*, part 2, 6-7 November 1989, 67.
41 See James Fallows, 'Containing Japan,' *Atlantic Monthly* 263(May 1989), 40-54.

ailments of the Japanese economy; Japan responded, in effect, that it wasn't broke and thus there was no need to fix it. The United States team expressed publicly its frustration and impatience after the second and third rounds, in November 1989 and February 1990.[42] This impatience arose from the fact that the administration was negotiating on a timetable set by Congress. By the end of March, the 1990 National Trade Estimates Report was due, and by the end of April the administration's 1990 list of priority countries and practices under Super 301 would be required.

Administration officials, in particular Hills, clearly wished to avoid any further use of Super 301. The 1989 designation had earned the United States widespread criticism in multilateral forums, and the final bargaining to complete the Uruguay Round was to begin in the summer of 1990.[43] Super 301 would be a major distraction, an excuse for recalcitrant governments not to make concessions in that forum. Without a strong interim SII agreement, however, the administration feared that it would be politically impossible to resist the pressure to name Japan again. Thus, as one USTR official put it privately, the United States really could not 'walk away' from the SII.

Obviously, Japan wished to avoid being singled out again as a Super 301 target. The price, however, was high, for the United States was demanding not just trade concessions but profound changes in long-standing domestic institutions and relationships. Moreover, Japanese negotiators were irritated at being forced to accept responsibility for a set of problems they believed to be caused by the mismanagement of the American economy. They were all the more irritated because the United States also expected them simultaneously to concede in the three Super 301 negotiations from 1989, negotiations in which they initially refused even to take part.

---

42 See Charles Smith, 'Fear and loathing,' *Far Eastern Economic Review*, 8 March 1990, 53.

43 See William Dullforce, 'US faces fusillade of censure in GATT council,' *Financial Times*, 22 June 1989, 8.

Breaking the sii deadlock required intervention at the highest level. Early in March President Bush called for a meeting
with Prime Minister Kaifu. The two leaders agreed on the urgent
need to co-operate, and Kaifu agreed to give guidance to the
Japanese team to that effect.[44] An important electoral victory for
the Liberal Democratic Party in March strengthened the prime
minister's hand. The problem remained, however, that the
United States was demanding hundreds of changes in Japan's
political economy. Clearly, Japan would not be willing to concede on everything; to conclude the sii required the United
States team to abandon its initial strategy and set priorities.
American negotiators continued to push for change in all areas,
but as the deadline for an interim agreement approached, three
issues emerged for special emphasis – bolstering Japan's anti-
monopoly enforcement, reforming its Large Retail Store Law,
and increasing its government's spending on public infrastructure. Each was a difficult issue for the Japanese government. The
first required an increase in the power of the relatively impotent
Japan Fair Trade Commission, at the expense of the Ministry of
International Trade and Industry and powerful corporations.
The second would alienate small shopkeepers in Japan, a key
source of the government's electoral support. The third infringed
upon a critical area of sovereign autonomy – the Japanese
budget process – which was guarded by the powerful Ministry of
Finance.

How did the Bush administration select its endgame priorities? The key factor remained the maintenance of inter-agency
harmony and cohesion. Each area was of special concern to one
of the three co-chairs of the negotiating team and their agencies,
none of which, in light of the massive commitment of time and
effort, could afford to walk away from the sii empty-handed.
Both Hills and her deputy, Lynn Williams, were experts in anti-
trust law and believed it was crucial to induce a shift in Japan

44 Comments of the assistant secretary of the treasury, Charles Dallara, and Lynn
   Williams in *U.S.-Japan Structural Impediments Initiative*, part 3, 5 March
   1990, 27.

away from its traditional pattern of market-distorting business-government collusion. The Japanese government should resemble its United States counterpart in seeking out and destroying concentrations of corporate power. To the State Department, the Large Retail Store Law was a dramatic example of all that was wrong with the Japanese distribution system – entrenched interests blocking the free play of market forces at the expense of the Japanese consumer. To the Treasury Department, long the champion of macroeconomic 'reflation' strategies for Japan and the Federal Republic of Germany, a significant increase in Japanese government spending would help to reduce the gap between savings and investment in Japan – the enabling factor for Japan's trade surplus and Treasury's principal sɪɪ concern. The Justice Department strongly supported the USTR's emphasis and worked closely with it in devising proposals for anti-trust reform. Finally, the Council of Economic Advisers was satisfied that the proposals emphasized market mechanisms rather than market-sharing arrangements or 'affirmative action' programmes for American firms.[45]

Thus, in setting priorities, the administration managed to avoid the bureaucratic dissension that might lead Congress to question the efficacy of its trade policy. That bureaucratic politics, rather than relative gains concerns, drove the American endgame strategy is readily apparent. For example, infrastructure has been a weak link in Japan's otherwise powerful economy; while helping to close the savings-investment gap, the increased spending demanded by the Treasury would also improve Japan's communications and transportation sectors, making its industrial economy more efficient in the process. The *Wall Street Journal* noted that in this regard, Washington was 'unintentionally doing Tokyo a big favor.'[46] Similarly, many observers noted that reforming the Large Retail Store Law was likely to enhance the

---

45 United States negotiators did welcome an import incentive programme from Japan's Ministry of International Trade and Industry but stressed that it would not 'count' as a structural change. See Amy Borrus, 'Tokyo unveils this year's "buy American" plan,' *Business Week*, 15 January 1990, 38-9.

46 'Prompted by the U.S., Tokyo slates trillion in domestic spending,' *Wall Street Journal*, 3 January 1991, 1.

position of Japanese corporate conglomerates which had been restrained by it. To the extent imports were facilitated, the likely beneficiaries would be European retailers at the high end of the market and Asian ones at the low end. A senior Japanese official noted the 'paradox' that 'the u.s. is expending great energy to change the structure of our retail system in a way that will have little effect on imports in general and none at all on American goods.'[47] Arguably, the focus on anti-trust issues served a relative gains purpose, to the extent that government-business and inter-firm collusion enhanced the position of Japanese firms at the expense of their foreign counterparts. If relative gains had been stressed, however, other items on the USTR's agenda – administrative guidance, government targeting and procurement strategies, and the exclusionary procurement habits of Japanese manufacturing firms – would also have been granted priority in the endgame.

If absolute gains had been the priority, the United States team would have sought in the endgame to bring together the American and Japanese proposals likely to maximize trade and payments adjustment. Instead, the endgame focused, under the watchful eye of Congress, on the scope and extent of Japanese concessions. In the interim report, the United States dutifully acknowledged the structural impediments pointed out by Japan but offered little in the way of new steps or initiatives to be taken.[48] Subsequent to the agreement, Japan complained publicly that the United States had broken even its modest pledges of good intentions – for example, in the area of federal budget deficit reduction.[49]

In an exhausting eighty-hour negotiating session over four days, the United States and Japan reached an interim SII agreement in April 1990. Japan made concessions in principle in each of the three priority areas (as well as in many other areas) and

47 Russell, 'America's hollow victory,' 34.
48 'Interim Report and Assessment of the U.S.-Japan Working Group on the Structural Impediments Initiative,' joint press release, 5 April 1990.
49 Steven Weisman, 'Trade talks with Japan face stormy reopening,' *New York Times*, 13 January 1991, 14.

promised to flesh out more specific concessions by the signing of a final agreement in June. At roughly the same time, American and Japanese negotiators reached agreement in each of the three Super 301 negotiations – satellites, supercomputers, and forest products. Hills went before Congress and announced her satisfaction with the 'blueprint and downpayment' she had received from Japan. She also made clear her intention not to name Japan, or any other country, a Super 301 target for 1990.[50]

The reaction of Congress was mixed. Some senators publicly supported Hills, arguing that Congress must grant the nation's trade negotiator the discretion to choose the means she deemed most appropriate in pursuit of United States interests. Others remained unconvinced. Senators Danforth and Lloyd Bentsen told Hills it would be a serious mistake to emphasize the Uruguay Round at the expense of enforcing the law of the land. Hills stood firm and stated that Congress must give her 'just a little longer tether.' 'Give me eight months,' she said, pointing ahead to the anticipated completion of the Uruguay Round, 'to achieve the objectives you and I can agree on.'[51]

The Super 301 deadline passed without any designations. After several more rounds of talks, the United States and Japan completed the final SII agreement in June 1990. The United States achieved most of what it wanted in the way of more specific commitments, and the two sides agreed to a series of meetings, over three years, to monitor implementation of the agreement.[52]

CONCLUSION

This chapter began by posing the manner in which decisions are framed as an intervening variable between the dependent variable of co-operation and the independent variables usually

---

50 Statement of Carla Hills in United States, Congress, Senate, Committee on Finance, *United States-Japan Trade Relations*, hearings, 101st Cong, 2nd sess, 25 April 1990.
51 *Ibid*, 1, 7, 22.
52 *Joint Report of the U.S.-Japan Working Group on the Structural Impediments Initiative*, 28 June 1990.

advanced to explain it. The case-study suggests that framing is a reasonably important variable. The Bush administration framed the relationship of the United States with Japan, and in particular the problem of trade and payments imbalance, in terms of loss avoidance. Consistent with the expectations of prospect theory, administration officials initially exaggerated the scope and magnitude of their potential losses. They also proved willing to adopt a risky strategy to avert those losses. The SII, given its scope and timetables and the expectations it created, was a considerable gamble for an administration that had earned an early reputation for conservatism in foreign policy. The focus on loss avoidance prompted American officials to initiate this co-operative venture and to work with Japan to ensure its successful conclusion.

This is not to suggest that framing, by itself, explains the co-operative outcome of the SII. Two other factors proved critical: the high-level intervention of Bush and Kaifu, which broke the negotiating deadlock, and the constant pressure from the United States Congress, which pushed the two sides to co-operate and helped each to resist the temptation to hold out for more in the negotiations. In the end, the executive both feared Congress and used it effectively as a source of leverage, convincing the Japanese that they would suffer along with the executive if Congress took control of United States trade policy. Such threats were credible because the United States controlled what was vital to Japanese security – access to the American market and the maintenance of an open world economy. Framing facilitated co-operation but does not provide a necessary and sufficient explanation for it.

If American officials had framed in terms of relative gains, the outcome would have been different. If the SII had still been pursued, it would have been negotiated differently and the endgame would have been harder to complete successfully. The issues likely to have been given priority in such a scenario – Japan's targeting of advanced technology, the exclusionary procurement of Japanese firms, the very existence of *keiretsu* – would have generated a set of endgame proposals which the Japanese government and Japanese industry would have found much harder to swallow. Moreover, the United States government would have been less inhibited about walking away from the table without an agreement.

The Bush administration had already framed several issues with Japan in terms of relative gains, in particular negotiations over satellites, supercomputers, and the FSX.[53] Those cases, however, involved fractious debate within the executive, and agencies sympathetic to relative gains concerns such as Commerce and the USTR enjoyed strong positions. In the SII, consensus within the executive was a key concern, and at least one strong advocate of relative gains thinking, the Commerce Department, was relegated to a secondary role.

Framing in terms of absolute gains might have altered the prospects for co-operation, though less significantly. Negotiations on the SII would have been more genuinely a two-way street, and the United States would have been more inclined to respond positively to Japan's agenda. Trade-offs across issues might have enabled American officials to extract even more concessions from Japan. Overall, the potential was greater for an agreement that led to meaningful change in the trade and payments imbalance. An absolute gains strategy, however, would have required the executive to confront directly the difficult problems of domestic adjustment. It was easier to focus on changing Japan than on changing the United States. Equally important, maximizing absolute gains would have required United States officials to recognize the legitimate right of their 'junior' negotiating partner not only to advance criticisms – in itself a significant step – but also to expect the United States government to accept proposed changes and carry them out, even if that were costly in terms of domestic politics. That is, American officials would have had to grant Japan what the United States routinely expected of Japan, and they were simply unprepared to do that.

Domestic structure best explains the Bush administration's

---

53 Mastanduno, 'Do relative gains matter?'

willingness to frame in terms of loss avoidance and to embrace the SII. The executive conducts trade policy under the watchful, constitutionally mandated eye of the Congress. During the 1980s, Congress posed an increasing threat to the executive's control of the trade policy process and to its preferred global trade strategy. Relations with Japan served as the lightning rod of that congressional challenge. The SII was perceived as an effective, albeit risky, way to cope with the threat, in both the short and long term.[54]

Domestic structure provides general incentives for United States officials to frame trade policy in terms of loss avoidance. In its pursuit of a consistent, coherent policy, the executive must be wary of challenges from Congress, from a business community with multiple points of access to the system, from within because of profound inter-agency divisions, and even from the general public. At the outset of the Structural Impediments Initiative, officials were cognizant of polls suggesting that 68 per cent of Americans felt Japan was a greater threat to United States security than the Soviet Union, 69 per cent favoured limiting the amount of Japanese goods allowed into the United States, 59 per cent favoured restricting technology transfer to Japan, and 79 per cent favoured requiring a certain amount of American products to be allowed into Japan.[55] It is not surprising that the temptation was great to dispel such attitudes and provide for United States economic security by launching an effort to remake Japan in the image of the United States – just as American officials had long sought to remake the Soviet Union in the American image in the interest of national military security.

54 As this paragraph suggests and as Timothy McKeown notes explicitly in the concluding chapter of this collection, the decision to pursue the SII and to emphasize unity in the negotiating strategy can be understood plausibly within the framework of utility maximization. At the same time, prospect theory and its focus on the cognitive dynamics of loss aversion plausibly explain why the administration adopted a risky strategy and tended to exaggerate its potential losses. The evidence of this case-study does not suggest the supremacy of either approach.

55 The complete results are found in Business Week/Harris Poll, *Business Week*, 7 August 1989, 51.

Framing matters. And in thinking about how decision-makers frame, it is important to consider the avoidance of loss as well as the pursuit of gain. The emerging debate over the conditions under which states pursue relative or absolute gain is important, but it may be too narrowly focused. While obviously not supplanting expected utility theories, prospect theory and its emphasis on loss avoidance yields insights into the foreign policy decision-making process that should not be ignored.

Three

Co-developing the FSX fighter: the domestic calculus of international co-operation

DEBORA SPAR

THE PUZZLE OF THE FSX

In November 1988 the United States and Japan formally agreed to co-operate in the development and production of a new breed of aircraft, a sophisticated fighter dubbed the FSX (Fighter Support Experimental). Under the memorandum of understanding that was signed, the two sides were to collaborate on all aspects of the aircraft's development, sharing the revenues, the risks, and virtually all of the technology. Barring technical difficulties, the agreement provided for the 'co-development' of Japan's next generation of fighter aircraft, with production to commence in 1997. In many respects, the FSX agreement was a classic case of co-operation for mutual gain. The agreement promised to strengthen an alliance that both sides deemed critical, to enhance the security of the Pacific region, and to provide both countries with cutting-edge technology. In addition, co-development was attractive because it was, to a large extent, merely an extension of a co-operative relationship that had existed since the end of World War II.[1]

The specific decision to co-operate on the FSX is not, there-

Assistant Professor, Graduate School of Business Administration, Harvard University, Boston, Massachusetts.

1 Soon after the United States dismantled Japan's aircraft industry, American firms began transferring technology to Japan and entering into technical partnerships with Japanese firms. For a description of some of these early arrangements, see David C. Mowery, *Alliance Politics and Economics: Multinational Joint Ventures in Commercial Aircraft* (Cambridge MA: Ballinger 1987), esp. 52-6.

fore, particularly surprising from a theoretical point of view. On the contrary, it might be seen as entirely consistent with the expectations of either conventional realist or liberal theory. A realist, for instance, could argue that military co-operation between the United States and Japan is explained by their mutual desire to reduce the threat of a Soviet attack. By the same token, a liberal could explain the decision in terms of an institutionalized relationship, a desire for mutual gain, and a reduction of transaction costs. In either case, co-operation on the FSX does not pose a puzzle.

What is entirely puzzling, however, is how close the final agreement came to being scuttled. Repeatedly, various groups in Japan and the United States tried to veto the co-development option and replace it with a unilateral policy. Voicing their claims largely in terms of national pride and economic competitiveness, these groups vehemently opposed co-development and, in a series of incidents described below, nearly gained sufficient strength to topple the programme. In the end, the co-operative option prevailed, but we are left with two distinct questions. Why was the co-operative solution very nearly overturned? And how did it finally survive?

This chapter will suggest that both questions can be addressed by focusing on the decision-making process and, in particular, on the way in which the situation was framed by those involved. Either realism or liberal institutionalism can explain why the decision to co-operate was in the interests of both parties, but neither can adequately explain why this decision was still so difficult to make. Standard theories of interest group behaviour and public policy can help to explain how co-operation was hampered by domestic battles, but they are not wholly satisfactory in explaining how relevant actors perceived their interests, and why they ultimately accepted the decision to co-operate.

I will argue that some of the observations provided by prospect theory help to fill these explanatory gaps in the story of the FSX. More specifically, it appears that domestic groups chose to enter the policy-making process precisely because they had framed the problem of the FSX project in a different way from the central decision-makers. This different frame, in turn, led them to a very different evaluation of the benefits of co-operation. In this sense, the act of framing can be seen as a variable that intervenes between political structures and the actual process of decision. Similarly, the domestic debate was resolved in part by the ability of one coalition to frame the problem more compellingly – that is, to offer a more powerful and persuasive description of the costs and benefits at stake. And in this case the most powerful domestic arguments were framed in terms of maintaining the status quo and avoiding absolute losses. While a number of internal groups initially defined the FSX issue primarily in terms of relative gains, and thus had distinctly different policy preferences, their definitions as well as their preferences were eventually overruled.

In the discussion that follows, I divide the decision-making process into two overarching phases. The first describes the initial negotiations between the United States and Japan and the subsequent decision to co-develop the FSX. The second describes the events that unfolded once American negotiators brought the memorandum of understanding home. The story itself is a messy one, filled with bureaucratic infighting, personal vendettas, and high-level arm-twisting. The central questions, however, should remain clear. Why was co-operation on the FSX project so nearly scuttled? And how was it finally revived?

FRAMING THE DECISION TO CO-OPERATE
The decision in Japan
Initially, the FSX project had nothing to do with co-operation. It was entirely the brainchild of the Japanese air force,[2] which determined in 1981 that its aging F-1 fighter needed to be replaced by a newer and more sophisticated model. Specifically,

---

2 Officially, the air force is known as the Air Self-Defence Force, and the division that specifically concerned itself with the FSX decision was the Air Staff Office. Both of these agencies are subordinate to the Japanese Defence Agency.

officials in the Japanese Defence Agency (JDA) calculated that
they needed to acquire a state-of-the-art fighter, one that could
be used 'to prevent the enemy from landing in our country and
to support our ground forces by attacking from the air the enemy
units that have landed, with a secondary role as an air combat
interceptor.'[3] On technical grounds, there were a number of aircraft that fitted the Japanese criteria, including the F-16 of General Dynamics, the F-18 of McDonnell-Douglas, and the Tor-
nado of Panavia. All of these aircraft were relatively inexpensive,
extremely well regarded, and capable of providing the close
ground support that the Japanese forces needed. This time, however, it gradually became clear that the top decision-makers in
the JDA explicitly did not want to buy a foreign model despite
the obvious benefits of doing so. Instead, they were determined
to replace the F-1 with a domestically developed fighter.

The reasons for this decision are not entirely clear, but several
factors appear to have been important. To begin with, the Japanese simply wanted to ensure that some share of their military
hardware was being built at home. The F-1 had been the product of indigenous development, and even though it was widely
regarded as an inferior aircraft, it was still a source of some pride
to officials in the JDA, who saw it as one sign of Japan's independence from the United States. Accordingly, they were
extremely reluctant to replace the F-1 with a foreign-built
fighter. In addition, these officials recognized the technological
importance of a fighter programme. They were anxious to test
the applicability of recent Japanese advances in electronics and
composite materials and to take advantage of the new technolo-
gies that would undoubtedly be derived from the development of
an advanced fighter. Finally, and perhaps most importantly, the
JDA wanted to use the fighter programme to foster Japan's nas-
cent aviation industry. Japanese firms had been assembling aircraft and supplying components, but they had never built a

3 Cited in Otsuki Shinji, 'Battle over the FSX fighter: who won?' *Japan Quarterly*
35(April/June 1988), 139-45.

sophisticated aircraft by themselves and had yet to gain significant experience with systems integration – the process by which
all of the intricate workings of an aircraft are made to fit
together. If Japanese firms could get the experience of developing the FSX by themselves, then they would be well positioned to
break into competitive international aviation markets.[4] Taken
together, these factors suggest that the JDA initially conceived of
the FSX almost entirely in terms of the relative gains that the
project was likely to yield.

Other agencies in the Japanese government, however, were
more circumspect about the military's ambitious plans and more
concerned about maintaining the status quo. While they all
shared the ultimate goal of building a competitive aerospace
industry in Japan, many highly placed officials and influential
bureaucrats were wary of going too fast and of taking any action
that might be perceived as a direct affront to American industry.
In particular, the JDA's proposal for the development of an indigenous fighter ran into some significant opposition from the Ministry of Finance and the Ministry of Foreign Affairs. Citing the
importance of Japan's special relationship with the United States,
both of these agencies argued that the FSX project would be seen
as an arrogant gesture, a sign that Japan was edging away from
its co-operative relationship with the United States and – even
more importantly perhaps – that it was not serious about reducing its burgeoning trade surplus. On political grounds, they
argued, the FSX project simply did not make sense.

Under normal circumstances, such weighty opposition would
have been sufficient to stop the FSX initiative in its tracks, especially because most domestic groups in Japan recognized the
absolute benefits of the alliance with the United States. In this

---

4 The full story of the JDA's decision is considerably more complicated than this
abridged version would suggest. For a more detailed account, see Richard J.
Samuels and Benjamin G. Whipple, 'The FSX and Japan's strategy for
aerospace,' *Technology Review* (October 1989), 43-51, and Masaru Kohno,
'Japanese defense policy making: the FSX selection, 1985-1987,' *Asian Survey*
29(May 1989), 457-79.

instance, however, a number of factors combined to strengthen the JDA's position and to support its proposed initiative. First, the success of earlier indigenous projects such as the T-4 and F-1 made the Japanese reluctant to return to a programme of off-the-shelf purchases. Second, the debate over the FSX played into broader questions of nationalism and national security policy in Japan; with the Japanese economy rapidly becoming a world leader, there was a resurgence of national pride and a growing sense that Japan was becoming a leader and was entitled to greater independence in the international realm. To those espousing this view, the FSX programme promised to provide a tangible symbol of Japan's new status.

Finally, the JDA found a powerful ally in the Ministry of International Trade and Industry (MITI) and in the corporations that form the backbone of Japan's aerospace industry. From the start, the FSX proposal had had the support of MITI's Aircraft and Ordnance Division and of senior MITI officials who viewed military research and development as the catalyst for a competitive civilian aircraft industry. In their eyes co-production was no longer a favoured option, because it did not allow Japanese industry to gain the relative benefits of technological leadership. As long as Japan bought aircraft that were developed in the United States, Japanese firms would remain subcontractors to the powerful aerospace industry. If these firms could develop their own aircraft, however, they could make the leap to prime contractor status and could eventually hope to challenge American dominance of the international aviation market. For these firms, as for the JDA, the absolute gains of the long-term relationship between Japan and the United States were outweighed, momentarily at least, by the relative gains of indigenous development.

Eventually, the JDA and MITI were able to cast the situation largely in terms of their own concerns and to focus the domestic debate on the relative gains of an indigenous programme. In January of 1985, the JDA formally requested a feasibility study of the domestic development of a fighter aircraft; the study, released in September, concluded that, with the exception of the engine, the fighter could indeed be developed within ten years. From that point on, the FSX became the choice of the Japanese government. Although the newly established FSX programme office continued to review outside options, and although it examined a host of American and European aircraft as possible models, it is generally acknowledged that the JDA had made its decision: Japan was going to build a new fighter, and all of the design, technology, and engineering was to be developed in Japan.[5]

Thus, the first phase of the decision on the FSX was framed largely in terms of relative gains. The JDA wanted Japan to demonstrate its independence from the United States, to gain a technological edge over American firms, and – possibly – to pose a challenge to American dominance of the international aviation market. With the FSX project conceived and framed in these terms, a co-operative strategy simply was not a viable option.

The decision in the United States

The news of Japan's desire to develop an indigenous fighter did not come as a complete surprise to defence officials in the United States, who had known for some time that Japan would need a new second-tier fighter and who had suspected that industrial interests would push for the development of an indigenous aircraft. Indeed, because Japan had co-produced the F-15 since 1978, and because the F-1 was an indigenous project, United States officials viewed the FSX as a rather natural progression and as a fairly standard decision in light of Japan's political, economic, and security objectives. What the Pentagon had not expected, however, was the magnitude of the new project and the explicit desire of its planners to eschew any off-the-shelf purchases from the United States. When the option of indigenous

5 The one exception was the fighter's engine, which the Japanese always planned to purchase from abroad. In addition, they acknowledged from the start that the new aircraft would incorporate a significant number of foreign-made components.

development was formally codified in the Japanese cabinet's Mid-Term Defence Plan of 1985, American officials became more concerned about the apparent shift in the tenor of the military relationship between Japan and the United States and about the implications of this shift for the American defence industry.

The first American official to deal formally with the FSX programme was Gregg Rubinstein, the deputy director of the Mutual Defense Assistance Office in Tokyo. Rubinstein, who acted as a liaison officer for both the State Department and the Pentagon, sent a cable to Washington in October 1985, suggesting to his superiors that Japan's plans for an indigenous fighter did not necessarily serve either the security or the military interests of the United States. In his cable, Rubinstein reviewed the three options that had been laid out by the Japanese: to co-produce an F-16 or an F-18; to modify an F-4; or to develop a new aircraft. None of these options, he argued, was truly feasible. Japanese industry would weigh in strongly against the co-production option, because it would not allow industry any wider role than it already had. Likewise, the second option – modification of an existing model – would fall short of the military's demand for a fighter that would meet its specific mission requirements. And finally, Rubinstein argued, for the Japanese to build a fighter wholly by themselves would risk both getting an inferior aircraft and damaging the security relationship with the United States.

Faced with these three alternatives, Rubinstein suggested a fourth course, a middle path between co-production, which the Japanese disdained, and indigenous development, which the United States saw as unlikely. In his cable, he referred to this option as co-development. Rather than acquiescing in Japan's plan to build an indigenous fighter, the United States would instead suggest that the aircraft be built jointly, with Japanese and United States firms collaborating in both the development and the production phases. In this way, Japan would still get the technical experience and the national symbolism that it desired, but the United States would be able to ensure that the fighter met its own defence requirements and that the alliance was not unduly strained by such an overt signal of Japanese autonomy.

Apparently, Rubinstein's cable struck a chord with high-level policy-makers in the Department of Defense and the State Department, and before long, co-development had become the Pentagon's official position on the FSX. Specifically, by late 1985, Pentagon officials had decided that the FSX should be a co-operative project, one which could work to the benefit of both the United States and Japan. The aircraft need not be bought directly off the shelf of an American manufacturer, but neither should it be made entirely by the Japanese. Rather, like the alliance itself, it should be the product of a co-operative effort.

Thus, unlike their Japanese counterparts, United States officials began by conceiving the FSX as a joint project and set their sights on finding a collaborative means of achieving it. In theoretical terms, they were framing the problem in a different way from the Japanese and therefore projected an entirely different set of policy outcomes. To a large extent, of course, this difference in frames can be accounted for by an underlying difference in interests: the Japanese wanted to build their own aircraft, and the Americans preferred to have some part in the action. Still, the precise calculation of interests here is not evident. Did Japan's interests lie primarily in the relative gains of indigenous development or in the enhanced security of its alliance with the United States? Likewise, was the United States more concerned about maintaining security in the Pacific or preserving the international market share of its aviation firms?

The Japanese calculation as of 1985 is fairly clear. Prodded by the JDA and MITI, they had decided to frame the FSX programme largely in terms of relative gains and thus to pursue an independent, non-co-operative solution. In the language of prospect theory, the Japanese had clearly framed their decision with reference to an aspiration level. Their explicit goal was to change the status quo and to push Japan to a higher level of technological expertise and military autonomy. The United States, by contrast, was framing the FSX decision in terms of the status quo. Because its decision-makers were generally pleased with the course of the United States-Japan alliance, they saw no reason to change it and sought only to ensure mutual gains in security. When faced with the idea of the FSX, therefore, their primary concern was to ensure that Japan got the very best fighter possible in order to protect allied forces against Soviet air capabilities in the Pacific.[6] The best way to get such a fighter, in their view, was to base it on an existing American one, presumably the F-16 or the F-18. Thus, in so far as enhanced security was a benefit to both the Japanese and the Americans, they saw co-operation on the FSX as a way to promote absolute gains.

At the same time, however, planners in the Pentagon were not unaware of Japan's desire for relative gains and of the consequences for the United States of a Japanese-built FSX. They realized that an indigenous FSX would mean a loss of business for American firms and a potential challenge to the American share of the international aviation market. They acknowledged, both publicly and in private, that the ideal situation from the American point of view would be for Japan to buy its next generation of fighter aircraft directly from an American manufacturer. Nevertheless, all of the decision-makers concerned were convinced that the Japanese would never agree to do this. As James E. Auer, the Pentagon's special assistant for Japan, put it: 'If this were 1947, we could have done that [convinced the Japanese to buy from the United States]. In 1987, we couldn't. They did have other options.'[7] Or, as another observer noted, 'there [was] no way in hell they were going to buy the plane right off the shelf.'[8] Thus, decision-makers were convinced that the 'buy American' option simply was not feasible; as Rubinstein explained: 'Japan

6 See, for instance, Eduardo Lachica, 'Bush bid to alter U.S.-Japan jet plan ends separation of trade, arms issues,' *Wall Street Journal*, 17 March 1989, A 12.
7 Quoted in Pat Towell, 'U.S.-Japanese warplane deal raises a welter of issues,' *Congressional Quarterly*, 11 March 1989, 535.
8 Michael W. Chinworth, quoted in Bruce Stokes, 'Beat 'em or join 'em,' *National Journal*, 25 February 1989, 461.

was going to develop its own jet plane. The question was whether the United States would participate.'[9]

Given these parameters, co-development seemed the next best thing. While any Japanese involvement in the fighter's development would undoubtedly help boost Japan's relative economic position, at least co-development would enhance co-operation between the two countries, make Japanese technology available to the United States, and reduce the aircraft's cost. Moreover, Pentagon officials recognized that indigenous development of the FSX would set off a storm of criticism in the United States. By developing the plane jointly, they concluded that they could forestall this criticism and still maintain the integrity of the alliance with Japan.

Thus the Americans had a number of very good reasons for wanting to co-operate with the Japanese. Co-development would mean business for American firms, technology for American industry, and enhanced security for United States forces. In theoretical terms, it is not immediately evident which kinds of gains Pentagon officials were most concerned with; presumably, there was no need to consider any trade-offs because co-development would satisfy both relative and absolute gains concerns. If the decision-makers had been completely motivated by relative gains concerns, of course, they might have been expected to insist on an off-the-shelf purchase. But all of the decision-makers seemed to agree that this simply was not a viable option for the Japanese.[10] Thus, the American decision to co-operate is fairly simple to understand and fits rather well within an orthodox utility maximization framework: decision-makers reviewed the options and chose the one that best satisfied their interests. What is somewhat novel about the decision, however, was the creation of

9 Cited in Peter Ennis, 'Inside the Pentagon-Commerce turf war,' *Tokyo Business Today* (October 1989), 23.

10 This is a contentious point. Many observers continue to insist that the Pentagon simply did not push the Japanese hard enough. See, for instance, the description offered in Clyde V. Prestowitz, *Trading Places: How We Are Giving our Future to Japan and How to Reclaim It* (New York: Basic Books 1989), introduction to the paperback edition, 5-58.

a new option rather than just choosing from among those on the table. Even so, this facet of the decision-making process is still largely understandable in an expected utility context.

The next stage

At this point the Japanese and American choices were fundamentally opposed: framing the decision in terms of the status quo, the Americans wanted co-development; framing it in terms of a level of aspiration, the Japanese wanted an indigenous FSX. What United States officials were subsequently able to do, however, was to persuade the Japanese to see the FSX decision in a different light and thus to choose co-operation over indigenous development. The array of interests did not change, and the process did not change. What changed during the next phase of the story was the way in which the Japanese defined the situation and the criteria by which they made their ultimate decision.

Negotiations over the FSX began in earnest in November 1985, when Auer went to Tokyo and floated the idea of co-development with his counterparts at the JDA. Several months later, at a security conference in Hawaii, high-ranking American officials again suggested co-development as a compromise solution for the FSX. The Japanese, as might be expected, were noticeably cool to any suggestion of collaboration. They never explicitly rejected the option; indeed, they claimed to be seriously considering using an American aircraft as the model for the FSX. But in numerous ways they made it clear to United States officials that an indigenous fighter was still their overriding objective. For most of 1986 and 1987, therefore, the two sides went back and forth, each acknowledging publicly that a compromise was desirable, but neither knowing how to obtain one. There were no formal negotiations during this time, and no established agenda. Instead, there was a sporadic series of mid-level discussions and high-level arm-twisting.

Throughout these various encounters, the Japanese maintained their willingness to 'buy American' but repeatedly claimed that no existing American model could meet their specifications.

Meanwhile, the Americans stressed the political importance of co-operation on this issue and the military necessity of 'interoperability.' As the discussions proceeded, however, they grew increasingly convinced that Japan was still determined to develop an indigenous FSX. For United States officials, the final straw came in April 1987, when reports from the 'Sullivan mission,' a technical team sent to Japan, suggested that any one of four American aircraft could meet the JDA's mission requirements better and more cheaply than any Japanese alternative. Japanese intransigence, the Americans were beginning to conclude, had as much to do with industrial goals as with military needs. From that point on, therefore, the Pentagon tightened its negotiating position. In June 1987, Richard L. Armitage, the assistant secretary of defense for international security affairs, told Seiki Nishihiro, the vice defence minister and the top career official in the JDA, that neither domestic development nor joint production of a new aircraft would be acceptable to the United States. In addition, Armitage emphasized that any new Japanese fighter would have to be based on an existing American model. In June, the secretary of defense, Caspar Weinberger, formally proposed co-development to Japan's defence minister and reiterated that the question of the FSX 'went to the heart of the U.S.-Japan relationship.'[11]

Until this point, Pentagon officials had been making the case for co-development largely in terms of mutual gains – stressing, for example, the benefits of military co-operation and the lower cost of using an existing model. By the summer of 1987, however, the language of persuasion changed dramatically. While not denying the gains accruing from co-operation, United States negotiators began to focus overwhelmingly on the costs of indigenous development. They began explicitly to warn the Japanese of the political consequences that were likely to befall them if they insisted on building the aircraft without American participation. In particular, they pointed to the growing force of anti-

11 *Ibid*, 29.

Japanese sentiment in the United States and warned of the back-
lash that was likely to ensue if Japan refused to 'buy American'
in the one area where United States firms still undoubtedly held
the comparative advantage.

This argument acquired special force following revelations
that Toshiba Machine Corporation, a subsidiary of the Toshiba
Corporation, had sold propeller-milling machinery to the Soviet
Union, helping the Soviet Union to make its submarines quieter
and less detectable.[12] At this point, with 'Japan-bashing' at an
all-time high in the United States, the leverage of the Japanese
had been drastically reduced. It is still unclear precisely how
American officials linked the FSX decision to the Toshiba case,
but, at a minimum, they undoubtedly warned their Japanese
counterparts of the importance of doing something to prevent a
serious rupture in the alliance. At a maximum, their warnings
may well have been issued as threats. During a summer visit with
Prime Minister Yasuhiro Nakasone, the secretary of defense
openly lobbied for co-development of the FSX, stressing the
importance of maintaining good relations between the United
States and Japan and pointing to the outburst of anti-Japanese
legislation in Congress.[13] By the autumn, such high-level pressure
from United States officials finally forced the Japanese to come
around to the American position, and in October 1987 the JDA
formally announced that the F-16 would be the model of the new
FSX fighter and that General Dynamics would be an active participant in the development and production of the FSX fleet.

To the American officials concerned, the deal was a good one
in all respects. Not only would the United States maintain its
close alliance with Japan and ensure the security of its forces in
the Pacific, but it would also ensure business for American firms.
As Armitage described it: 'This was a brand new airplane. We
would get money, we would get jobs ... We saw the agreement in

---

12 See the Toshiba case in Raymond Vernon, Debora Spar, and Glenn Tobin, *Iron
Triangles and Revolving Doors: Cases in U.S. Foreign Economic Policymaking*
(New York: Praeger 1991).
13 See, for instance, Kohno, 'Japanese defense policy making,' 468-9.

all its aspects, and we thought we had a deal.'[14] For the Japanese, by contrast, co-development seemed to offer far fewer benefits. As Yuko Kurihara, the director-general of the JDA, told reporters: 'From the point of view of Japan's national interest, this was a difficult choice to make, and it represented a substantial concession on our part.'[15] What the Japanese had very clearly done was to sacrifice the relative gains of indigenous development to preserve their alliance with the United States. As Kurihara explained: 'Japan gave up the idea of domestic development of the FSX because [we] thought a decision aimed at maintaining good relations with the U.S. based on the Japan-U.S. Security Treaty was important.'[16]

In theoretical terms, it appears therefore that American officials were able to convince the Japanese of the importance of minimizing absolute losses. Faced with the threat of a rupture in their alliance with the United States, Japanese decision-makers ignored the temptation of relative economic gains and focused instead on the risk of absolute political losses. In the end, the way in which the decision was framed by the Americans had a considerable impact on the decision that the Japanese finally made. The decision to co-operate, never conceived by the Japanese as a particularly attractive option, turned out in such a context to be preferable to an even less attractive alternative. To be sure, in this sense, it is possible to see Japan's decision in terms of standard realist theory: Japan's capitulation would simply be attributable to the superior power of the United States. Such an explanation, however, misses much of the substance of the story. In particular, it fails to consider how critical the presentation of the situation was to its final outcome. Nothing, after all, changed between 1985 and 1987 except the way in which United States officials were presenting the case for co-development. When it was presented to the Japanese as a way of boosting their overall security and reducing their long-term costs, they simply

14 Interview, 10 July 1990.
15 Quoted in *Asahi Shimbun*, 3 October 1987.
16 Quoted in *Japan Times*, 4 October 1987.

were not interested. When, however, it was presented as a way of forestalling a rupture in their most important alliance – that is, as a way of minimizing absolute losses – Japanese officials were much quicker to concede. It is particularly ironic, therefore, that it was this same presentation that nearly scuttled the FSX agreement, when American officials brought it home.

THE DOMESTIC DEBATE IN THE UNITED STATES

Once Japan had agreed to use the F-16 as the model for its FSX, officials from the Pentagon and the JDA, together with representatives from General Dynamics and Mitsubishi Heavy Industries (the prime Japanese contractor) worked together for nearly a year to hammer out the specific details of the co-operative venture. In November 1988 a memorandum of understanding was signed which formalized the terms of co-development and established a timetable for production of the FSX. As far as the White House and the Pentagon were concerned, the FSX was now a done deal. The problem, however, was that not all groups in the United States chose to see the FSX programme in the same terms. In particular, there were a number of groups which saw co-development primarily in terms of relative gains and which calculated that the United States was giving to the Japanese far more than it was getting in return. One of the first and loudest opponents of the FSX deal was the Commerce Department. As standard models of bureaucratic politics would predict, Commerce evaluated the deal in terms of its own concerns – that is, it calculated what co-development was likely to mean for the United States business community and for the overall industrial position of the United States. And on these grounds it found the deal sorely lacking.

Specifically, almost as soon as they learned about the FSX and co-development, a group of concerned officials in Commerce argued that the Pentagon had sold out American economic interests. They claimed that co-development would mean giving Japanese firms critical technology that they could otherwise never obtain and that this technology, in turn, would allow those firms to make serious inroads into the international aviation market, one of the few market sectors where United States firms still had a substantial lead. In addition, they argued that the agreement did little to ensure that any technology derived from the production of the FSX would subsequently be transferred back to American industry; as a consequence, Japan would gain far more from the deal than the United States would. And, finally, they insisted that the entire course of the negotiations demonstrated the Pentagon's total lack of concern for economic security – that is, for the relative strength of the American economy and the health of American industry.

The Commerce Department was not therefore disputing the Pentagon's claims that co-operation on the FSX would be good for United States security and good for the alliance with Japan. Rather, they were arguing that these were the wrong criteria to employ in this case. Co-development, they contended, was not about security and alliances. It was about technology transfer and industrial advantage. And from this point of view co-development would be a relative gain for the Japanese and a relative loss for the United States. Thus, the Commerce Department was evaluating the FSX project in a wholly different context and against a wholly different set of criteria. It was concerned with economic rather than military costs and with relative rather than absolute gains.

A similar set of concerns, meanwhile, began to emerge from within Congress. Once again, the opposition came mostly from groups that brought a different perspective to the FSX deal leading them to evaluate it by largely economic criteria and to see it mainly as a relative gains problem. For instance, one of the first complaints against the FSX came from powerful members of the Senate Armed Services Committee who had been engaged in a long-standing battle to eliminate 'offset agreements' under which United States defence manufacturers which sold arms to foreign countries would agree that a certain percentage of the sale would be 'offset' by production facilities constructed in the purchasing country or by components purchased from local suppliers.[17] To the companies that used offsets, they were an integral part of doing business abroad. To some senators, however, they were nothing but a giveaway of American technology and jobs. Thus, for several years these senators had been trying not only to eliminate offsets but also to force the Defense Department to consider the economic ramifications of all arms sales and technology transfer agreements.[18] To these senators, the FSX deal stood as a concrete example of the evils that could result when economic criteria were not given sufficient consideration in the negotiation of an ostensibly military agreement.

The FSX agreement also attracted the interest of congressmen who were concerned about the trade deficit, and particularly about the growing trade imbalance between the United States and Japan. For some time, people such as Richard Gephardt, a Democrat from Missouri, and Senator John Danforth, a Republican also from Missouri, had been arguing that the deficit had to be addressed directly and that Japan had to co-operate with the United States in setting the balance aright. In particular, these congressmen insisted that Japan had to remove its internal barriers to trade and buy more products from the United States. In their eyes, the FSX deal was a flagrant example of Japan's unwillingness to play by the rules of free trade, and evidence that the Japanese were not negotiating in good faith whenever they promised to buy American goods. As one representative put it: '[The FSX agreement] is not in accordance with free trade principles by which the Japanese should be purchasing this product,

---

17 In some cases, the amount of the offset was considerably more than the entire purchase price. In one well-publicized case, for example, a sale of the Boeing Airborne Warning and Control System to Great Britain included offsets worth over 100 per cent of the system's price. See Ethan B. Kapstein, 'Losing control: national security and the global economy,' *National Interest* (winter 1989/90), 86.

18 For instance, the 1989 Defense Authorization Bill included a provision that required American firms to report all offset agreements to the Defense Department and a provision that required the president to enter negotiations with those countries that customarily demand offsets.

fighter aircraft, for which the United States has a tremendous competitive advantage. At a time when we are facing a $55 billion bilateral trade deficit with Japan, Japanese officials should be particularly willing to abide by free trade principles and to purchase quality, cost-competitive u.s. products.'[19]

In addition, the FSX provided a good case for those who had been struggling to draw attention to the problem of the declining industrial base of the United States. Centred largely in the House Subcommittee on Economic Stabilization, these congressmen had watched the United States lose manufacturing share to the Japanese in a number of critical markets. To them, the FSX threatened to be another case in which American firms would transfer their technology abroad, only to find out several years later that they had also transferred their competitive advantage. As one representative argued: 'Common sense ... dictates that we not give away the store in this vital aerospace industry, whether it is military or commercial. We must remember that economic security is also national security. Let's not do as Abraham's son Isaac did, and give away our future for a mess of pottage, by selling out our aerospace industry.'[20] Or as another put it: 'It seems to me that five years from now, as sure as the day is long, that the aerospace industry is going to be coming to us, including [General Dynamics] and saying "boy, did we make a terrible mistake in 1989 by accelerating the development of the competition".'[21]

Clearly, what all of these congressional groups had in common was a concern for the relative economic position of the United States and a belief that this position was being compromised by Japan's economic success. While their specific interests were quite diverse, they were united by a similar focus on relative economic gains and by a sense that Japan was gaining too rapidly

19 Testimony of Representative Mel Levine (Democrat, California) before the House Committee on Foreign Affairs, 3 May 1989, 113.
20 Testimony of Representative Helen D. Bentley (Republican, Maryland) before the House Committee on Foreign Affairs, 9 May 1989, 122.
21 Levine testimony, 144.

at the expense of the United States. In the FSX case, moreover, they all saw a relative gain for Japanese industry and a devastating blow against the American position in the international aviation market. In essence, congressional opponents of the deal were evaluating it on very different terms from those that had been employed by policy-makers in the Pentagon. None of the opponents of the FSX project was denying that co-development would strengthen the military alliance between the United States and Japan or that it was better for the United States than allowing Japan to build an indigenous fighter. Rather, they were arguing against the project on the basis of an entirely different set of criteria: that it allowed the Japanese to benefit economically without forcing them to pay a price. The FSX deal simply gave the Japanese a relative economic gain and inflicted a corresponding loss upon the United States.

Faced with this growing opposition to the FSX agreement, the newly installed Bush administration quickly decided to reopen the deal for further consideration. Thus, on 6 February, the National Security Council sent a memo to all cabinet departments requesting them to answer a series of questions concerning the FSX project and inviting them to a meeting on 10 February.[22] For the first time, the negotiations were opened to officials beyond the Pentagon and the State Department, and, for the first time, Commerce explicitly brought commercial concerns into the discussion of United States security policy.

As the internal discussions got under way, the parameters of the debate became immediately obvious. On one side stood a coalition led by officials from the Commerce Department and including representatives from Office of the United States Trade Representative, the Treasury, the Department of Labor, and the Department of Energy. Their position was that the deal was not an unmitigated good, that it raised troubling questions about Japan's willingness to purchase American goods, and that it risked undermining the competitiveness of domestic industry by giving away its most advanced technology. In the immediate

22 Ennis, 'Inside the Pentagon-Commerce turf war,' 25.

term, the group wanted to delay notification of the deal pending a more thorough review of its commercial and technological provisions. In the longer term, they wanted to ensure that economic issues were added to the security policy calculus and that their agencies – and in particular the Commerce Department – would be included in the policy-making process.

Against this group stood the initial coalition of the Pentagon and the State Department, convinced that the FSX agreement was a good deal and worried that any last-minute efforts to change it would only serve to sabotage relations with Japan. Primarily, this group urged that the security relationship between the two countries remained the paramount concern and that the United States would be getting technology back, not just giving it away. In addition, however, the Departments of Defense and State argued that they had given great weight to economic considerations but that there simply was no way that the Japanese government was going to buy an American fighter off the shelf. Under those circumstances, co-development offered the best alternative for the American aircraft industry.

In theoretical terms, the differences between these two positions are especially stark. The Commerce Department and its allies were framing their arguments entirely in terms of relative gains: they saw the FSX deal as a relative loss for the United States and thus wanted to prevent it. The Pentagon and its allies, meanwhile, were framing the situation in terms of absolute losses, arguing that to step away from the deal at this point would be to threaten the overarching alliance between the United States and Japan. As it turned out, the latter argument won the day. After an extensive review of the FSX programme, the Commerce Department asked that certain critical provisions of the agreement be 'clarified' and that Commerce officials be included in negotiation of all future co-development schemes. Once the Pentagon agreed to these terms, Commerce dropped its outright opposition, and the FSX deal proceeded as originally planned.

To a certain extent, therefore, the resolution of this portion of the FSX debate bears out the predictions of prospect theory. Most importantly, it appears that an appeal to loss avoidance proved the most persuasive way of framing the situation. At the same time, however, it is important not to overlook the larger dynamics of the decision-making process. For instance, it is clear that bureaucratic politics goes a long way in explaining the outcome of the internal debate. All of the agencies involved were framing the decision in a way that was entirely consistent with their bureaucratic interests; 'framing' can thus be treated simply as the presentation of a bureaucratic position. Moreover, in this case, the losing side in the battle was not necessarily convinced of the superiority of the other side's argument. Rather, it seems that the Pentagon was just a more powerful internal player. Like Japan at an earlier stage in the process, then, Commerce changed its 'frame' when political imperatives demanded that it do so. The evidence therefore is mixed. While there are some grounds on which to argue that the notion of framing helps to explain the decision outcome, so too is there ample reason to point to the usual 'pulling and hauling' of bureaucratic politics.

A similar combination marks the final phase of the FSX debate, although here the appeal to loss avoidance appears to have been the more decisive factor. After the Japanese reluctantly agreed to the tightened demands of the 'clarified' agreement,[23] the memorandum was sent to Congress for its formal review.[24] As expected, the debate was heated and focused on the relative gains that the FSX would generate for the Japanese. A number of congressmen, for instance, urged that the United States should force Japan into 'giving us a bigger piece of the pie'[25] and reiterated their concern that co-development would only allow Japan to compete more efficiently against American

23 The clarifications provided that the aircraft's fire-control software remain in black boxes, that United States firms be guaranteed a 40-per-cent share of both production and development, and that the procedures for technological flowback be assured and specified.

24 Under the provisions of the Arms Export Control Act, both houses of Congress are given thirty days in which to review all arms export licences. During that time, they can either simply let the agreement pass back to the authority of the executive branch, or they can stall it by passing a formal resolution of disapproval.

25 Towell, 'U.S.-Japanese warplane deal,' 537.

exporters.[26] The concerns that had initially motivated the Pentagon – ensuring Japan's role in the Western security alliance, building the best defensive aircraft possible, and building a fighter that would be compatible with United States forces – were largely absent from the debate.

As the hearings ran their course, however, the relative gains concerns that animated the opposition were once again gradually eroded by the administration's appeal to avoid absolute losses. In particular, it appears that many legislators were ultimately convinced that the deal had gone too far to stop and that efforts to halt it at this point would prove counterproductive. As an editorial in the *Washington Post* put it: 'If the United States now tried to back out of its fighter aircraft deal with Japan, it would do severe damage both to the Japanese government and itself ... The point is, this government should keep its word.'[27] By the time that the agreement was actually put to a vote, a majority of Congress had been convinced. Although many members continued to insist that the deal was not a good thing for the United States, the general sentiment was that the alternative – letting the Japanese go it alone and risking a rupture in the alliance – was worse. In June 1989, Congress approved the so-called Byrd proposal, which registered Congress's official displeasure with the FSX agreement but stopped short of actually disapproving it. The FSX, at last, was really a done deal.

PROSPECT THEORY AND THE FSX

In reviewing the overall story of the FSX, it is clear that no single decision-making theory is sufficient to explain either the process or the outcome. By way of conclusion, however, I will consider the extent to which prospect theory can fill in the gaps left by other, more traditional, explanations.

The first question is how well prospect theory fares against expected utility models with regard to the search process. Here,

---

26 See, for instance, *New York Times*, 11 May 1989, D1.
27 *Washington Post*, 17 March 1989.

as elsewhere, the results are mixed. At many points in the story, the rational and calculated process described by orthodox approaches does appear to have been approximated. The Japanese, for instance, conscientiously reviewed all of the aircraft that could fit their specifications, and they evaluated each one on its merits. To be sure, their evaluation was heavily influenced by their desire to develop an indigenous aircraft and by their selection of an ambitious aspiration level, but this kind of interest-based calculation is still easily handled within a subjective expected utility framework. Likewise, Rubinstein's initial cable is virtually a model of search and evaluation. Not only did he identify and weigh the obvious options, he also searched for and developed a new option that better served the interests of the United States. Although the decision-making process did not explicitly assign estimates of costs and benefits, it too seems well within the parameters of a standard rational choice model.

By the same token, however, the FSX case also offers evidence of truncated search. For example, there were groups within the Japanese bureaucracy that never took seriously the idea of co-development, insisting from the start that the FSX had to be an indigenous project. Similarly, the deal's opponents in the United States clearly were engaging in a less-than-complete review of the possible options; indeed, many of them seem to have reacted in a knee-jerk fashion. As one might expect, moreover, where we find evidence of truncated search, we see a greater reliance on heuristics and aspiration levels. The Japanese opponents, for example, consistently defined the FSX as a question of nationalism and a test of Japan's independence from the United States. Inherently, their arguments seemed to be fixed on an 'aspiration level' that defined the minimally acceptable pay-offs in this situation: they wanted to be independent of the United States and were wary of any option that would only serve to maintain the status quo. Once the situation was described in these terms, co-operation necessarily entailed capitulation. In the United States, meanwhile, much of the opposition to the FSX deal can be traced to a reluctance to adjust to changes in the status quo. Specifically, opponents of the project were mourning the loss of American economic dominance and set their sights on doing whatever was necessary to restore the status quo ante. In their arguments, these opponents framed the deal almost entirely in terms of economic security. And, once again, defining the situation along these lines made co-operation particularly unpalatable.

Thus, although prospect theory does not explain all of the decision-making process, it does describe some of the elements that fall beyond the scope of expected utility models. It is interesting to note, moreover, that those aspects of the process that are better described by prospect theory are also those that pushed towards a non-co-operative outcome. In particular, the fact that the opponents of co-development were the ones who gave evidence of truncated search and reliance on heuristics might suggest that this type of reasoning tends to preclude co-operation. If decision-makers define a situation in terms of some particular analogy or paradigm, they may well limit their ability to think creatively or to evaluate all of the possible options. This is a conclusion that fits well with the propositions of prospect theory, and one that receives support from the FSX case.

A second aspect of prospect theory that receives some support from this case is the broad notion of framing. For instance, we saw how various groups managed to frame the situation in different ways and how these frames in turn shaped their willingness to co-operate. As long as the Japanese framed the decision in terms of economic and military autonomy, they naturally preferred the non-co-operative option of indigenous development. Likewise, those groups in the United States that conceived of the FSX as a case of 'economic security' were also unwilling to co-operate. It was only when the decision was framed in terms of alliance preservation – that is, of avoiding absolute losses and maintaining the status quo – that co-operation became the policy choice.

This raises two central points. The first concerns the extent to which framing in this case can be largely subsumed into more traditional models of interest group behaviour and bureaucratic politics. Clearly, in the case of the FSX, an assumption of consistent and transitive preferences is completely denied by the facts that different groups had very different preferences and that these preferences evolved and changed over time. Differences of preference, however, need not be linked to the effects of 'framing,' as prospect theory would lead us to suspect. On the contrary, these differences can simply be attributed to the different interests of sub-national groups. In the FSX case, for example, the opposition of the Commerce Department is easily explained by its bureaucratic role as the defender of American industry. That it framed the decision in terms of economic security has less to do with perception than with institutional mandate. Similarly, we would expect that the State Department and the Department of Defense would be more concerned with alliance relations than with economic competitiveness. Allison's well-worn dictum that 'where you stand depends on where you sit' thus goes quite a long way in explaining difference of preferences among sub-national groups. This is not to argue that framing is unimportant. On the contrary, we might be able to use the notion of framing as a means of explaining how bureaucratic interests are defined and promoted. In particular, frames might be helpful in understanding the background against which institutions set their goals and how these goals affect their perception of a wide range of policy issues.

Where prospect theory is even more directly applicable, however, is in its emphasis on the importance of loss aversion. At two separate points in the story, co-operation emerged after one of the parties was able to frame the debate in terms of avoiding absolute losses. In the summer of 1987 the Pentagon convinced the Japanese to agree to co-development by making it clear that anything less would seriously rupture the alliance between the two countries. Likewise, in the spring of 1989, the Bush administration used the threat of a breach in the alliance to prevent a congressional resolution of disapproval. In both cases, a debate over relative gains was overwhelmed by a focus on absolute losses.

In both cases, the ability to frame the decision in terms of loss avoidance was instrumental in obtaining a co-operative solution.

Turning to the questions raised at the outset, therefore, we can suggest that what allowed co-operation ultimately to prevail was a focus on loss avoidance. Once all the parties conceived of the decision in terms of avoiding absolute losses, they all could accept co-development as the best of the available alternatives. In this respect, prospect theory contributes significantly to our understanding of the dynamics of co-operation in this case. By the same token, what nearly scuttled the co-operative accord was the ability of sub-national groups to define the situation in terms of relative gains and to push their own concerns onto the political agenda. This is an element of the decision-making process that is entirely absent when orthodox expected utility models are focused at the national level and that is only vaguely alluded to by prospect theory.

What, then, are we to conclude about the explanatory power of prospect theory in the case of the FSX? The theory throws light on some key aspects of the process but does not mount a completely successful challenge to an expected utility perspective, especially when the latter is combined with a bureaucratic politics approach. Indeed, although not entirely explaining the full range of behaviour that occurred in the course of the FSX deliberations, a model that combines bureaucratic politics and an orthodox utility maximization perspective offers a compelling account of how the process unfolded at several critical junctures. It works well, for example, in describing the initial positions taken by both the Japanese and the Americans and in accounting for much of the subsequent debate in the United States. Where prospect theory is most useful, it seems, is in underlining the dramatic appeal of loss avoidance and in drawing our attention to the importance of reference levels in setting the parameters of any decision-making process.

Going one step further, there is certainly ample evidence in the FSX case to suggest a strong link between co-operation and loss avoidance. Whenever the FSX project was framed in terms of relative gains, co-operation proved exceedingly difficult to obtain. When it was framed in terms of absolute losses, co-operation emerged. One case, of course, is far too limited a basis upon which to generate any far-reaching propositions. Nevertheless, the existence of the link in the FSX instance at least suggests the potential for future investigation.

Four

The political foundations
of multilateral economic
surveillance

LOUIS W. PAULY

Following World War II, the states that built a new world monetary order made a novel commitment. As the system designed in principle at the 1944 Bretton Woods Conference evolved in practice, in the words of Robert W. Cox, 'the notion of international obligation moved ... to a general recognition that measures of national economic policy affect other countries and that such consequences should be taken into account before national policies are adopted.'[1] Exchange rates, the economic variables

Associate Professor of Political Science, University of Toronto, Toronto, Canada; author of *Opening Financial Markets: Banking Politics on the Pacific Rim* (1988).

Earlier drafts of this chapter were presented at the 1991 World Congress of the International Political Science Association, Buenos Aires, and the 1991 meeting of the American Political Science Association, Washington, DC. For assistance and constructive comments at various points, I am grateful to Ralph Bryant, Robert Bryce, Philip Cerny, Margaret de Vries, Richard Friman, Stephen Gill, Joseph Gold, Eric Helleiner, C. Randall Henning, Miles Kahler, Peter Katzenstein, Michael Mastanduno, Timothy McKeown, Jacques Polak, Michael Schechter, Robert Solomon, Janice Gross Stein, Susan Strange, David Welch, and Robert Wolfe. My interest in this topic was sparked in 1989 when I spent a year as a visiting fellow at the IMF under the auspices of the International Affairs Fellowship Program of the Council on Foreign Relations. Subsequently, as a guest scholar in the Economic Studies programme of the Brookings Institution, that interest deepened. Research for this paper was supported by a grant (410-91-1308) from the Social Sciences and Humanities Research Council of Canada. Responsibility for the final text is, of course, mine alone.

1 Robert W. Cox, *Production, Power, and World Order* (New York: Columbia University Press 1987), 256. The earlier gold exchange system of the 1880-1914 period involved the heroic assumption of an external constraint on domestic policy but created no binding obligation. It is commonly held that the system essentially involved states accepting a single external price constraint and then allowing their domestic money supplies automatically to be affected when payments imbalances arose. In practice, the system never worked so neatly and

most immediately reflective of such policy interdependence, provided the initial focus of that obligation, and the central institutional mechanism for overseeing compliance was embodied in what came to be known as the surveillance function of the International Monetary Fund (IMF). Over time, the mandate of that broadly based multilateral organization expanded beyond narrowly defined exchange rate issues to encompass a range of national macro-economic and structural policies that had systemic consequences. Concurrently, analogous surveillance roles were built into the operations of other bodies with more restricted memberships, more limited mandates, or less formal organizational structures, such as the Organization for Economic Co-operation and Development (OECD) and the forum of leading industrialized nations known as the Group of Seven (G-7).

Notwithstanding the innovative nature of multilateral economic surveillance by an international organization like the Fund, one needs only to delve briefly into the literature to discern a widespread sense of scepticism about its actual utility. The advice resulting from surveillance activities can be controversial and is frequently ignored, not only by great powers resistant to policy adjustment but by smaller states as well.[2] If anything, dissatisfaction with the mechanism has deepened since Susan Strange characterized it in 1971 as 'the pantomime of multilateral surveillance.'[3] Supporters of international organizations bemoan its inefficacy; analysts informed by realist or structuralist assumptions depict it as a transparent cover for underlying power relations; students of economic adjustment in developing

states jealously guarded their sovereign rights to determine the actual scope and extent of domestic adjustment. For background, see Barry Eichengreen, ed, *The Gold Standard in Theory and History* (New York: Methuen 1985).

2 Alan Milward scathingly depicts the inefficacy of the Fund even in its earliest days when its principal focus was on European economies recovering from the war. See *The Reconstruction of Western Europe 1945-51* (London: Methuen 1984).

3 Susan Strange, *Sterling and British Policy* (London: Oxford University Press 1971), 292. For background, also see Susan Strange, 'IMF: monetary managers,' in Robert W. Cox, Harold Jacobson, et al, *The Anatomy of Influence* (New Haven CT: Yale University Press 1973).

countries criticize its asymmetry and apparent inflexibility.[4] Nevertheless, substantial international and national resources continue to be devoted to economic surveillance in general and to the surveillance function of the Fund in particular. At various times during the formal and informal discussions on international monetary reform that have taken place since 1944 the function could have been abandoned. At moments of decision, national policy-makers have instead continually reaffirmed their Bretton Woods commitment and re-emphasized their support for multilateral surveillance. The consequent puzzles are obvious. If the principle behind the function is meaningful, why have states not matched the Fund's mandate with more substantial authority? If the principle is meaningless, why have they not simply abandoned the function?

In theoretical terms, scholars of international relations would typically answer such questions by referring to the idea that states must balance conflicting goals in the monetary arena; most simply, they seek to reap the benefits promised by economic interdependence without forsaking their political independence.[5] In seeking to comprehend the manner in which that balance has been recalibrated during the postwar era, analysts typically assume that states calculate their interests here within a framework that emphasizes the gains promised by monetary stability. In this vein, realists or structuralists stress the effects of hegemonic power in restraining the types of relative gains calculations associated with earlier periods of systemic monetary disorder.[6] In

4 The conventional criticism is that Fund advice is only effective when it is tied to conditional balance of payments lending. The evidence is mixed, at best. Herman Schwartz ably surveys the literature in 'Can orthodox stabilization and adjustment work? Lessons from New Zealand, 1984-90,' *International Organization* 45(spring 1991), 222-56. For a thorough analysis of the issues, see Jacques J. Polak, *The Changing Nature of IMF Conditionality*, Princeton Essays in International Finance 184 (Princeton NJ: Princeton University, September 1991).

5 See, for example, Robert Gilpin, *The Political Economy of International Relations* (Princeton NJ: Princeton University Press 1987), 167.

6 Gilpin (*ibid*), for example, argues that the Bretton Woods system worked 'because of responsible American leadership and the willingness of other nations

contrast, analysts informed by essentially liberal premises point to the fundamentally common state interests that arise from the condition of economic interdependence and persist despite changes in systemic power structures.[7] Such analytical approaches shed light on the character of multilateral surveillance, but, with their system-level focus and emphasis on abstract calculations of relative or absolute gains, they obscure the decision-making processes that have actually moulded the mandates of such organizations as the IMF. This chapter approaches the subject at the level of the policy-makers acting in the name of states and contends that both the endurance and the weakness of the surveillance function of the Fund, in particular, are best accounted for by understanding the manner in which relevant constitutive decisions were framed.

Despite the deepening interdependence that has characterized international monetary relations throughout the post-World War II era, the institutional structures for encouraging co-operation have not been easy to create.[8] Not surprisingly, given the

---

to subordinate their domestic policies to international norms. Its successor, the regime of flexible exchange rates, functioned poorly because of policy autonomy and the massive financial flows that followed currency convertibility.' With a less instrumental view of hegemony, Cox (*Production, Power, and World Order*, 256) sees accommodating national polices as arising from an 'internationalized policy process' that 'presupposed a power structure, one in which central agencies of the U.S. government were in a dominant position.' External pressures were also internalized, Cox continues, 'through ideological osmosis.'

7 Robert Keohane, for example, argues that the persistence of monetary order after the turbulence of the early 1970s 'is not explained by the theory of hegemonic stability ... It is partially accounted for by the continued strength of the United States, which had an interest in liberalism [but] also partially by the continuation of shared interests in the efficiency and welfare benefits of international economic exchange.' *After Hegemony: Cooperation and Discord in the World Political Economy* (Princeton NJ: Princeton University Press 1984), 209.

8 See Ralph Bryant, *Money and Monetary Policy in Interdependent Nations* (Washington: Brookings Institution 1980), 475-81. During earlier periods as well as in the contemporary period, international monetary history is filled with examples of states refusing, in practice, to subordinate domestic economic policies to the cause of external monetary stability. This raises problems for arguments that characterize monetary relations as unusually co-operative in

doctrinal basis of the state system, there has never been a mechanism for ensuring consistent and mutually constructive monetary behaviour. Large states have always been capable of shifting burdens of adjustment onto others, and small states, even financially dependent ones, have often found ways of resisting unwanted policy change. The acceptance of multilateral economic surveillance, in this light, thus represents a minimal level of co-operation among states unwilling or unable to submit to a truly supranational order – a rough analogue to the modicum of co-operation entailed in the opening of weapons sites to external oversight which provides the fundamental basis for future arms control agreements. The obligation to consult on the systemic implications of domestic economic policies, to hold those policies up to external scrutiny, supports, at best, a modest mechanism for aggregating and sharing information, building trust, and fostering confidence.[9] Despite its limitations, achieving the minimal level of co-operation that multilateral surveillance represents has been difficult. But the states that created it have persisted in maintaining it despite the vicissitudes of international monetary relations in the nearly fifty years since Bretton Woods. To understand why, this chapter concentrates on the two central points of decision that laid the legal and institutional foundations for IMF surveillance: 1944-6, when the oversight mandate of a broadly based international organization was initially conceived, and 1975-6, when that mandate was revived and extended. The essential argument is that at both points the constitutive deci-

---

comparison with other areas of inter-state contact – owing, for example, to centralized and insulated decision-making, cross-nationally–shared ideological commitments and personal relationships among relevant national élites, or technical arcana that render it difficult to discern or trace the political effects of monetary policies. Joanne Gowa reviews such issues in 'Public goods and political institutions: trade and monetary policy processes in the United States,' *International Organization* 42(winter 1988), 15-32.

9 Its efficacy cannot therefore be 'tested' by looking for examples of Fund advice decisively altering domestic policies. But understanding its origins provides a basis for assessing the aspirations and the limits of more ambitious efforts to co-ordinate monetary and other economic policies.

sions were framed not in terms of the potential future gains accruing from co-operation but in terms of the potential future losses threatened by the failure to co-operate. The decisions were modest, but they held promise for future institutional innovation. Had they been framed in other terms, it is quite conceivable that they would not have been taken.[10]

The preferences of key national policy-makers in both the 1940s and the 1970s were constructed by their assessments of the potential economic and social losses associated with a reversion to international monetary turmoil and of the potential political losses associated with acceptance of a novel infringement on their traditional policy autonomy. At both points, assigning oversight responsibilities to an international organization was seen by many, especially in national legislatures, as politically risky; at both points, such fears were overcome, partly by the negotiation of safeguards limiting the actual authority of the Fund but more significantly by continual reference to the analogy of the monetary 'anarchy' of the interwar period. Long after the actual risks of competitive currency depreciation had faded, the spectre of the economic and social effects of monetary disorder during the Great Depression continued to cast its pall over the negotiating table and the legislative chamber. In retrospect, the value of that analogy in simplifying calculations of interest is striking, especially since recent research casts doubt on the conventional wisdom concerning the consequences of generalized currency

10 The theoretical context for this argument is set out in Janice Stein's introduction to this volume. Note that in between and after these 'constitutive' decisions, the function was elaborated and refined through a series of other actions, the most significant of which will be noted. But in compressing the long, complicated, and essentially evolutionary history of IMF surveillance for present purposes, some simplification is unavoidable. My reading of the historical record convinces me that this simplification is not only justified by events at the crucial points of decision but also desirable in order to elucidate a subject usually wrapped in an opaque fog of specialized knowledge. Finally, for present purposes I have intentionally traded off comprehensiveness for parsimony: I have concentrated on the state that has clearly had the preponderant influence on the development of the Fund, the United States, and I have made the judgment that at the crucial decision points on Fund surveillance the focus deserves to be on central state policy-makers rather than sub-national or bureaucratic actors.

manipulation during the 1930s.[11] In short, the analogy made vague prospects of future losses from the failure to co-operate seem more certain. By doing so, it helped policy-makers in key states build the domestic political support they needed to breach traditional resistance to the principle of external accountability.

THE INCEPTION OF MULTILATERAL ECONOMIC SURVEILLANCE

The development of the surveillance function of the IMF should be viewed against the backdrop of the broader consensus that arose from the ashes of World War II. Mainly crafted in the course of arduous debate between the United States and Great Britain, and most clearly expressed in the 1944 Bretton Woods agreement, that consensus sought to reconcile increasingly liberal external economic relations with the retention by individual states of their right to intervene in their internal economies.[12] Grounded in the basic liberal premise that expanding international trade held the key to stable economic reconstruction and development, the agreement sought to create a set of supportive monetary arrangements. The common understanding was that the durability of those arrangements depended on adept management of the problem of economic adjustment, the scope of which was regularly quantified and summarized in national balance of payments accounts. Because, in one way or another, confronting this problem was inevitable, there was a need to design mechanisms to facilitate adjustment in ways that would not dis-

11 See Barry Eichengreen and Jeffrey Sachs, 'Exchange rates and economic recovery in the 1930s,' *Journal of Economic History* 45(December 1985), 925-46. On the basis of systematic empirical analysis, the authors argue that currency depreciation was clearly beneficial to the initiating country and, moreover, that recovery from the Great Depression would have been hastened if depreciation had been practised more widely and co-ordinated.

12 See John Gerard Ruggie, 'International regimes, transactions, and change: embedded liberalism in the postwar economic order,' *International Organization* 36(spring 1982), 195-231. Also see Eric Helleiner, 'American Hegemony and Global Economic Structure: From Closed to Open Financial Relations in the Postwar World,' doctoral dissertation, London School of Economics, 1991, chaps 2 and 3.

rupt the restoration and progressive liberalization of international trade.

At the heart of the Bretton Woods design were open current accounts and fixed but adjustable exchange rates supervised by a multilateral arbiter. With a degree of hyperbole, Fund documents liked to refer to this as a 'regulatory' role. In essence, states acceding to its Articles of Agreement provided the Fund with a threefold mandate: to monitor and discourage restrictions on current payments, to provide short-term financing to ease the adjustment of imbalances, and to oversee orderly changes in exchange rates in cases of 'fundamental' payments disequilibria. To enable such a mandate to be fulfilled, signatory states agreed to 'collaborate with the Fund to promote exchange stability, to maintain orderly exchange arrangements, and to avoid competitive exchange alterations.'[13] In institutional terms, this commitment eventually entailed participation by all members in the 'consultations' process of the Fund, a process that comprises the practical core of the Fund's surveillance function. Although accepting an obligation to submit to Fund surveillance is hardly as substantive as, say, establishing a common currency, an irrevocably fixed exchange rate, or a joint central bank, the record indicates that the Fund's member-states have never taken that obligation lightly nor treated it as inconsequential, despite periodic derogations. The precedent was established at Bretton Woods.

The historiography on the 1944 agreement is substantial and complex, as is the jurisprudential literature on its later elaboration.[14] For present purposes, we need only focus on what that literature indicates about the motivations of those individuals who had the most impact on the negotiation and ratification of

---

13 Article IV, section 4(a), of the Articles of Agreement.
14 G. John Ikenberry provides a fine orientation, particularly on the broader negotiating context, in 'A world economy restored: expert consensus and the Anglo-American postwar settlement,' *International Organization* 46(winter 1992), 289-321. For an introduction to the legal literature on this topic, see Joseph Gold, 'Duty to collaborate with the Fund and development of monetary law,' in *Legal and Institutional Aspects of the International Monetary System: Selected Essays* (Washington: IMF 1979), 390-409.

the agreement. Concentrating on John Maynard Keynes, the chief spokesman for the British, and on Harry Dexter White, his American counterpart, Richard Gardner's classic account of the Bretton Woods negotiation makes a case for viewing the initial mandate of the IMF as the product mainly of the clash between the expected postwar interests of Britain and of the United States in an environment widely forecast to be deflationary.[15] On the one hand, Keynes anticipated a pressing need for external financing after the war but also a deep aversion in parliament to external interference in the domestic stimulative policies needed to restore economic growth. White, on the other hand, was clearly cognizant of pressures that would be directly reflected in Congress to open foreign markets for American exports, end preferential trading arrangements such as that which prevailed within the sterling bloc, and limit enduring external financial commitments. Linking the two chief negotiators and biasing them towards some kind of agreement, as Gardner's account underlines, was their mutual concern about a reversion to 1930s-style monetary policies.

In accordance with British interests, and moving away from an opening position that gave central emphasis to monetary arrangements organized around rigidly fixed exchange rates, Keynes began in 1943 to push proposals for greater exchange rate flexibility that would render it easier for states to transfer the burden of economic adjustment away from the domestic and towards the external sector, thus easing potential pressures for ultimately harmful policy responses. For his part, White originally promoted the idea that a multilateral referee should be able to require changes in the internal policies of member-states but later retreated when it met implacable British resistance. To simplify what was actually a complex compromise, in the end White reluctantly agreed to a system that in effect permitted large adjustments in the declared 'par values' of exchange rates but only under what were expected to be exceptional circum-

---

15 Richard N. Gardner, *Sterling-Dollar Diplomacy in Current Perspective* (rev ed; New York: Columbia University Press 1980).

stances and only when concurred in by the referee. The system also permitted the referee to express its views to members on issues related to exchange arrangements. White also agreed that the referee was not to object to an exchange rate change considered necessary to deal with a 'fundamental disequilibrium' or justified in light of 'domestic social and political policies.'[16] During the subsequent political battles over confirmation of the Bretton Woods agreement, it became clear that neither negotiator had underestimated the depth of concern about their handiwork among their political masters.

Keynes faced the broadest possible antipathy to the agreement in the parliamentary debate that preceded British assent. As an American embassy official put it at the time: 'The outstanding psychology of the debate seemed to be, first, that a postwar slump in the United States is inevitable and second, the fear that the United States does not allow Britain and other countries to adopt the necessary measures of self-defense and that, consequently, the United States will drag the whole world down with her into the abyss.'[17] Although there was a widespread sense that such measures had proven self-defeating in the interwar years, the oversight role assigned to the Fund aroused particularly acute sensitivities. Because many parliamentarians suspected that that role would in effect provide a means for the United States to insist on domestic policy changes, Keynes took special pains to minimize its intended scope. Emphasizing the variability of exchange rates in the proposed system and the automaticity of borrowing rights, he even went so far as to assert that those policies would be 'immune from criticism by the Fund.'[18]

White, for his part, confronted quite different concerns in Congress during the American ratification debate, and he emphasized quite different interpretations. Although somewhat wary of a provision of the agreement (the 'scarce currency' clause) that could under certain circumstances allow countries to

16 IMF, Articles of Agreement, article IV, section 5(f).
17 Quoted in Gardner, *Sterling-Dollar Diplomacy*, 124.
18 *Ibid*, 127.

restrict United States dollar payments, and therefore to discriminate against imports from the United States, many legislators were more concerned that financing provided by the Fund might come with no strings attached. In subsequent hearings, White and other administration spokesmen traversed a fine line as they sought to reassure their critics that 'conditionality' would develop in practice and that Fund-promoted policies abroad would ensure that the United States was not held responsible for any future shortage of dollars.

Despite these doubts the agreement was ratified on both sides of the Atlantic. Economic prostration and the negotiation of safeguards surely helped to tip the balance in Britain. But concerns about the ultimate consequences for the domestic economy, and for the sterling bloc, of the liberal internationalist vision at the core of the IMF agreement were finally eclipsed by the prospect of severe economic dislocation if renewed depression and American isolation followed the war. A substantial body of opposition, both from the nationalist left and the traditionalist right, nevertheless fought the agreement, and promoted alternative plans, until the bitter end. Final assent was contingent on the Americans going first.

American opinion eventually swung decisively behind the agreement in the anti-isolationist euphoria that greeted the end of the war. As Gardner notes, in the end the administration relied heavily on the argument that the Bretton Woods proposals presented the same opportunity for ensuring future world peace that the League of Nations had offered in 1921. Having missed the earlier chance, at such dreadful human and financial cost, the United States could not afford to miss this second chance. 'However exaggerated these arguments may seem in retrospect,' recounts Gardner, 'they paid rich dividends at the time ... This feeling that "we must take a chance" – that however imperfect, the Bretton Woods institutions must be tried – played a decisive role in winning final approval.'[19] In other words, casting the

19 *Ibid*, 142.

decision in terms of the seemingly certain prospect of future losses proved crucial. From the start, however, the scope of the agreement was limited by safeguards responsive to concerns about another kind of loss – the loss of domestic political authority occasioned by the working out of liberal internationalism in practice. The result was a novel experiment that made a first limited inroad into the hitherto sacrosanct right of sovereign states to craft their economic policies without external interference.

The historical record indicates that the oversight role assigned to the IMF reflected a widely shared desire to avoid a reversion to monetary anarchy. The analogy of the interwar period helped to build a supportive political coalition in the key states by making the potential costs of non-co-operation appear more certain. Neither the United States nor Britain would be entirely satisfied with the way in which the principle of external accountability would be implemented. But an innovative institutional structure with the potential for encouraging co-operative monetary behaviour had been put in place. Other outcomes were of course possible. Had the decision to accede been framed simply in terms of the absolute economic gains potentially accruing from cross-national policy collaboration, for example, it seems doubtful that a coalition of support could have been structured either in Britain or in the United States. British policy-makers had little interest in moving quickly to non-discriminatory arrangements in money or trade, and bailing out the world from the bankruptcy of the war years in order to achieve such gains held little attraction on Capitol Hill. Conversely, had the decision been framed by American policy-makers in terms of an unambiguous need to secure relative political gains now and in the future – perhaps by minimizing the safeguards that allowed other countries room for manoeuvre – it seems evident that the agreement would have foundered in Britain. The way in which the decision was framed, in short, may plausibly be seen as making a difference.

THE INITIAL DEVELOPMENT OF THE FUND'S MANDATE

In its first years the oversight function of the Fund was associated most directly with those member-states availing themselves of article XIV of the agreement, which permitted them to retain, during the 'post-war transitional period,' restrictions on payments and transfers for current international transactions. On the assumption that this membership status would be temporary, and to encourage members to embrace as quickly as possible the full obligations of 'article VIII status,' which entailed complete freedom for current payments and transfers, article XIV required members maintaining exchange restrictions to consult regularly with the Fund.[20] The form of such consultations was actually presaged during the Bretton Woods negotiations.

Focusing on the expected length of time required to return to normal economic relations in the wake of the war, Keynes sought to preserve the maximum flexibility for Britain to decide for itself when that point had been achieved, while White originally sought to restrict the transition to an explicit three years in order to limit the risk that postwar protectionism and discriminatory payments arrangements would become permanent.[21] A British participant in the final negotiations reported that White 'tried hard to persuade us to abandon the idea of an indeterminate transitional period [and] Keynes threatened to walk out if

20 To the extent that other members considered feasible or desirable any further 'pressures' for payments liberalization and currency convertibility, articles XIV and XV also included sanctions provisions. In short, following Fund 'representations' that particular restrictions could be withdrawn, persistent reliance on those restrictions 'inconsistent with the purposes of the Fund' could lead to a declaration of ineligibility to use Fund resources and ultimately to a requirement to withdraw from membership. In practice, following a 1947 episode involving France, the Fund has typically eschewed such tactics. For background, see Joseph Gold, 'The "sanctions" of the International Monetary Fund,' *American Journal of International Law* 66(October 1972), 737-62. An amendment to the Fund's articles, proposed by the United States in 1990, reopened consideration of such matters by providing for the suspension of voting and related rights for members in arrears to the organization: see *Proposed Third Amendment of the Articles of Agreement* (Washington: IMF 1990).

21 Gardner, *Sterling-Dollar Diplomacy*, 178-87.

he is pressed ... on this matter.' But, according to the Fund's official history, the report of the American delegation on this particular meeting is 'less dramatic, but makes it clear that strong views were expressed': 'It reads that Keynes was asked if "the British recognized that in joining the Fund they were accepting some obligations to modify their domestic policy in light of its international effects on stability;" he replied that they did – but at their own discretion. "He finally seemed to admit," the minutes went on, "that it might be helpful to have an obligation to the Fund to back up those who were working for some modification of domestic policy, providing the Fund did not issue orders on some specific phase of domestic policy such as wages."'[22] The final compromise, codified in article xiv, provided that the Fund would begin to report internally on members' exchange restrictions three years after the start-up of operations and would begin to consult directly with such members after five years. Significantly, the outer time limits of the transitional period were not defined. It is fair to say, however, that most contemporary participants and observers assumed that period would be reasonably short. They were mistaken. The practical difficulties involved in both removing restrictions under article xiv and accepting the full obligations of article viii were generally underestimated, especially for developing states. Britain itself, and most of its continental neighbours, only accepted article viii obligations in 1961. By 1991, only 70 of the Fund's 155 members had successfully made the transition.[23] Article xiv consultations therefore came to assume an extent and importance that was not anticipated at the end of the war.

Prior to the start of the first round of such consultations, deep divisions were present in the Fund's Executive Board. Consistent with its strategy at Bretton Woods and aiming at the creation of a non-discriminatory international economic regime, the United States obviously saw those consultations as a mechanism for put-

22 J. Keith Horsefield, *The International Monetary Fund, 1945-65*, vol I
    (Washington: IMF 1969), 85, and 311-15.
23 *IMF Survey*, September 1991, supplement.

ting pressure on states maintaining restrictions, which often translated into restraints on dollar-based imports. With a different view on the necessity of such restrictions, the states to be consulted did not welcome the attention. Indeed, the cleavage lines demarcated in struggles over the breadth of Fund authority and the juridical status of its advice continually reappeared during the Fund's early years, with the United States and Canada frequently trying to broaden the interpretation of the Fund's mandate under article XIV, and Britain, Australia, India, and others fighting for a narrower interpretation. Far from being overcome in a series of bitterly divided votes, this split prevented the board from ever adopting a clear definition of exchange restrictions or a clear boundary marker between financial restraints and trade impediments. Through interpretations actually articulated, definitions left unstated, and, eventually, a tacit consensus on the need to limit board votes on sensitive policy matters, the constraints on the Fund's authority implied in the articles became established in practice.[24]

Nevertheless, throughout the 1950s what might be termed the quality of consultations gradually improved.[25] In 1960 the board was able to agree on the necessity and appropriateness of

24 The most significant of these decisions sought to amplify the interpretation of the Fund's mandate. While certain members, notably Australia, wanted to narrow the Fund's scope and allow it to comment only on the financial aspects of particular restrictions, the United States pushed for broader Fund authority to inquire into the underlying factors necessitating their retention. On an important procedural point, the Americans also fought to ensure that consultations would result in the Executive Board taking a formal position on issues raised therein. In explicit board votes, the United States got its way on both counts. The bitterness left in the wake of these and other votes, however, eventually led the United States to back off from its hardline stance and the Fund's staff to couch the draft conclusions of consultations in extremely cautious language. After these early debates, formal votes at board level on such questions became rare and consensus decision-making the norm. See Margaret Garritsen de Vries, 'The consultations process,' in de Vries et al, *The International Monetary Fund, 1945-65*, vol II (Washington: IMF 1969), 230-5.

25 The venue of consultations also shifted. Initially having taken place with local representatives of member-states in the Fund's Washington headquarters, they later took place with higher-level officials directly in national capitals and ended with board discussions of resulting staff reports.

the Fund collecting data on restrictive trade practices adopted
for balance of payments purposes, a subject of acute sensitivity a
decade earlier. When the United States now lobbied for a broad-
ening of the Fund's scope in the area of exchange restrictions,
consensus was readily achieved. This was not due solely to the
liberalizing trade environment. By then the limits of what was
actually involved in Fund assent or dissent were evident. This
realization was undoubtedly in the background when the board
later agreed to the inclusion in consultations of general fiscal and
monetary policies as well as other domestic policies having a
direct or indirect impact on payments balances. As the Fund's
historian puts it: 'Agreement was eased by the understanding
that no general precedents were being set ... and that comments
from the Fund might be helpful to the authorities of some countries in putting through politically unpopular policies.'[26] The
actual practice of Fund surveillance, in essence, ameliorated earlier fears that domestic political authority would be intolerably
eroded.

As the surveillance function evolved, the most significant
move to expand its scope and breadth came when the United
States and Canada agreed to establish a precedent for consultations under article VIII, a move unanticipated in 1944 and not
required under the agreement. Following discussion on new procedures, in 1960 the board adopted a decision to begin regular
annual consultations with article VIII members to enable the
Fund 'to provide technical facilities and advice ... or as a means
of exchanging views on monetary and financial developments.'[27]
Relevant to the central argument of this volume concerning the
importance of loss avoidance thinking, the fundamental reasons

---

26 *Ibid*, 241. Note, however, that Fund comments, both informally from the staff
and formally from the board, have always been treated as confidential.
27 E.B. Decision 1034-(60/27), 1 June 1960. In this regard, the central question
that gave rise to some disagreement was whether an article VIII consultation
should conclude with a board decision putting forward an official Fund position
on the affairs of the member concerned. In the end, the board deferred to the
sensitivities of members agreeing to engage in the consultations on an essentially
voluntary basis.

for the consequent expansion of the Fund's role are implicit in the recently declassified minutes of the first article VIII consultation with the United States.[28]

The consultation began on 5 March 1962 with a meeting between the Fund's managing director, Per Jacobsson, and the interdepartmental National Advisory Council on International Monetary and Financial Problems, the top-level official co-ordinating group created by the United States Congress when it ratified the Bretton Woods agreement. Jacobsson's opening remarks harked back to the consultations initiated in the 1920s by the Financial Committee of the League of Nations and tactfully decried their restricted nature, limited as they were to those countries in need of stabilization programmes and rejected even by a few countries that fell into that category. Clearly hoping to reinforce the message that the international community had a legitimate right to voice opinions about national policies that had systemic implications, Jacobsson stated: 'Naturally, the attitude of the United States is in this, as in other matters, of the greatest importance since what the United States does becomes respectable for any other country.'[29] He went on in a subtle and diplomatic way to express concerns about, among other things, wage inflation in the United States that threatened to exacerbate international payments imbalances. In this vein, he opened the door to a discussion of problematic trends in United States fiscal and monetary policy. The American officials followed with detailed explanations and generally sought to demonstrate the complexities of the economic challenges then facing the United

28 Office of the Secretary of the Treasury, Records of the National Advisory Council on International Monetary and Financial Problems, Minutes, #62-1, National Archives of the United States, box 3 of 61 (RG 56). The first consultation with Canada actually preceded this meeting. Beginning late in 1961, it concluded at the Fund's board meeting on 16 February 1962. See Central Files, Department of Finance, National Archives of Canada, file 1041-37-7-3-3. For commentary, see A.F.W. Plumptre, *Three Decades of Decision: Canada and the World Monetary System, 1944-75* (Toronto: McClelland and Stewart 1977), 127-8.

29 National Advisory Council on International Monetary and Financial Problems, Minutes, #62-1, attachment, 2.

States. Jacobsson concluded the meeting by observing 'how var-
ied the problems being faced by the u.s. were ... [and that] the
problems were well in hand.'[30] Although later events would make
this judgment seem wildly optimistic, Jacobsson did get across his
central message about the fundamental value of Fund consultations by reawakening the memory of the interwar period.

THE REBIRTH OF IMF SURVEILLANCE

If the consultations process under both article VIII and article
XIV established the machinery for international monetary collaboration, that machinery did not prove powerful enough to prevent the demolition of the central pillar of the Bretton Woods
order in the early 1970s. The story of the breakdown of the
pegged exchange rate system and the failure of subsequent
attempts to craft a replacement on the basis of a new and comprehensive global bargain has spawned a substantial analytical
literature.[31] For present purposes, it is sufficient to note that
when the crisis point came after a protracted and frustrating
series of negotiations, national policy-makers decided not to
abandon the institutional innovation of Fund surveillance. To
the contrary, they significantly expanded its scope and legal
force. That they did not match that expansion with substantive
political authority, or refrain from experimenting with new
mechanisms for policy co-ordination outside the Fund, only
makes more puzzling the question of why they bothered.

Despite a radically changed international environment, the
answer lies in the same set of perceptions of loss that they faced
at Bretton Woods. Key policy-makers came to believe that a truly
anarchical outcome to the 1971-3 débâcle – monetary arrange-

30 *Ibid*, 3.
31 See, for example, Benjamin J. Cohen, *Organizing the World's Money* (New
   York: Basic Books 1977); John Williamson, *The Failure of World Monetary
   Reform, 1971-74* (New York: New York University Press 1977); Fred L. Block,
   The Origins of International Economic Disorder (Berkeley: University of
   California Press 1977); John Odell, *U.S. International Monetary Policy*
   (Princeton NJ: Princeton University Press 1982; and Joanne Gowa, *Closing
   the Gold Window* (Ithaca NY: Cornell University Press 1983).

ments without a modicum of broadly accepted rules – would create an intolerable risk of a reversion to a 1930s-style environment of competitive exchange manipulation. This fear did not translate into their willingness to restore a pegged exchange rate system. But it did translate into their acceptance of a renewed obligation to avoid currency manipulation and into their willingness to open their domestic systems more fully and more formally to the surveillance apparatus of the Fund. Although less than satisfactory from the point of view of optimizing economic gains, Fund surveillance came to be seen, once again, as a feasible and necessary compromise between interdependence and autonomy. In a decision-making context that continued to emphasize prospective losses, it was better than nothing.[32]

Following the trauma of the 1971-3 period, the Fund and its member-states struggled mightily to provide some agreed order for the floating exchange rate arrangements that ensued. In 1974, the Executive Board agreed on a set of Guidelines for the Management of Floating Exchange Rates.[33] In the lengthy debate preceding that decision, a range of executive directors from countries that were letting their exchange rates float indicated a reluctance to grant the Fund any binding authority over their exchange rate policies, even to the point of refusing to go

32 An obvious question is why such a concern about losses did not motivate policy-makers, especially in the United States, when they took decisions in the early 1970s to break the exchange rate mechanism of the Bretton Woods system.
    Still the subject of much scholarly debate, the refusal of the United States to subordinate its own domestic interests to the needs of the system seems to me to be inadequately encompassed in a straightforward relative gains framework. By 1971 there was a deep sense even among 'liberal' policy-makers in the United States and elsewhere that the mechanism itself had long since been fatally compromised by the linkage between international liquidity needs and the United States payments deficit as well as by asymmetrical adjustment burdens. It is certainly likely that American authorities underestimated the ultimate costs of throwing the system into disarray, but having made the 1971-3 decisions, for better or for worse, the subsequent record indicates the rather rapid emergence of a consensus on the need to restore 'the rule of law.' Discounting associated rhetoric, my point is that this consensus was fundamentally shaped not by prospects of gain but by a fixation on prospects of loss.

33 E.B. Decision 4232-(74/67), adopted 13 June 1974. The guidelines themselves were published in the Fund's annual report for 1974, at 112-16.

along with a regime of prior consultation, that is, consulting with the Fund before moving, for example, from a fluctuating to a pegged exchange rate. Ultimately, they agreed in the decision only to 'use their best endeavors' to observe the guidelines. Despite their weakness and ultimate failure, the guidelines did establish precedents that would later be central to the revived surveillance role of the Fund. After specifying that members should act to 'prevent or moderate' sharp and disruptive fluctuations in their exchange rates through intervention in exchange markets, they attempted to ensure that policies having the intent of manipulating rates over a longer term were discouraged. Significantly, the guidelines also made it clear in principle that Fund oversight extended beyond narrow intervention practices to broader policies that had the same effect when adopted for balance of payments purposes, such as capital restrictions, various types of fiscal intervention, and monetary or interest rate policies.[34] However novel this effort to restore some kind of order, the guidelines were clearly no substitute for the multilateral treaty that had broken down.

As policy-makers struggled to craft a new treaty, mainly outside the established structures of the Fund, they had to deal with a number of interrelated complexities. The nature of the exchange rate system, the future monetary role of gold, the maintenance of a liberal payments system, the regulation of rapidly expanding international capital flows, increased financing for developing countries, the future role and financial size of the IMF, and other international liquidity and adjustment issues – all were on the table. Although this agenda proved too ambitious and the global reform effort foundered, a consensus did eventually arise among the leading monetary powers sufficient to foster

---

34 For discussion, see Kenneth W. Dam, *The Rules of the Game* (Chicago IL: University of Chicago Press 1982), 196-9. It is significant that this was stated explicitly. Under its Articles of Agreement, Fund authority was specifically limited to restrictions on the current account. This tentative step towards extending that authority to the capital account in certain circumstances represented an important concession.

the second-best solution of codifying what could be codified and leaving other matters to evolve outside the code. Loss avoidance thinking proved critical in this regard.

With the central pillar of the IMF articles essentially voided by state practice, and the 1974 guidelines of the Fund's board widely viewed as insubstantial, the spectre of monetary anarchy loomed again. For this reason the United States, which had taken the final steps that broke the Bretton Woods order, also took the lead in pushing for the restoration of legality on whatever minimal basis could be found. In the end, that restoration hinged on an agreement among the Group of Five leading industrial states, with key IMF staff members playing a facilitating role.

Unable to craft a comprehensive reform deal in a fully multilateral setting, the finance ministers and central bank governors of the United States, the United Kingdom, France, the Federal Republic of Germany, and Japan attempted to reach agreement among themselves on three key issues: IMF quotas, the future role of gold, and the nature of the exchange rate system. By August 1975, they had reached a consensus on the first two issues. Only the third remained. Because France and the United States had previously articulated the most divergent positions on that issue, the G-5 officials collectively agreed on 30 August to go along with any agreement on exchange rates that those two countries were able to hammer out.

Although their positions had been moderating over time, France was known as the key proponent of a return to some version of a fixed rate system while the United States insisted on maintaining its ability to let the dollar float. Often depicted as a doctrinal dispute, differing positions on the appropriate distribution of the costs of adjustment between deficit and surplus countries were obviously central to the negotiations. The search for a middle ground essentially came down to a series of secret meetings in the autumn of 1975 between the under secretary of the treasury of the United States, Edwin H. Yeo III, and the deputy finance minister of France, Jacques de Larosière. From the little that has been written about these discussions, and from their context, it is possible to make reasonable inferences about the influences that led to the final agreement and, especially, to the place of IMF surveillance within it.[35]

French policy-makers had long complained that the Americans enjoyed an 'exorbitant privilege' in their ability to finance international payments imbalances with dollar liabilities. In contrast to a compulsory 'asset settlement' system that could have required the United States to draw down official reserves to cover current account deficits, thereby subjecting it to some external discipline on its internal policies, the key role the dollar played in the Bretton Woods system allowed the United States, in effect, to shift adjustment costs abroad. After that system broke down, floating the dollar essentially allowed it to do the same. The interest in restoring some version of a fixed rate system, so prominent in long-standing debates over international monetary affairs inside France, may also be understood in this light.[36] Opening the door to greater flexibility on this issue, however, were more mundane considerations concerning gold. Given the high stock of gold known to be held in private hands inside France, and given the agreed 'restitution' (to member-states) of some of the IMF's gold stock (in a context where the fixed official price of gold would eventually be abandoned), French policy-makers had an evident incentive to reach agreement on the exchange rate issue.[37]

35 The literature consists of Margaret Garritsen de Vries, *The International Monetary Fund, 1971-1978*, vol II (Washington: IMF 1985), 743-9; Robert Solomon, *The International Monetary System, 1945-1976* (New York: Harper & Row 1977), 307-10; Dam, *The Rules of the Game*, 256-9; Robert D. Putnam and Nicholas Bayne, *Hanging Together* (Cambridge MA: Harvard University Press 1987), 39; F. Lisle Widman, *Making International Monetary Policy* (Washington: International Law Institute, Georgetown University, 1982), 52, and Joseph Gold, *Exchange Rates in International Law and Organization* (Np: American Bar Association, Section of International Law and Practice, 1988), chaps 2 and 3. My own insights have also come from a series of background interviews with five former officials who were close to the negotiations.

36 As late as the October 1975 annual meeting of the IMF, the French finance minister criticized floating rates as 'a dangerous phenomenon that disturbs world order': Dam, *The Rules of the Game*, 257.

37 Aware that the agreement on gold was particularly important to France, the

For their part, American policy-makers generally supported a discretionary exchange rate regime, at least for the dollar and at least for the time being, precisely in order to mitigate the costs of adjustment that could have arisen under an asset settlement system. The conviction that it was not only appropriate but essential that other countries, especially those with persistent payments surpluses, should bear more of those costs had long since become an article of faith. Within Congress, such a view had been advanced energetically by the respected and influential Henry Reuss, who embellished that conviction with the view that constraints on the ability of the United States unilaterally to redistribute those costs should be resisted.[38] As Reuss and others sought to justify that stance, however, they had to confront the widespread fear that uninhibited floating rates could destabilize the world trading system by making it easier for countries to manipulate their currencies. As Kenneth Dam notes, this attitude may have been 'an illogical carry-over from the very different conditions of the interwar period,' but it remained widely held.[39]

The way around the conundrum was to advocate not stable exchange rates, as the French preferred, but a 'stable system of exchange rates,' wording that would be included in the final agreement. But how would a stable system be maintained in the absence of a binding rule? The American answer was twofold: by leaving it up to individual countries to create the conditions

secretary of the treasury let it be known that the agreement would not be submitted to Congress for authorization until a deal was struck on the exchange rate regime. Solomon, *The International Monetary System*, 316-17.

38 For an insight into the connection between this view and the future role of the Fund, see United States, Congress, House, Subcommittee on International Finance of the Committee on Banking and Currency, *International Monetary Reform*, Hearings, 93rd Cong, 1st sess, 13 November and 5 December 1973. Note that during the hearings, Reuss had become extremely exercised about the word 'surveillance' and objected strongly to the possibility that floating by the United States might at some point be constrained by the Fund. Paul Volcker, under secretary of the treasury, riposted: 'Now I do not object to "surveillance." I think a country operating on a floating rate should be subjected to some international rules and surveillance' (p 22).

39 Dam, *The Rules of the Game*, 257.

for domestic price stability and by renewing and expanding the
mandate of the IMF to 'exercise surveillance over the adjustment
process.'[40] Thus, contrary to the earlier assumption that the
necessity of defending a fixed exchange rate overseen by the
Fund would encourage internal policy adjustments, this new
rationale effectively assumed that international market forces
supplemented by the peer pressure embodied in Fund surveillance would discipline countries and foster domestic stability. In
the end, in the face of United States intransigence and accepting
the infeasibility of pegging rates at a time when wide differences
existed in national inflation rates, French policy-makers were
prepared to accept this thinking, but they insisted that the word
'firm' precede the reference to Fund surveillance and that the
eventual restoration of pegged rates not be precluded. Assenting,
once again, to IMF surveillance, including now the formal legal
obligation to consult with the Fund, the United States accepted
the principle that a pegged rate system might someday be
restored, but it was careful to negotiate safeguards, including an
effective veto, that protected its right to determine for itself
whether and when it would revert to greater exchange rate
fixity.[41]

The text of the agreement between France and the United
States was blessed in November 1975 at the Rambouillet summit
(of the G-5 heads of government plus Italy) and refined by Fund
staff and board members. Following the January 1976 meeting
of the IMF's policy-making Interim Committee in Jamaica, it
became the key item in the Second Amendment to the Articles
of Agreement of the Fund, the multilateral treaty that finally
restored the monetary system to legality. The new article IV
enjoined the Fund to 'oversee the international monetary system

---

40 *Ibid*, 239. The word 'surveillance' was again chosen with careful thought. At a
meeting of G-10 central bankers and top finance ministry officials in December
1975, Arthur Burns, chairman of the Board of Governors of the United
States Federal Reserve Board, explicitly considered and rejected the term
'management.' His counterparts agreed that 'surveillance' had the preferred
'connotation.' Background interview, February 1990.
41 The plan for a return to pegged rates was embedded in what eventually became
schedule C of the Fund's articles as amended.

in order to ensure its effective operation' as well as to 'exercise firm surveillance over the exchange rate policies of members, and ... adopt specific principles for the guidance of all members with respect to those policies.' Moreover, those principles were to 'respect the domestic social and political policies of members, and when applying these principles, the Fund shall pay due regard to the circumstances of members.' Those members, for their part, were required to 'provide the Fund with the information necessary for such surveillance, and, when requested by the Fund, [to] consult with it on ... exchange rate policies.' Among other things, they also agreed to 'avoid manipulating exchange rates or the international monetary system in order to prevent effective balance of payments adjustment or to gain an unfair competitive advantage over other members.'

During the ratification debate that followed in the United States, Yeo provided insight into the reasons behind the agreement when he defended it before the Foreign Relations Committee of the Senate. He began his testimony by emphasizing the need 'to restore the legal framework that is necessary ... to reduce the risk that nations will pursue selfish policies which pay too little regard to the effects on others.' In the face of sceptical questioning, he amplified this theme:

We feel [the legislation] is important because interdependence ... has to be governed by a body, a structure of law. I think we can all ... feel fortunate that coming out of recession we have not in any significant degree seen or observed restrictionist tendencies or beggar-thy-neighbor tendencies. This legislation will provide a framework to insure that that performance continues ... The best example of what happens when countries as a group follow beggar-thy-neighbor policies was uncovered in the 1930s. Each individual country pursued its narrow interests in the most circumscribed manner imaginable — tariff barriers, competitive devaluations — and we all lost.

The testimony continues:

SENATOR CASE. This isn't just a question of state of mind, is it? MR YEO. No. It is a question of state of mind and of hard economic interests. The example, if we could just go back to the 1930s where we have a concrete test case of what happened — SENATOR CASE. You don't remember that; you read about it. I was there at the time. MR YEO. ... no, you are right. I read about it. I have studied it. I like to say I have studied it.

Following up on this line and querying the expanded role proposed for the IMF, a key member of the committee, Senator Jacob Javits, continued: 'Basically I agree that we have to be multinational, and multilateral, and that the IMF is the key instrument ... and that this is a promotion the Fund deserves — to assume a greater role.' But he then pressed for some indication of the urgency of the legislation. Yeo replied:

More important [than companion legislation to increase the resources of the Fund] ... I hesitate to use the word urgent — but [it is] quite important that we go back to the rule of law in terms of the international monetary system. I would direct your attention to ... section 1 of article IV, which colloquially has become known as the 'Thou shalt not manipulate' item. That relates directly to section 3 of the same article which gives the Fund additional powers ... It says that the Fund shall maintain firm surveillance over members' exchange rate practices.[42]

It is noteworthy that this testimony was provided by a spokesman for a strongly market-oriented administration. The treasury secretary, William Simon, for example, was well known for his passionate advocacy of the disciplinary power of market forces. Nevertheless, it had obviously become the accepted view that market discipline alone was not adequate to the task of stabilizing international monetary relations in the contemporary environment.[43] A new legal structure, however soft its actual rules,

---

42 United States, Congress, Senate, Committee on Foreign Relations, *International Monetary Fund Amendments*, Hearings on S. 3454, 94th Cong, 2nd sess, 22 June 1976, 5, 27-8, and 32-3.

43 Looking back fifteen years later on the assumptions concerning floating rates widely held at the time, Paul Volcker labelled them 'pretty naive': *Wall Street Journal*, 28 November 1988, A 12, quoted in Joseph Gold, *Legal Effects of Fluctuating Exchange Rates* (Washington: IMF 1990), 17.

was considered to be worth the expenditure of so much time, negotiating effort, and political capital. To secure congressional assent to that structure, including its central surveillance provisions, it obviously seemed useful to raise the potential threat of exchange rate manipulation such as had occurred in the 1930s.[44] At the same time, however, it was considered important to build significant flexibility into that structure. As constrained as ever, despite the adjective 'firm,' the commitment to IMF surveillance by the leading monetary power once again rested on a choice between potential economic losses in the future if competitive impulses reasserted themselves in the arena of exchange rates and an immediate, if measured, infringement on domestic political authority. National economic policies that had a systemic impact would not be 'constrained' by supranational authority, but many who might initially have agreed with Henry Reuss on the sanctity of national authority had eventually come to agree on the necessity of a limitation expressed in terms of external accountability. A supportive political coalition ultimately rested on a sense of disquiet concerning the viability of the status quo, a world without a modicum of agreed monetary order. The 1930s analogy, despite its arguable inappropriateness in the context of the 1970s, gave that sense a clearer meaning.

On paper, and broadly interpreted, the new Articles of Agreement seemed to give the Fund a significantly expanded role. In practice, the resistance of member-states to granting effective new powers to the Fund was intense. During the post-

---

44 I do not doubt that key policy-makers sincerely believed that the analogy was appropriate. Subsequently, Yeo and Sam Cross, the American executive director at the Fund during the Second Amendment negotiations, continued to emphasize the importance of preventing states from gaining unfair competitive advantage through exchange rate manipulation. See chapters by both officials in Jacob S. Dreyer et al, eds, *Exchange Rate Flexibility* (Washington: American Enterprise Institute 1978), 181-90. Note, however, that no evidence existed then, nor has any subsequently come to light, that systematic exchange rate manipulation on any significant scale was being practised. Exchange rate volatility and enhanced export competitiveness have generally been viewed by informed observers as having other sources. See Gold, *Legal Effects*, 16.

Jamaica discussions of the Executive Board on the design of a substantive code of conduct that would make the new article IV operative and replace the unsatisfactory 1974 guidelines on floating, deep divisions immediately became apparent. To simplify somewhat, three major bodies of opinion initially emerged among the principal monetary powers. In a series of background papers, the managing director and staff of the Fund subtly pushed for a broad interpretation of the new article IV to revive the notion of prior consultation before a member-state changed its exchange rate, to permit the Fund to take a view on whether an exchange rate was 'wrong' or creating 'disorderly' market conditions, and to facilitate Fund inquiries into a wider range of domestic policies.[45] A second approach, identified with continental European members, rejected prior consultation but called for the Fund to promote broad policy objectives – for example, by taking a view on the correctness of particular exchange rates.[46] Countering both of these views, the United States, Canada, and Britain favoured an approach that would defer to market forces, narrowly construe the meaning of market disorder, and concentrate the Fund's mandate on the avoidance of rate manipulation by governments.[47] In the face of these differences, it was obvious that a set of clear or encompassing principles would be impossible to design. On the basis of a suggestion from Canadian and British officials, therefore, all that could be agreed at this initial stage was that specific new rules should evolve out of practice. Along these lines, the 'First Surveillance Decision' finally emerged from the Fund's board in April 1977.[48]

Echoing themes expressed at Bretton Woods, the 1977 deci-

45 de Vries, *The International Monetary Fund, 1971-1978*, II: 840.
46 West Germany and France, in particular, retained the strongly held view that countries (read, the United States) should not be able to maintain exchange rates that had the effect of exporting inflation abroad.
47 The critical concerns of this group were that countries should defer to market forces and, in particular, that low-inflation countries should not be able to assist their export industries by resisting upward valuations in their exchange rates.
48 E.B. Decision 5392-(77/63), 29 April 1977, in IMF, *Selected Decisions* (15th

sion really articulated only one formally binding principle (already stated in the articles) – that members *shall* avoid manipulating exchange rates or the system as a whole to avoid adjustment or to gain a competitive advantage. Two non-binding principles complemented this one: that members *should* intervene in exchange markets to counter disorderly conditions and that in deciding upon intervention policies members *should* take into account the interests of other members. To encourage adherence to these principles, members agreed in the decision to consult with the Fund annually under the new article IV. In view of the key objective of encouraging the adjustment of international payments imbalances, the decision specified a series of developments that would suggest the need for Fund discussion with a member, including protracted large-scale intervention, unsustainable levels of borrowing, the introduction or substantial modification of restrictions on capital flows, the use of monetary and other domestic financial policies that gave abnormal encouragement to capital flows, and so on. To appraise such developments, the Fund was, significantly, formally empowered to enquire into a range of policies that had an impact on exchange rates. But in exercising those powers, it was to recognize that members' objectives included not just international adjustment but also 'sustained sound economic growth and reasonable levels of employment.'[49] Additionally, in a weak replacement for the former requirement that a member consult with the Fund prior

---

issue) (Washington: IMF, 30 April 1990), 10. For commentary, see John H. Young, 'Surveillance over exchange rate policies,' *Finance & Development* 14(September 1977), 17-19.

49 On the logical inseparability of exchange rate matters from other aspects of macro-economic policy, see Richard Cooper, 'IMF surveillance over floating exchange rates,' in Cooper, *The International Monetary System* (Cambridge MA: MIT Press 1987), 149. On the basis of such reasoning, the Fund's surveillance mandate with respect to certain developing member-states expanded in a novel way in the 1980s. Procedures for 'enhanced surveillance' were developed in connection with certain debt rescheduling operations. In this way, the Fund at times became a mediator between indebted member-states and international banks.

to changing its exchange rate, the decision gave the managing director the authority to question, at his own initiative, the exchange rate policies of members and report to the executive directors on the answers.[50] The decision also authorized periodic reviews of exchange rate and other international economic developments in general, a task that now culminates in the annual publication of the Fund's *World Economic Outlook*, an exercise which has come to be viewed by the Fund as a central component of its surveillance role.

The Second Amendment to the Fund's Articles of Agreement replaced the Bretton Woods regime with what has been called 'soft law.'[51] The new approach to multilateral economic surveillance actually extended the formal jurisdiction of the Fund but did not reinvest it with real regulatory power. Consultations formerly voluntary under article VIII were now required, and every article IV consultation was to end with a summing up by the managing director which, after any amendments by directors, was to be considered a formal legal decision of the board. And despite the apparent narrowness of the 1977 surveillance decision, the explicit recognition that broader macro-economic policies had an important impact on exchange rates in a freer environment actually widened considerably the scope of the legitimate concerns of the Fund. That this more ambitious mandate would meet continued resistance from critics and disappointment from supporters was certain. But generally ameliorating that resistance and assuaging that disappointment was the tacit acceptance of the view that although the world might not actually be worse off if a mechanism for broadly based multilateral surveillance ceased to exist, it was better not to find out.

50 On the implementation of the 1977 decision and its aftermath, see Eduard Brau, 'The consultation process of the Fund,' *Finance & Development* 18(December 1981), 13-16, and David Burton and Martin Gilman, 'Exchange rate policy and the IMF,' *Finance & Development* 28(September 1991), 18-21.
51 Joseph Gold, 'Strengthening the soft international law of exchange arrangements,' in *Legal and Institutional Aspects of the International Monetary System*, vol 2 (Washington: IMF 1984), 515-79.

Since 1977 the main institutional challenges to Fund surveillance have arisen as states have sought better to accommodate their shifting monetary interests through more limited arrangements.[52] Indeed, almost as soon as the Second Amendment came into effect, states intensified their efforts to supplement Fund surveillance. European states, for example, moved to tighten financial linkages among themselves and to seek greater exchange rate stability through the European Monetary System and eventually through plans for monetary union.[53] Simultaneously, the United States and other major industrial states sought to create more restricted forums for the discussion of macroeconomic policy issues, most prominently the G-7 summit meetings.[54] Building on the narrow jurisdictional base provided in the 1977 decision, the IMF began playing a limited role in the summits after 1982, when its managing director was first invited to participate in the economic overview discussions of the finance ministers, though not in their substantive policy-making sessions. Over time, the G-7 deputies began to rely more heavily on Fund staff for an increasing amount of technical assistance, particularly related to the use of economic indicators to monitor and evaluate overall policy trends. At the Tokyo Summit in June 1986, the Fund's role was emphasized, at least in principle, when

52 Miles Kahler cogently surveys this subject in 'Organization and cooperation: international institutions and policy coordination,' *Journal of Public Policy* 8(July-December 1988), 375-401. Also see Kahler, 'The United States and the International Monetary Fund: declining influence or declining interest?' in Margaret P. Karns and Karen A. Mingst, eds, *The United States and Multilateral Institutions* (Boston: Unwin Hyman 1990), 91-114.

53 See Louis W. Pauly, 'The politics of European monetary union: national strategies, international implications,' *International Journal* 47(winter 1991-2), 93-111.

54 Wendy Dobson provides a comprehensive and balanced analysis of this development in *Economic Policy Coordination: Requiem or Prologue?* (Washington: Institute for International Economics, April 1991). Also see Robert Solomon, 'Background paper,' in *Partners in Prosperity* (New York: Priority Press 1991); Putnam and Bayne, *Hanging Together*; and I.M. Destler and C. Randall Henning, *Dollar Politics* (Washington: Institute for International Economics 1989).

the G-7 leaders reaffirmed their undertaking 'to co-operate with the IMF in strengthening multilateral surveillance.'[55] Regular surveillance-style discussions also continued among the two dozen industrialized states of the OECD.[56] While their proponents see benefits coming from the informal or restricted nature of these alternative vehicles for surveillance, others see them eroding the overarching normative order of multilateralism.[57]

CONCLUSION: MULTILATERAL ECONOMIC SURVEILLANCE AND ITS LIMITS

The constitutional base of the Fund's surveillance function has been constructed by the decisions of policy-makers struggling to find alternatives to a status quo believed to contain the seeds of economic catastrophe. Placing outer boundaries on those decisions were perceived limits on their capacities to accept infringements on national political authority. In both the 1940s and the 1970s, prospects of loss more than prospects of gain appear to have moved states to accept external accountability in principle. The fundamental character of multilateral economic surveillance, in turn, has been crucially shaped by their reluctance to

55 Quoted in Andrew Crockett, 'The role of international institutions in surveillance and policy coordination,' in Ralph Bryant et al, *Macroeconomic Policies in an Interdependent World* (Washington: IMF 1989), 357. Pronouncements to this effect have been made regularly, albeit with disputable intentions and doubtful effects. Even as unlikely a supporter as Donald Regan, President Ronald Reagan's first treasury secretary, was moved in 1984 to say: 'The United States is prepared to move ahead decisively to strengthen international surveillance. We believe that such measures as increased public awareness of Article IV consultations with member countries, and a greater use of ad hoc consultations between the Managing Director and Finance Ministers, would be very useful. We hope others support proposals such as these for a stronger IMF role.' Speech of 24 September 1984; quoted in Ralph Bryant, 'Alternative futures for the International Monetary Fund,' unpublished manuscript.
56 Since 1961 the main forum has been the regular meeting of Working Party 3 of the OECD's Economic Policy Committee. For background, see Robert W. Russell, 'Transgovernmental interaction in the international monetary system, 1960-1972,' *International Organization* 27(autumn 1973), 431-64.
57 See, for example, Fabrizio Saccomanni, 'On multilateral surveillance,' in Paolo Guerrieri and Pier Carlo Padoan, eds, *The Political Economy of International Cooperation* (London: Croom Helm 1988).

put that principle fully into practice. In the last major reformu-
lation of the Fund's mandate in this area, policy-makers essentially restated the Bretton Woods formula, albeit with a more
complex understanding of the systemic consequences of national
policies in a system of flexible exchange rates. Under conditions
of tightening interdependence, the policies of a state that have
an impact on the system are the legitimate concern of all others;
that concern can legitimately be expressed by the international
community through a broadly based multilateral organization,
but final decisions on those policies remain the prerogative of
individual states themselves.

But have perceptions really mattered in the evolution of Fund
surveillance, or do straightforward economic and political interests, rationally conceived and rationally interpreted, offer an
adequate explanation? The claim of the American under secretary of the treasury in 1976 that both 'states of mind' and interests were involved seems unexceptionable to me. At the level of
policy-makers themselves, the role of perceptions cannot be
ignored. In the 1970s, as in the 1940s, the analogy of interwar
monetary anarchy certainly captured the imaginations of key
American policy-makers, the leaders in the movement to refor-
mulate the Fund's mandate. In view of radically altered systemic
conditions, the absence of evidence of competitive currency
manipulation, and the natural receding of memories, this is
somewhat surprising. Surely it is conceivable that another analogy, another set of perceptions, or a straightforward 'rational'
calculation of interests could have focused attention on prospective gains of either the absolute or the relative variety. In such an
alternative framework, it is easy to imagine the Fund's surveillance mandate either being markedly strengthened, as Fund staff
consistently advocated, or abolished entirely, as stalwart proponents of 'market discipline' have long championed.[58] The man-

---

58 Note here that such a strengthening of multilateral surveillance implies no
    necessary view on the wisdom of the actual 'co-ordination' of economic policies,
    a subject of considerable scholarly controversy. It might, as some have
    suggested, merely entail the clearer articulation of the right of the international

date actually designed did not clearly maximize the absolute gains that could conceivably accrue from a more efficient and effective organization of the world economy, nor did it clearly maximize relative gains for any one country. Instead, the character of that mandate appears to have been defined at critical junctures within decision-making frameworks that heightened perceptions of potential future losses.

The interwar analogy, an image that crystallized fears of the consequences of non-co-operation, was in the atmosphere at Bretton Woods. Despite completely different international economic conditions in the 1970s, and despite the more nuanced understanding of the actual history of the interwar period that might have been expected to be current by then, that analogy remained prominent as the architects of the Fund's Second Amendment laboured to restore 'the rule of law' to a broken monetary system. Without its influence in sharpening perceptions of the costs of maintaining the status quo, resistance to multilateral surveillance, as bounded by safeguards as it was, might easily have proved overwhelming.[59]

During the past fifteen years, states have increasingly moved to supplement multilateral surveillance with limited or regional experiments in policy co-ordination. The exclusivity and/or informality of these experiments have attracted both critical and supportive comment. It seems clear, nonetheless, that they represent a retrenchment from any vision of the progressive development of durable and broadly based collaborative institutions. As we have seen, however, since Bretton Woods that develop-

---

community to express consensus views about the inappropriateness of a particular state's policies in light of the needs of the payments adjustment process and the obligation of that state to respond to such criticism in a public forum. See Jacques J. Polak, 'Strengthening the role of the IMF in the international monetary system,' in Catherine Gwin, Richard E. Feinberg et al, *The International Monetary Fund in a Multipolar World: Pulling Together* (New Brunswick NJ: Transaction 1989), 45-68.

59 Obviously, American administration officials found the analogy useful in dealing with Congress. This connection between domestic structure and loss avoidance strategies in this case reinforces Michael Mastanduno's argument in this volume.

ment was never to occur along an uncomplicated trajectory. As the prospect of catastrophic systemic losses fades along with actual memories of the 1930s, and as the economic history of the interwar period itself is reinterpreted, national policy-makers and their constituents seem ever more reluctant to expand the scope of truly multilateral institutions. It would be ironic, indeed, if a new global disaster were required to convince them otherwise.

Five

The politics and psychology of restraint: Israeli decision-making in the Gulf War

DAVID A. WELCH

> Two horses were sitting at a bar reminiscing about the day's races. 'The strangest thing happened today,' said the first horse. 'I was waiting for the start of the fifth race at Rockingham Park, when I felt this odd twitch in my hind leg. As soon as the race started, I sprinted to the lead, and never looked back. I won by four lengths.'
>
> 'What a coincidence,' said the second horse. 'The same thing happened to me in the third race at Suffolk Downs. I felt the same twitch just before the race, and I ran faster than I ever have in my life. I won by six lengths!'
>
> Just then a greyhound sitting at the far end of the bar put down his beer and approached the two horses. 'Pardon me, boys,' he said, 'but I couldn't help overhearing your conversation. You'll never believe this, but I felt a strange twitch in my leg, too, just before the start of the second race at Wonderland today; I set a course record, winning by eight lengths!'
>
> 'Now there's something you don't see every day,' said the first horse to the second: 'A talking dog!'

From time to time an event may involve so many puzzles at once that when our attention is drawn to one in particular, we tend not to notice others that may be just as important or perplexing. The Gulf War of 1991 is a case in point. Who in January 1990 could have predicted that, within a year, American and Syrian troops would be fighting side by side in the Middle East, that the Soviet Union would staunchly support a massive American mili-

Assistant Professor of Political Science, University of Toronto, Toronto, Canada.

The author would like to acknowledge the invaluable assistance of Colonel Bruce F. Williams (ret.), former United States defense attaché to Israel; Mende Meron, former director general, Israeli Ministry of Defense; Oded Eran, deputy chief of mission, Israeli embassy, Washington; Itamar Rabinovich, rector, Tel Aviv University; Yehuda Ben Meir and Dore Gold of the Jaffee Center for Strategic Studies, Tel Aviv University; Zvi Levy; Michael Mastanduno; Robert Matthews; Timothy McKeown; Louis Pauly; Timothy Prinz; Debora Spar; Janice Gross Stein; Melissa Williams; and the Connaught Fund, University of Toronto.

tary operation in the Third World, that the United Nations Security Council would authorize a collective security action, that the Iraqi air force would seek refuge in Iran, or that Israel would weather a sustained ballistic missile attack against two of its largest cities without responding? Any one of these developments would seem to qualify as a talking dog.

Of all these features of the Gulf War, the last may be the most remarkable. For the first time in history, one state employed its military forces against the metropolitan territory of another without eliciting so much as a single shot in return. It may be that this was also the first time in history that a state attempting to goad another into war failed to do so. Moreover, by not responding to Iraq's assault, and by accepting the deployment of American Patriot air defence missiles and crews to intercept Scud missiles, Israel forsook two cardinal tenets of its security policy: (1) swift and decisive retaliation to any and all armed attacks; and (2) military self-reliance – a policy reinforced less than a week before the outbreak of war by the statement of Prime Minister Yitzhak Shamir that Israel's defence 'always was and always will be the sole and exclusive responsibility of the government of Israel.'[1] To add to the sense of wonder, it may be noted that for several months – indeed, right up to the eve of war itself – Israel's highest officials had stated repeatedly and unequivocally that Israel *would* respond if attacked.[2] There can be

---

1 *Jerusalem Post*, 14 January 1991, 1. Editorially, the *Post* acknowledged that Israel's dependence on American forces during the Gulf War set a dangerous precedent: 20 January 1991, 4.

2 Shamir, for example, stated: 'Saddam Hussein knows that if he tries to attack Israel, we shall strike back. Our allies are aware of our position and of our state of readiness.' The foreign minister, David Levy, warned of a 'strong response' and 'very painful' retaliation, a point he stressed repeatedly, including to a group of visiting American congressmen. The minister of defense, Moshe Arens, likewise made several similarly definitive statements. On this issue, the cabinet was unanimous. See, eg, *Jerusalem Post*, 2 January 1991, 1; David Makovsky, 'Scenarios: will Israel hit Iraq?' *Jerusalem Post*, 4 January 1991, 9; and *Jerusalem Post*, 14 January 1991, 1. Prominent Israeli military figures echoed the theme. For example, Shlomo Gazit, former head of Israeli military intelligence, wrote (*Jerusalem Post*, 8 January 1991, 4): 'Saddam is no fool; he undoubtedly knows that were he to launch an unprovoked attack against Israel,

little doubt of Saddam Hussein's confidence both that Israel would respond and that by doing so it would tear apart the coalition arrayed against him. Indeed, this confidence may explain yet another major puzzle: the failure of compellence under near ideal conditions (Saddam Hussein refused to yield in the face of overwhelming military force, an unprecedentedly effective trade embargo, and almost total diplomatic isolation).[3]

The decision-making process that led Israel to forbear is fascinating and instructive because the decision itself was neither pre-determined nor over-determined; it touched issues at the very core of the value system of most states; and it directly posed the 'co-operate or defect dilemma' that lies at the very heart of the dominant realist analysis of international politics and of several current debates in international relations theory. I will attempt to argue that at its present level of development, international relations theory is poorly equipped to explain Israeli behaviour. Each of the explanations that seem *prima facie* most plausible from various theoretical standpoints has at least one glaring weakness. A system-level explanation couched in terms of Israeli dependence upon the United States does not fit the general pattern of American-Israeli relations and cannot explain why (as seems virtually certain) Israel would have retaliated under fairly well specified conditions that, through sheer luck, simply never materialized. A state-level explanation couched in

---

Israel would have to respond.' Not until 16 January did the government modify this policy, when, on Israeli television, Shamir denied that Israel was committed to 'automatic' retaliation, noting instead that Israel merely reserved the right to decide whether and how it would respond: *Jerusalem Post*, 17 January 1991, 1.

3 The virtual certainty in the United States and Canada that Israel would respond if attacked was reflected in an informal poll I conducted in the months between the Iraqi invasion of Kuwait on 2 August 1990 and the beginning of Operation Desert Storm on 17 January 1991. Of several dozen political scientists, current and former government officials, and military officers surveyed, only one (Colonel Williams) believed it even conceivable that Israel would weather an Iraqi attack without a military reaction of some kind. A similar informal survey after the war yielded a different result, however: a slim majority claimed not to have been surprised at Israel's restraint. I suspect that this may be a function of the same bandwagon effect that leads a far larger proportion of respondents in post-election polls to claim to have voted for winners than actually did.

terms (for example) of strong domestic support for a policy of restraint is inconsistent with Israeli decision-makers' manifest disregard of public opinion. And an individual-level rational actor explanation fails to account for important aspects of Israel's behaviour that are inconsistent with the assumptions and expectations of orthodox cost-benefit analysis. Insights from prospect theory, however, enable us to understand a number of otherwise puzzling features of the Israeli decision-making process. While they cannot account for all, they nonetheless permit, on balance, a more satisfying and more persuasive explanation of Israeli behaviour than do more traditional theoretical perspectives.

Unfortunately, the task of explaining Israeli behaviour poses a number of methodological challenges. Relatively few details of the Israeli decision-making process have been published, and some published accounts are suspect. Many important details will remain diplomatically or militarily sensitive for some time, and government documents will be sealed for several decades. The dearth of reliable public information has enabled many unsubstantiated and contradictory rumours to circulate. These obstacles make it impossible to provide a detailed history of Israeli decision-making; fortunately, this is not necessary. Enough may be gleaned from the published record and from informed testimony to provide a *characterization* of the process adequate to the tasks at hand. With that goal in mind, this study is based primarily on interviews conducted in Israel and the United States in May, June, and July 1991. Israelis interviewed included current and former members of the cabinet, foreign ministry, ministry of defense, and the Israeli Defense Forces (IDF). Americans interviewed included senior officials in the National Security Council and the Department of State, some of whom accompanied the deputy secretary of state, Lawrence Eagleburger, on his two pivotal diplomatic missions to Israel in January 1991. Although willing to discuss sensitive matters, only one of those interviewed – the Israeli minister of agriculture, Raphael Eitan – consented to speak on the record, and several requested that they not be identified as having been interviewed at all.[4]

I proceed first by relating what currently appear to be the key features and events of the Israeli decision-making process, in approximate chronological order, covering Israel's pre-crisis goals, its policy to January 1991, and its policy during the war itself, concentrating on Israeli-American interactions. I then briefly discuss the aftermath of the war in order to elucidate the Israeli perception of the costs and benefits of their restraint and finally turn to the theoretical issues alluded to above.[5]

THE PRE-WAR SITUATION

In the 1970s and 1980s, Iraq began to loom large in Israeli threat assessments. Iraq's leader, Saddam Hussein, was at once ruthless, megalomaniacal, and anti-Zionist. He commanded an enormous military force and, most importantly, actively sought to develop nuclear weapons. The 1981 attack on Iraq's Osirak reactor demonstrated the seriousness with which Israel regarded that threat, even though, with Iraq's nuclear programme seemingly in its infancy and the Iraqi armed forces bogged down in a costly war with Iran, the danger to Israel was neither immediate nor acute.

---

4 Those who consented to be identified as having spoken off the record include Colonel Hanan Alon, director of foreign affairs, Israeli Ministry of Defense; Colonel Shimon Hefetz, aide de camp to Moshe Arens; Major General Musa Peled (ret.), chief executive officer of Rafael Armaments Development Authority; Yitzhak Rabin, former prime minister and minister of defense; Richard N. Haass, special assistant to the President and senior director for Near East and South Asian affairs, National Security Council; William R. Brew, director, Office of Israel and Arab-Israeli Affairs, Department of State; William Brown, ambassador of the United States to Israel; and Steven N. Simon, director, Policy Analysis, Bureau of Politico-Military Affairs, Department of State.

5 A few procedural points: to avoid excessive use of adverbs such as 'reportedly,' I will employ a straight narrative form; the reader should be aware that unreferenced claims are based on oral testimony. My presentation of Israeli military options is my own interpolation from the very guarded remarks of knowledgeable individuals, but I am relatively confident that it is accurate because several people have confirmed its key features while no one has contradicted it. Finally, I have chosen to develop important but distractingly technical points in footnotes rather than in the text.

More threatening in the short run were Iraq's chemical weapons, particularly in view of Saddam Hussein's demonstrated willingness to use them, first against Iranian troops and then against his own people. He also possessed two weapons systems with which he might at some point be able to launch a nuclear or chemical attack against Israel itself: a crude ballistic missile (the 1950s-vintage Soviet ss-1c, the Scud B) and the Soviet Union's best supersonic low-level attack aircraft, the Sukhoi Su-24).[6]

Learning from the Osirak incident, Saddam Hussein decentralized his nuclear programme, sending much of it underground into well-fortified bunkers. Identifying research sites and monitoring the progress of Iraq's programme became a priority for Israeli intelligence. Aware of Israeli concern, but uncertain how much Israel knew, Saddam Hussein made several threatening statements early in 1990 which were apparently intended to deter an Israeli pre-emptive strike. On 1 April, for example, he vowed to 'make the fire eat up half of Israel if it tries to do

6 The range of the basic Scud missile, designed as a battlefield support weapon, was insufficient to reach Israel from western Iraq. To strike targets in Teheran during the Iran-Iraq War, however, Iraqi technicians developed two modifications of the Scud with longer ranges (but proportionately smaller payloads) known as the Al-Hussein and the Al-Abbas. Both were capable of reaching targets in Israel. At the outbreak of the Gulf War, there was no evidence that Iraq had yet developed a nuclear weapon of any kind or that it had developed chemical warheads for the longer range Scud modifications. Iraq was known to be capable of delivering chemical weapons by air, however, because of its 1988 attack on Kurdish rebels. For this reason, and because the Su-24 could carry a payload of 4,000 kilograms compared with only 180 kilograms for an Al-Hussein, Israeli military intelligence considered Iraq's 16 Su-24s the greater of the two threats. See, eg, *The Military Balance 1990-1991* (London: Brassey's for the International Institute for Strategic Studies 1990), 106, and Edward Luttwak, 'Saddam's missile-rattling,' *Jerusalem Post*, 11 January 1991, 7. However, in 1991 Israel did not yet possess the capability to intercept Scuds. Its own intermediate-range anti-ballistic missile weapon, the Arrow, was in an early stage of development under an arrangement with the United States and its funding was still very much up in the air. Israel *did* have the capability to intercept the Su-24, but there was no guarantee that it could do so with 100-per-cent reliability. The commander of the Israeli air force stated publicly that the Su-24's advanced low-level radar capability greatly complicated interception but noted also that the aircraft was new enough to the Iraqi air force that its pilots might not yet have mastered its capabilities: *Jerusalem Post*, 11 January 1991, 1.

anything against Iraq.'[7] Such remarks heightened Israeli concern
that Iraq's nuclear programme was approaching a critical phase.
Israel began detailed contingency planning for possible operations against Iraq's unconventional military capability and for
countering the Scud and Su-24 threats. Another source of Israeli
concern was the increasing scope and degree of military co-operation between Iraq and Jordan, including a joint air force squadron operating in Iraq, a planned joint mechanized division,
advance planning for co-ordinated air operations, and intelligence sharing. Israel especially feared that Iraq might use Jordan
as a springboard for a surprise attack, an alarming prospect
because an attacking Su-24 could reach Tel Aviv from the Israeli-
Jordanian border near the Dead Sea in 2.5 minutes.[8]

Iraq's invasion of Kuwait on 2 August 1990 strongly reinforced the Israeli impression that Saddam Hussein harboured
hegemonic ambitions and illustrated once again his willingness
to use armed force to achieve his political objectives. The action
confirmed the views of many in the Israeli defence and political
establishments that Saddam Hussein had to go and that Iraq's
unconventional military capability had to be destroyed.[9] As the

7 For further discussion of the speech and the American reaction, see Bob
  Woodward, *The Commanders* (New York: Simon & Schuster 1991), 200-2.
  Saddam Hussein made similar remarks in February and also at the Arab
  League's meeting in Baghdad in May.
8 Hence the government's insistence after the Iraqi invasion of Kuwait that Israel
  absolutely would not tolerate a movement of Iraqi troops into Jordan and
  Israel's concern over Jordan's 'defensive' mobilization during the war itself. See,
  eg, Makovsky, 'Scenarios: will Israel hit Iraq?' 9. Some Israelis have indicated
  that the former declaration was intended largely to protect Jordan from being
  the next victim of Iraqi aggression; they insist that King Hussein would not
  willingly have allowed Iraqi troops into Jordan, fearing that they would not
  leave and knowing that his own regime could not long survive an Iraqi presence.
9 See, eg, the remarks of Levy, *Jerusalem Post*, 9 January 1991, 1. There was
  consensus in Israel on the need for eliminating Iraq's chemical and nuclear
  capability, with on-site verification. There was also wide agreement that Iraq's
  more destabilizing delivery systems would have to be eliminated. However, there
  were differences of opinion on whether the removal of Saddam Hussein from
  power was absolutely necessary for Israeli security and on the best course of
  action for the United States in the present situation. Some were convinced that
  there was no alternative to military action; others claim that they would have
  been satisfied with a diplomatic solution that included restrictions on Iraqi arms
  in addition to the unconditional evacuation of Kuwait.

United States responded with a rapid build-up of forces in Saudi Arabia in Operation Desert Shield, some Israeli officials began quietly lobbying the Americans to seize the opportunity to act; as one senior air force officer put it: 'If you don't take care of Saddam Hussein now, then in a year or two we will have to do it, and you'll wish you had.' But Israel maintained a low profile in the crisis, in accordance with American requests. The two countries agreed to consult closely as the crisis unfolded, however, as provided in the 1984 agreement governing their strategic relationship.

As part of his strategy to sow dissension in the ranks of the multinational coalition arrayed against him and to bolster his support in the Arab world, Saddam Hussein repeatedly threatened to strike Israel if attacked by the United States and its allies. Precisely to deter such an action, Israeli leaders made a series of strong statements to the effect that Israel would retaliate decisively if attacked.[10] Because of the danger that Israeli participation in a regional conflict might disrupt the coalition or trigger a geographical escalation, American officials spent considerable time and energy in the weeks prior to the war attempting to secure an agreement from Israel not to attack Iraq pre-emptively and, in the event of war itself, to refrain from retaliating if attacked.[11] In January, Eagleburger did secure an agreement from Shamir not to pre-empt, as well as a pledge to stay out of a military conflict 'if at all possible,' but Shamir made it clear that under no circumstances could Israel definitively undertake *not* to retaliate if attacked by Iraq, although he promised to 'consult' the United States before taking action.[12]

As the 15 January deadline decreed by the United Nations for Iraq to pull out of Kuwait approached, Israel pushed hard for an American commitment to give top priority in the event of

10 See note 2, above.

11 See, eg, the story in the *Jerusalem Post*, 11 January 1991, 1. Israeli doctrine called for pre-emption, where possible, in the face of imminent threat and was largely responsible for Israel's success in the 1967 war. American officials feared that Israel might stick too closely to its script.

12 *Ibid*, 14 January 1991, 1; Woodward, *The Commanders*, 363. By 'consult' Shamir made it clear that he meant more than 'notify.'

war to eliminating the Iraqi threat to Israel, noting that the only sure way to prevent Israel from entering the conflict was to prevent or defeat Iraqi attacks against it. The minister of defense, Moshe Arens, pushed for early and massive strikes at two airbases in western Iraq (designated H-2 and H-3) from which Su-24s could operate and where Israeli intelligence had identified 10 fixed Scud sites.[13] Arens also pressed for an intensive effort to locate and destroy the estimated 25 to 50 mobile Scud launchers deployed in the desert of western Iraq.[14] To this end, Israel gave the United States 'most of its intelligence secrets regarding Iraq'[15] and shared with the American military the results of exercises Israeli forces had conducted to perfect Scud-hunting techniques in the desert.

American officials were quite willing to give these targets high priority. Indeed, American aircraft hit the two airbases and their associated fixed Scud sites in the opening phase of Operation Desert Storm. But Israel also insisted on full access to American targeting intelligence and bomb damage assessments, real-time battlefield intelligence on western Iraq, and the IFF (Identification Friend or Foe) codes that would have enabled Israeli aircraft to operate in western Iraq without running the risk of being mistaken for hostile aircraft and engaged by coalition interceptors.[16] These requests posed a dilemma for Washington: the more it conceded to Israel, the easier it made an Israeli mil-

---

13 *Aviation Week & Space Technology*, 21 January 1991, 26.
14 Cf *Jerusalem Post*, 15 January 1991, 1. It is interesting to note the pre-war expectation that the Scuds could be dealt with fairly easily; the *Post* opined that 'more than one strike' would be needed at the start of the war, with follow-ups as the mobile launchers revealed themselves.
15 *Ibid*, 7 January 1991, 1. These secrets evidently included information on the locations and defensive arrangements of several suspected Iraqi nuclear, chemical, and biological weapons facilities.
16 As the Israelis put it (not without a smile): 'We didn't want to be put in a position where we were shooting down American or British planes.' Israel first raised the question of sharing IFF codes on 2 August but did not lobby strongly for them until January. The Israelis made clear, however, that the lack of the codes would not stop them if they chose to launch a military operation. They consistently represented their request to the United States as intended to facilitate *American* air operations.

itary operation; yet the more it resisted, the more difficult it would be to demonstrate to the Israelis that the United States was making every possible effort to find and destroy the Scuds. According to American officials, managing this dilemma was 'the key problem' from their perspective both immediately before and during the war.

The Bush administration went a considerable distance towards meeting Israel's requests, although it stopped short of providing the IFF codes. Most notably, it despatched a flag officer to Tel Aviv from Central Command in Riyadh to serve as an operational liaison officer with the IDF, and it authorized the establishment of a dedicated secure voice link from headquarters in Riyadh to IDF headquarters via the Pentagon operations centre in Virginia and the American embassy in Tel Aviv. The system, operating under the code name Hammer Rick, became operational on 13 January.[17] During the war, the system enabled the United States to give Israel a minimum of 90 seconds' warning of an impending Scud attack – enough time to broadcast a national alert and enable the Israeli population to take cover.[18] Through the same channel, the United States secretary of defense, Richard Cheney, and the Israeli defense minister could reach each other at any time.[19] In addition, to help defend Israel against missile attack, the president authorized in December a

17 Woodward, *The Commanders*, 363-4.
18 Before the war, the United States manoeuvred two military satellites into geosynchronous orbit over the equator. The satellites took an infra-red image of Iraq with every twelve-second rotation. A series of stereoscopic images of a Scud plume would be transmitted instantaneously to Alice Springs, Australia, and via military communications satellite to the United States Space Command's Warning Centre in Colorado Springs, where computers would use them to calculate a likely impact zone. It took a maximum of two minutes from the moment of detection to the calculation of the impact zone; approximately three additional minutes were needed to transmit the warning to IDF headquarters. Because the flight time of a Scud from western Iraq to Israel was approximately 7 minutes, Israeli authorities had a minimum warning time before impact of 90 to 120 seconds. *Aviation Week & Space Technology*, 21 January 1991, 60.
19 Cheney could access the line both at home and at the Pentagon; Arens could do so from his office. Apparently, there was never an occasion when one wanted to talk to the other but was unable to do so.

draw-down and transfer to Israel of two Patriot air defence missile batteries.[20] These arrived on 3 January; their Israeli crews, however, would not complete their training in Texas for another three months. The United States offered to send crews to operate the missiles in the meantime, but Arens declined the offer on 11 January so as not to set the precedent of having foreign soldiers defend Israeli territory.[21] Consequently, when the war began, these systems were not operational.[22]

It is evident that co-operation between the United States and Israel prior to the outbreak of war was extensive. Yet despite the closeness of the military relationship, there was considerable friction and tension at the political level. One source of friction was the fact that the United States was supplying its Arab coalition partners with advanced weapons systems that threatened to erode the qualitative edge upon which Israel relied to compensate for its numerical disadvantage. Another was Israel's refusal to commit itself to a policy of restraint despite American persistence. To help justify that refusal, and to argue that Washington exaggerated the fragility of the anti-Iraq coalition, Israeli officials pointed to statements from Egypt and Syria indicating that the two Arab countries would 'understand' if Israel undertook a 'one-time retaliation' in response to an Iraqi attack.[23] These

20 The original Patriot was designed as an anti-aircraft system but the PAC-2 hardware, software, warhead, and fuse modifications gave it the capability to intercept short-range ballistic missiles. Contrary to some reports, the batteries delivered to Israel prior to the outbreak of war apparently included a mix of original Patriots and PAC-2s. For a discussion of the Patriots and their operations, see *Aviation Week & Space Technology*, 28 January 1991, 26-8, and 18 February 1991, 49-51, and Theodore A. Postol, 'Lessons of the Gulf War experience with Patriot,' *International Security* 16(winter 1991/92), 124-6, 130-5.

21 *Jerusalem Post*, 27 January 1991, 1. He also refused an American offer to send *American* Patriot batteries and their crews in the week before the outbreak of war, for the same reason.

22 *Ibid*, 6 January 1991, 1. Arens and others vigorously deny a *Newsday* report that Arens held up delivery of Israel's Patriots for several months so as not to jeopardize the prospect of American funding for the Arrow. See, eg, *ibid*, 21 January 1991, 1.

23 Touring Arab capitals the week before the outbreak of war, the secretary of state, James Baker, received quiet assurances that the allies would permit such a

'green lights' were a mixed blessing, from the American perspective. While they raised the possibility that the coalition could survive some form of Israeli action, they also tempted Israel to act. The green lights themselves, therefore, quickly became an issue in American-Israeli relations.[24]

Americans could take heart, however, from the considerable debate within Israel about the wisdom of responding to an Iraqi attack under the rather unusual circumstances of the day.[25] In particular, American officials greeted Shamir's eleventh-hour modification of the government's hard line with an audible sigh of relief.[26] On the eve of Operation Desert Storm, the Bush administration held some hope that Israel would not jeopardize the coalition by responding to an Iraqi attack. In any case, it concluded that it had done everything possible for the moment to prevent such an action. It had no confidence, however, that those measures would be effective and braced itself for a major diplomatic struggle if the Scuds got through.

ISRAEL UNDER ATTACK

Between 17 January and 27 February, 39 Iraqi Scuds landed in Israel, many of them in crowded Tel Aviv suburbs such as Ramat

---

response. Egypt's statement was very clear; the signal from Syria, however, was ambiguous and – to American officials at least – unreliable. *Newsweek* (special commemorative issue, spring/summer 1991), 71; *Jerusalem Post*, 13 January 1991, 10, and 20 January 1991, 1.

24 According to some observers, one reason why the Israelis thought that the green lights were more reliable and the coalition more robust than did the Americans was their conviction that national interests were more important than ideology to the Arab states.

25 As early as August 1990, some senior Israeli military officers had quietly indicated to Americans that Israel might not respond to limited Iraqi attacks under conditions such as those that obtained during the war itself. Some, such as Rabin and Major-General Aharon Yariv, head of the Jaffee Center for Strategic Studies, openly voiced the opinion that Israel should not retaliate, thereby calling into question the wisdom of the government's declaratory policy. Rabin's remarks in particular came in for scathing criticism from Likud ministers on the ground that they undermined Israel's deterrent threat. Makovsky, 'Scenarios: will Israel hit Iraq?'; *Jerusalem Post*, 4 January 1991, 9, 17 January 1991, 8, and 11 January 1991, 5.

26 See note 2, above.

Gan, B'nai-Brak, and Ramat Aviv. Most hit in the first two weeks of the war, although Iraq managed to continue the attacks throughout. Miraculously, casualties were extremely light. Only one Israeli died as a direct result of a missile impact; three others died of heart attacks.[27] This fatality rate was at least two orders of magnitude below that expected for an assault of this size.[28] None of the Scuds carried chemical weapons: 38 were armed with conventional high explosives; one – a practice round – had a concrete warhead.[29]

The players

At no point did Israel decide as a matter of policy not to respond to Iraq's attacks. Instead, after each attack, Israeli leaders merely decided not to respond immediately. Thus the 'decision' was under constant review and subject to change at any time. An actual decision to respond, had it been made, would have been the prime minister's alone; but Shamir, Arens, and the foreign minister, David Levy, formed a de facto triumvirate which dom-

27 Postol reports evidence that the individual killed directly may in fact have been killed by the impact of a Patriot interceptor rather than a Scud: 'Lessons of the Gulf War experience with Patriot,' 140.

28 To forecast the likely fatalities from Scud attacks, the IDF used as a base rate the number killed in Teheran during the War of the Cities, where, on average, an Al-Hussein Scud modification killed between nine and ten people. While Israel could expect to enjoy greater warning time of an impending strike than did Iran, the decision to take precautions primarily against chemical attack (ordering Israeli citizens to don gas masks and lock themselves in above-ground sealed rooms rather than in below-ground shelters) theoretically increased the population's vulnerability to conventional attack. Estimates of the likely fatalities from chemical attacks were more difficult. With ample warning, they should have been minimal in view of Israel's extensive civil defence measures. Under a worst-case scenario (no warning and maximum gas dispersion), Israeli experts thought it conceivable that fatalities could run into the thousands for any given missile.

29 This remarkable fact is just one indication among several that the Iraqi troops firing Scuds at Israel were doing so at gunpoint. Apparently, they considered it more important to fulfil orders to launch missiles at Israel than to await the availability of a suitable warhead. Another indication is the remarkable fact that to minimize the time during which a mobile launcher had to expose itself in order to fire, Iraqi crews fuelled the missiles *before* transporting and erecting them. Given the volatility of the Scud's liquid fuel and the extreme danger of explosion, no knowledgeable crew would have done this willingly.

inated the deliberations. Together, they periodically consulted with the cabinet as a whole and on at least two occasions privately briefed prominent members of the opposition (most notably, Shimon Peres and Yitzhak Rabin of the Labour party). In addition, they discussed the question of retaliation within the appropriate parliamentary committees. There is disagreement as to whether Shamir, Arens, and Levy asked Israel's military leaders for their opinion on whether or not to respond. One rumour circulating widely in Israel holds that the chief of staff, Dan Shomron, and the chief of staff designate, Ehud Barak, met privately with Shamir and strongly advocated restraint. This claim is emphatically contradicted by Eitan, however, who insists that Israel's military leaders were asked only to present military options and evaluate their prospects of success.

The other key players in the Israeli decision-making process were Americans: most notably, President Bush, who spoke personally with Shamir three times in the opening days of the war; Cheney, through his direct channel to Arens; William Brown, the American ambassador to Israel; and the members of Eagleburger's team, who returned to Israel a second time on 20 January.[30] These men and others (such as officials at the National Security Council, embassy personnel, American military representatives) engaged in the diplomatic equivalent of a full-court press to hold Israel back. Their own impression – confirmed by most of the Israelis interviewed for this study – was that this diplomatic effort made the difference between Israeli action and restraint at several points, and at three moments in particular: immediately after the first and second Scud attacks on Friday and Saturday mornings (18 and 19 January) and on the following Tuesday after the first attack resulting in an Israeli death (22 January). These were among the occasions that Eitan characterizes as 'hair-trigger situations.'

30 These included the under secretary of defense for policy, Paul Wolfowitz, Eagleburger's senior adviser, Kenneth Juster, the deputy assistant secretary of state, Daniel Kurtzer, and the State Department's director of policy analysis in the Bureau of Politico-Military Affairs, Steven Simon.

The pressures

That Israel came closest to undertaking military action immediately after Scud attacks is hardly coincidental; indeed, both
Israelis and Americans indicate that the main source of pressure
to respond was emotive. Israeli leaders experienced a perfectly
normal phenomenological response to each and every strike: first
shock, then anger, followed by an intense desire for retribution
that would gradually subside over a period of hours to permit
reflection and calm deliberation.[31] During the periods of most
intense passion, American-Israeli relations were at their most
heated and most strained. Participants to the discussions
describe the interactions as 'games of chicken'; the Americans
involved refer to them as the most intense encounters of their
diplomatic careers, in which they played 'the hardest hardball'
of their lives and resorted to 'extremely blunt' and 'wholly undip-
lomatic' language to restrain Israel. Israelis generally concur in
this characterization but note as well that the two countries were
engaged in a curious form of 'mutual deterrence' which was free
of hostility and personal animosity but far more intense (and far
more successful) than Israel's attempted deterrence of Iraq.[32]

Emotional pressures were not the only ones inclining Israel to
respond, however, even though they were clearly the most important. In addition, many Israeli decision-makers feared that
Israeli restraint would be mistaken by present and future adversaries (Syria in particular) as weakness, undermining the credibility of Israeli deterrence. While most acknowledged this danger, however, it was clearly not a controlling consideration.
Shamir, Arens, and Levy bracketed off the issue and resolved to

31 This same sequence is evident in both Soviet and American decision-making
during the Cuban missile crisis. See James G. Blight and David A. Welch, *On
the Brink: Americans and Soviets Reexamine the Cuban Missile Crisis* (2nd ed;
New York: Noonday 1990), 312-14, for an argument that, in that instance,
successful crisis management hinged on the availability of sufficient time to
permit this phenomenological evolution to run its course.

32 While the United States may well have been attempting to deter Israel from
taking military action, Israel was attempting to *compel* the United States to do
more to stop the Scuds. 'Mutual deterrence' is an erroneous characterization.

deal with it at a later time.[33] American diplomats argued – as did some Israelis, such as Rabin and at least one anonymous spokesman for the government – that because Saddam Hussein clearly wanted Israel to respond, restraint *bolstered* rather than eroded deterrence in the long run. The gist of this argument was that a demonstrated willingness to suffer costs in order to resist complying with the will of an adversary enhanced credibility in general.[34] While restraint dramatically illustrated this willingness, the argument is not universally accepted in Israel. The effect of Israel's restraint on its deterrent posture has been the subject of considerable debate since the war in both official and academic circles.

The third source of pressure to respond stemmed from the simple imperative of stopping the attacks. Among other things, the attacks had brought the country to an economic standstill. Moreover, the government had an obligation to defend the people of Israel. Most importantly, the longer the attacks continued, the greater were the odds that they would do serious damage. The lighter than expected casualties considerably eased the pressure to respond immediately, but there was no guarantee that they would continue to be so light.[35] Those in the cabinet who actively advocated a military response – Ariel Sharon, Yuval Ne'eman, and Raphael Eitan in particular[36] – were confident that the IDF could do a better job of stopping the Scuds than the American forces could and argued primarily on the basis of such considerations that the IDF should be permitted to do so. They

33 After the war Israeli officials set about to do so with dispatch. Note, especially, Levy's remarks in Spain: 'We are very closely monitoring the increase of Syria's military arsenal of weapons of mass destruction, the improved Scud missiles delivered by North Korea ... Our restraint during the Gulf war should not be taken as applicable to any set of circumstances. Should Syria attack, we will defend ourselves, with all that implies.' *Jerusalem Post*, 26 June 1991, 1.

34 'A senior Israeli official' remarked on 19 January that 'Saddam Hussein is trying to drag us into this war, and we don't have to play into his hands.' *Ibid*, 20 January 1991, 1.

35 Indeed, some apparently feared that Saddam Hussein would interpret restraint as weakness and be emboldened to launch a chemical attack.

36 *Ibid*, 24 January 1991, 1.

appealed only secondarily to the importance of maintaining the credibility of Israeli deterrence.[37]

What American officials dreaded most was a chemical attack or a conventional attack resulting in 'substantial' fatalities. The Israelis had told American officials that these were circumstances under which they would have no choice but to take military action against Iraq – the 'red lines' with which Israeli leaders defined and constrained their decision space. While there was no universally agreed standard for what constituted 'substantial' fatalities, Israelis and Americans retrospectively discuss figures in the range of 30 to 300. 'Our greatest fear,' said one senior American official, 'was that a Scud would hit an apartment building and kill 100 people.' There is near unanimous agreement on both sides that a chemical attack – with or without casualties – would have elicited an Israeli response because of its symbolic implications: it would simply not have been possible for a state founded in the wake of the Holocaust to stand idle while its citizens were gassed.[38]

The military options
Well before the outbreak of war, the IDF had prepared and conducted exercises on a series of military options, including both retaliatory strikes and operations designed to serve specific mili-

---

37 It is interesting to note Eitan's observation that the ministers with military backgrounds were keenest to respond while those with non-military backgrounds were split.

38 The same senior official quoted in note 34 declared (*ibid*, 20 January 1991, 1): 'If [Saddam Hussein] thinks either Israel or the coalition will sit idly by if there's a gas attack, he's very much mistaken. The consequences would be extremely severe.' No question is more difficult to pin down than the precise nature of these red lines. As one Israeli put it, 'You can never know for certain where a red line is until you have crossed it.' Indeed, Arens stated to the cabinet on 27 January that Saddam Hussein had already 'crossed the red line' but that Israel would choose the time, place, and method of its response. *Ibid*, 28 January 1991, 1. Consequently, most Americans and Israelis are careful to suggest that 'substantial fatalities' or a chemical attack would not have resulted in *automatic* retaliation; but they also insist that they would have generated irresistible pressures to retaliate. This would seem to be as close an approximation to automaticity as a prudent forecast could bear.

tary purposes. Among the available options, according to Eitan, was one designed explicitly for use in the event of a chemical attack. I was completely unable to elicit any comment from any quarter on the details of this particular option. In view of the intensity of Israeli feeling about a chemical attack and the widespread perception among those interviewed that it would have constituted a 'crossing of the Rubicon,' this curious silence circumstantially suggests that this may have been a nuclear option. Reticence is not an Israeli trait; but the one subject on which Israelis will make absolutely no comment of any kind is their nuclear capability.

The retaliatory options seem to have fallen by the wayside in the early days of Operation Desert Storm, simply because coalition aircraft were saturating virtually every conceivable military target in Iraq. As one Israeli put it: 'Under those circumstances, a retaliatory strike would have been like a drop of water in an ocean. It might even have gone unnoticed.' The option the government was considering most seriously was a plan to find and destroy mobile Scud launchers in western Iraq. This plan had a number of variants, ranging from a pure air operation to a combined air/ground operation which one American official described as 'extremely ambitious.' The pure air option called for low-level sweeps of the Scud launch areas, two very narrow arcs several hundred kilometres long with Tel Aviv and Haifa as their geometrical centres.[39] The combined air/ground option

39 Iraq proved extremely resourceful in minimizing the period of time during which its mobile launchers were exposed to attack. In addition to pre−roll-out fuelling, the Iraqis calculated the optimal launch points prior to the outbreak of war by flight testing an Al-Hussein missile from eastern to western Iraq, measuring the distance travelled, and using that measure as the radius of two semi-circles in the Iraqi desert whose centres were Tel Aviv and Haifa. The transporters, carrying fuelled missiles, could then sprint to their launch positions, point themselves in the right direction, elevate the missiles for maximum range (44°), fire them, and hide again, before American planes arrived. By reducing the normal firing time from approximately 1 hour to 10 minutes or less, they could escape destruction even though the American satellites could pinpoint their locations to within several hundred metres within two minutes of firing. Cf *Aviation Week & Space Technology*, 28 January 1991, 26, 28, and *Jane's Weapon Systems 1983-84* (London: Jane's 1984), 65.

called for inserting several mobile lightly armed teams of soldiers into the Iraqi desert to scour the launch areas, call in and spot for air strikes, and even, if necessary, engage Scud crews directly. Israel's military leaders – especially Barak and the commander of the air force, General Avihu Bin-Nun – favoured the more ambitious variant because they believed it would be the most effective.[40]

Any of the variants in the Israeli plan would have entailed crossing Jordan. As far as the Israeli military was concerned, the prospect of a military clash with Jordan was a complicating though not a critical problem. The Israeli air force had no doubt of its capability to clear the necessary airspace.[41] Indeed, Israel's advanced F-15s and F-16s might have succeeded in crossing Jordan without being intercepted at all. But if Jordan had refused to allow the passage of Israeli forces, the more ambitious operation would have had to have been preceded by the suppression of Jordanian air defences.[42] It is evident that the Israeli government did not consider a possible clash with Jordan an important consideration, however; those interviewed insist that the decision whether or not to execute the IDF's plan would not have hinged on Jordanian acquiescence.[43] If anything, Israeli decision-makers

40 This is consistent with Richard K. Betts's finding that military leaders, while not appreciably more willing to employ force than civilians, tend to favour a greater application of force once a decision has been made to resort to arms: *Soldiers, Statesmen, and Cold War Crises* (Cambridge MA: Harvard University Press 1977), appendix A, 215-21.

41 A 'senior official' in the prime minister's office publicly dismissed Jordan as 'a marginal factor': Makovsky, 'Scenarios: will Israel hit Iraq?' 9.

42 Israel's C-130 Hercules and IAI-210 Arava troop transports were too slow, and flew too low, to avoid interception by Jordan's 32 Mirage F-1s and 14 Hawk surface-to-air missile batteries. They would have had to be neutralized prior to any overflight. Data from *The Military Balance 1990-1991*, 108, 107.

43 Israel asked the United States to approach King Hussein and secure permission for a quiet, unpublicized Israeli transit of Jordanian territory in case Israel chose to take military action. The king refused, and made his refusal public, pledging to defend Jordan from either side: *Jerusalem Post*, 16 January 1991, 1. Some senior Israelis believe that a second approach would have been attempted, once a decision to use military force had been made, and maintain that the king might well have turned a blind eye, particularly if he wanted to seize the opportunity to repair his strained relations with the United States. His biggest threat, of course, was Jordanian public opinion, and much would have depended on the possibility of keeping the Israeli operation secret.

considered the most serious drawback of the plan to be the possibility that it would fail to stop the Scuds, reflecting poorly on Israeli military capabilities.[44] But this, too, was far from a controlling consideration. As one senior American official put it: 'The Israelis made it clear that they were aware of the risks and would have accepted them, had they made the decision to go.'[45]

United States-Israeli diplomacy

Shortly after word reached Cheney that the first Scud missiles had hit Tel Aviv early on Friday morning, 18 January (local time), he sped to the Pentagon and called Arens on the secure line. Arens, in a fury, demanded the IFF codes and strongly indicated that Israel was considering an immediate military response. Cheney pleaded for time and rushed to the White House, where the president and his top advisers from the Pentagon and the National Security Council were setting the American diplomatic effort in motion.[46] Immediately, the group offered to send Patriot batteries with their American crews to Israel – an offer which Arens now quickly accepted – and dispatched Eagleburger to serve as the president's personal representative on the

44 At the time the greatest danger seemed to be the possibility that Iraqi manoeuvre groups were operating in the Scud launch zones. In retrospect, an additional factor – the Iraqis' remarkable ingenuity in launching the Scuds quickly – seems to have been grossly underestimated by both Israeli and American planners.

45 This point is confirmed by Israeli observers as well, who note Israel's long history of high-risk military operations, such as the opening pre-emptive strike in the 1967 war, the 1976 raid on Entebbe, and the 1982 invasion of Lebanon.

46 Contrary to the story widely circulated in the American press, United States and Israeli officials deny that Arens informed Cheney that 12 F-16s were already in the air ready to strike Iraq and that Arens insisted the United States clear the skies over Iraq for four hours in order to facilitate a response. See, eg, *Newsweek*, commemorative issue, 72. Arens did insist on the IFF codes, just in case Israel decided to respond. He apparently made it clear, however, that Israel would not be deterred from striking back if it did not get the codes or if the United States did not clear western Iraqi airspace. In a line American officials maintained throughout the war, Cheney refused to agree to facilitate an Israeli response. This, in part, was the 'game of chicken' the two countries played. Most Israelis assume – and some American officials are inclined to agree (but will not confirm) – that if Israeli aircraft had headed towards Iraq without the IFF codes, American AWACS planes would have been instructed to clear the area rather than risk a clash with Israel.

scene.[47] Thus began several weeks of an extremely difficult and delicate behind-the-scenes struggle between Israel and the United States played out through a wide variety of channels and at a wide variety of levels. The essence of the Israeli position, however, was quite simple: if the United States did not stop the Scud attacks, the IDF would. The essence of the American response was twofold: (1) that the United States was making every effort to do this and that Israel could do no better; and (2) that the costs of an Israeli action would be horrendous not only for the United States and the coalition effort but also for Israel.

Initially, Israeli military and political leaders were sceptical of the first American claim, insisting that the United States could devote more resources to the Scud-hunting campaign and frankly stating that Israeli forces could do the job more effectively. Many Israelis continue to believe this.[48] In response to Israeli pressure, Bush ordered General Norman Schwarzkopf to devote more assets to the Scud-hunting campaign, which, according to some, accounted for 15 per cent of the coalition air effort at its peak and prompted an angry outburst from Schwarzkopf that 'political sideshows' should not dictate allied bombing priorities.

As the Scuds continued to fall, Israeli frustration – and hence

---

47 Americans and Israelis alike agree that Eagleburger's extraordinary diplomatic skills played a major role in smoothing over disagreements.

48 The essence of the dispute concerned the reluctance of the Americans to conduct low-level sweeps. On the opening night of Operation Desert Storm, American aircraft *did* conduct low-level attacks at H-2 and H-3 airbases and over areas where mobile Scuds were suspected to be operating, but they encountered heavy anti-aircraft fire: *Aviation Week & Space Technology*, 18 February 1991, 61. American targeters did not believe that the potential costs of low-level sweeps in damaged and downed aircraft were worth what they considered to be their marginal or negligible advantages over higher altitude patrols. Israeli doctrine, however, held that low-level operations were considerably more effective. In addition to this tactical difference of opinion, Israel maintained that its pilots were more experienced in low-level ground attack missions and more highly motivated than their American counterparts. They would thus be willing to take the admittedly higher risks associated with low-level operations.

tension between the Americans and the Israelis – grew. According to one story circulating in the West, at some time within the week after the first Scud attack Israel took the unprecedented step of rolling a Jericho ballistic missile out into the open and then rolling it back under cover. Israeli officials will not comment on the story, in keeping with their strict code of silence on matters touching their nuclear capability. American officials, however, confirm that the event took place, although they disagree on its meaning. Some are inclined to interpret it as an Israeli attempt to deter Saddam Hussein from continuing the attacks. According to this interpretation, the Israelis hoped that Soviet satellites would detect the roll-out and relay word to Baghdad. Since a Jericho missile would have been completely ineffective in anything but a nuclear mode, the implication is that this was a nuclear deterrent threat. Other American officials are inclined to believe that the signal was intended for Washington's benefit: to demonstrate that Israel's patience was wearing thin. Still others are inclined to think the signal was intended for both audiences. A final group admits being baffled by the move, interpreting it primarily as a sign of Israeli frustration.

Whatever the case may be, Israel now began to insist on playing a role in hunting the Scuds. The United States initially attempted to deflect the request, arguing that there was nothing Israel could add to the effort and that any overt Israeli participation could disrupt the coalition. But Israel insisted, and the United States ultimately agreed, provided that Israel's role remained discreet.[49] Sometime within the first two weeks of the war, Israel began to help target mobile Scud launchers and to consult on tactical operational matters.[50] This participation was

[49] Ironically, therefore, the United States desperately sought to convince Israel to free ride, while Israel strongly resisted, and, in view of its covert participation, ultimately succeeded in refusing.

[50] Israelis insist that all aspects of their contribution were important, but Americans maintain that much of it was redundant, particularly the Israeli role in targeting mobile Scuds. Shortly after the first Scud attacks, Israel moved much of its testing equipment from its missile ranges in the Negev to positions

evidently crucial in easing Israel's pressure to respond, first, by satisfying Israel's need to play a role and, second, by undercutting the force of the Israeli argument that the IDF could do a better job than American forces. It did not, however, make a significant difference to the Scud-hunting campaign itself; the Iraqis managed to continue firing Scuds at Israel throughout the war at a regular if diminished rate.

The second track of the American diplomatic effort concentrated on convincing Israeli leaders of the enormous costs associated with Israeli military action. In this endeavour, the United States left few stones unturned, concentrating on (*a*) the possible damage to the coalition; (*b*) the possible disruption of Operation Desert Storm; (*c*) the danger of a geographical escalation; and

---

in and around Tel Aviv. By recording Scud trajectories from a variety of angles, using both video cameras and radar, the Israelis were then able to calculate their approximate launch positions using mathematical formulas describing the path of ballistic missiles. American officials consider the information redundant primarily because the United States had deployed two systems that could locate mobile Scuds quite precisely in real time: the two satellites (discussed in note 18, above) and two Joint Surveillance Target Attack Radar System E-8A aircraft, operating as the 4411th Joint-STARS Squadron, which were capable of detecting the movement of tracked and wheeled vehicles at ranges of 200 kilometres or more. *Aviation Week & Space Technology*, 14 January 1991, 24-5. The E-8As, however, proved more useful in detecting the movement of concentrations of vehicles (such as Iraq's Republican Guard units) than lone Scud launchers.

More helpful were Israel's tactical suggestions for hunting Scuds, which included inserting special forces (Green Beret and Delta Force) into western Iraq to spot for air strikes, in some cases laser-designating targets for precision-guided munitions. It is unclear whether Israel played a role in designing the 'box patrol' technique by means of which groups of two to four F-15E aircraft would comb the Scud launch zones. *Aviation Week & Space Technology*, 18 February 1991, 60.

A senior IDF official also claimed in July 1991 that Israel provided military equipment to the United States for operations in the Kuwaiti theatre – including bridges, mine-clearing equipment, surveillance equipment, and remotely piloted vehicles – that it was considering writing off as a draw-down from Israeli stocks. It is difficult to know what to make of this claim (which I have been unable to confirm) since matériel of this kind would have had to be deployed in Saudi Arabia, where the presence of IDF equipment could conceivably have triggered a political uproar. One knowledgeable American source is inclined interpret this claim as a misrepresentation of normal American procurement because the Pentagon routinely purchases the items in question from Israeli suppliers.

(*d*) the potential costs of violating Jordanian airspace in view of the precarious situation of King Hussein and the possibility that he could be succeeded by a militantly pro-Iraqi regime. None of these arguments carried much weight with the Israelis because they did not believe them to be serious or unmanageable risks.[51] More important was a consideration that American officials deny was under discussion: namely, the future of the American-Israeli relationship, which Shamir, Arens, and Levy were eager not to strain further if at all possible.[52] Shamir, in particular, seems to have gotten the message that unless Israel held back, the United States would reconsider its patronage. Whether Shamir was reading between the lines, or whether American officials made the point explicitly, the possibility of losing American diplomatic and material support in the postwar environment appears to have played a major role in convincing Shamir that, *until and unless the red lines were crossed*, Israel should forbear. What he needed, Shamir told Eagleburger, was a justification for inac-

[51] One notable exception was David Ivry, director general of the Defense Ministry, who stated that one reason not to retaliate was to avoid complicating the war aims of the anti-Iraq coalition: *Jerusalem Post*, 20 January 1991, 1. This, however, was a public rationale somewhat at variance with the main currents of the government's thinking. To the extent that Israeli leaders believed the coalition to be fragile at all, they thought Syria to be the only possible defector. From their perspective, this would hardly have been a fatal blow to the coalition, since (according to a senior Israeli official) 'Syria wasn't a real member of the coalition anyway.' Egypt and Saudi Arabia were thought to be far too committed to back out; by the time the ground war began, Israel concluded that even Syria would stay in. While in Israel, I expected to hear someone make the argument that a Syrian defection would have been *desirable*, since it would have damaged President Hafez al-Assad's respectability campaign and his search for a new military patron in the wake of the Soviet Union's withdrawal from the world stage. From both a diplomatic and a military-technology perspective, this would seem to have certain advantages for Israeli security. Curiously, I heard nothing of the kind, possibly because, as one Israeli put it, 'Syria wasn't the issue; Scuds were.'

[52] Relations between the United States and Israel had deteriorated under Bush, who did not share the categorical pro-Israeli sentiments of Ronald Reagan. In particular, Bush and Baker openly and repeatedly criticized Israel's policy of encouraging Jewish settlement of the West Bank. Some observers claim that personal animosity between Bush and Shamir explains the remarkable fact that the two did not speak to each other at all during one eight-month period in 1990.

tion: namely, proof that the United States was making every possible effort to defeat the Scuds.[53]

Israeli officials, therefore, constantly brought the conversation back to the question of the Scuds, their all-consuming concern.[54] The great success of the United States in restraining Israel
was a function primarily of its positive efforts to promote Israeli
security: the intensity of its effort to find and destroy the Scuds;
its rapid deployment of Patriot missiles to help protect Tel Aviv;
its generous sharing of intelligence, both on Scud launches and
on military operations in western Iraq; its willingness to maintain
round-the-clock dedicated communications; its willingness to
send to Israel high officials from the Departments of State and
Defense to maintain close communications; and its willingness to
give Israel an operational role. In addition, the impressive performance of the American military assuaged Israeli doubts about
American capabilities.[55] With perhaps the sole exception of the
implicit or explicit threat to reconsider its postwar support,
Washington's efforts to convince Israel of the costs of a military
response were generally ineffective because the Americans were
insensitive to the fact that Israel's attention was focused exclusively on the problem of stopping the Scuds.

Similarly ineffective were the various arguments to the effect

53 Most agree that of the three men at the apex of Israeli decision-making, Shamir
   was most eager not to be put in a position to have to take military action and
   Arens the least concerned by the prospect. But all three were sending mixed
   signals, belligerence alternating with co-operativeness, in approximate rhythm
   with the Scud attacks.

54 Towards the end of the war, Levy sought to broaden the agenda and begin to
   discuss the postwar peace process. When Arens travelled to Washington on 11
   February with David Ivry and Ehud Barak to discuss the Scud issue, Levy was
   not informed, precisely to keep the agenda focused. This triggered a serious rift
   in the triumvirate. *Jerusalem Post*, 12 February 1991, 1, and 13 February 1991,
   1.

55 Israelis were extremely impressed, for example, by the fact that the United
   States Patriot batteries offered on 20 January were transported, unloaded, and
   operational within 28 hours of being ordered to Israel. The efficiency of the air
   campaign, and later the ground war, also greatly bolstered the Israeli opinion of
   the American military. A major breakthrough came when former head of the
   Israeli air force, Benny Peled, publicly questioned whether the IDF could do a
   better job hunting Scuds than the United States was already doing: *ibid*, 20
   January 1991, 8.

that the war was of greater concern to the United States than to Israel and that therefore Israel should defer to American judgment. Likewise, the fulsome praise that the United States and other coalition countries heaped upon Israel for its restraint early in the war – intended to reward and reinforce Israel's good behaviour – merely struck Israelis as patronizing and offensive and did not play a role in Israel's decision to forbear. In addition, Israeli officials are virtually unanimous in denying that public opinion polls indicating that the vast majority of Israelis favoured restraint influenced their judgment, contrary to the American perception. Indeed, Eitan went so far as to say that public opinion 'played absolutely no role at all.' By all accounts, Arens greatly resented the civics lecture President Bush gave him on the subject while in Washington on 11 February.[56] Only once did an Israeli official suggest that restraint might be bought. On 22 January, on his own initiative, Yitzhak Moda'i, the finance minister, asked Eagleburger for $3 billion to cover the direct costs of the war and $10 billion in special aid for absorbing immigrants over the next four to five years. While he publicly denied this was an offer to sell restraint, his overture was so interpreted in both the United States and Israel, where it was universally dismissed as clumsy and inappropriate.[57]

No factor was more important to Israel's restraint, however, than pure luck. Israelis claim today with total seriousness that the light death toll was miraculous. The knowledge that, on any given night, a Scud could strike a crowded apartment building and kill hundreds of people meant that there was no lasting respite from the pressure to act.[58] Indeed, some Israelis claim that the cumulative effect of weeks of stress gradually increased the

56 Curiously, one of the few senior Israelis to suggest that public opinion played a role was Dan Shomron: *ibid*, 27 January 1991, 1.
57 See, eg, *ibid*, 23 January 1991, 1, 10, and 25 January 1991, 18.
58 Anecdotal evidence supports the miracle hypothesis quite strongly. Apparently, just before the outbreak of war, Israeli civil defence officials decided to conduct a limited number of checks on shelters in suburban Tel Aviv. They declared one of them unsafe and padlocked its door. That shelter took a direct hit from a Scud in the opening days of the war and was completely destroyed. The 230 Israelis who would normally have been in the shelter during the alert survived the attack unscathed in a temporary shelter next door.

pressure to take military action. Some – but not all – report that
the pressure eased for a few weeks in the middle of the war while
the country rejoiced in the illusory success of the Patriot missile.[59]
Still others endured the war convinced that as his final act of
defiance, Saddam Hussein would launch a massive chemical
attack against Israel. Not until the final ceasefire on 3 March
did Israelis – and American officials – breathe easily.

THE AFTERMATH

Most Israelis interviewed for this study reported surprise and
shock that the ground war came to an end so quickly – only 100
hours after it had begun – leaving Saddam Hussein in power with
a considerable portion of his army intact. Subsequent disclosures
that much of Iraq's nuclear programme survived only added to
their frustration with President Bush for not pursuing a more
decisive victory.[60] Less surprising was the reinvigoration of the

59 Press reports at the time indicated that Patriots were intercepting and destroying
a high proportion of Scuds. In fact, there is not a single documented case of a
Patriot missile destroying a Scud warhead launched at Israel, and
knowledgeable Israelis believe that, at most, Patriot missiles destroyed three. In
part, this was because the crude modifications Iraq made to the Scud to
increase its range had the effect of complicating interception. Iraqi technicians
cut Scuds in two and, cannibalizing others, stretched their fuel tanks and
welded them back together. This gave the Al-Hussein and Al-Abbas a longer
boost phase, and therefore greater velocity, higher peak altitude, and greater
range. But Iraqi technicians made no modifications to the Scud's primitive
stabilization system. The lighter warhead and extended length altered the
missile's centre of gravity and thus its flight characteristics. As a result, the
missile would tend to wobble or tumble upon re-entry and break up at an
altitude of 15 to 20 kilometres. Patriot missiles would engage the largest
fragments their radar systems detected – the Scud's engine or fuel tank – while
the warhead continued on to its target unmolested. During the war itself, the
Patriot's software was hastily modified to correct for this error, with unknown
results. Postol argues that Patriot missiles may actually have *increased* the amount
of damage on the ground in Israel. According to him, the first 13 Scuds uncon-
tested by Patriots killed no one, injured 115, and damaged 2,698 apartments; the
next 14 to 17 Scuds launched after Patriots had been deployed killed 1, injured
168, and damaged 7,778 apartments. 'Lessons of Gulf War experience with
Patriot,' 135n, 126-30, 140.

60 Some Israeli observers retrospectively argue that the government should have
known that the United States would not push the war beyond the liberation of
Kuwait in view of the constraints under which Bush was operating, which

Middle East peace process – orchestrated by the United States – that would obviously result in increased pressure on Israel to withdraw from the occupied territories.[61] Together, these two developments largely account for the Israeli perception that the war did not significantly improve Israel's security in the long run; at best, it bought time. While the Iraqi military had been dealt a serious blow, and therefore represented a less immediate threat, Israel had seen too many defeated Arab armies rise again to take much comfort from that fact. In several respects, the war worsened Israel's strategic position. Syria – Israel's most menacing adversary – emerged strengthened both diplomatically and militarily. Its acquisition of North Korean Scuds was a particularly threatening development, because Syria's proximity meant that it would not be plagued by the technical or operational difficulties experienced by Iraq.

The new ballistic missile environment created new challenges for Israeli security which place a premium on strategic 'height' and 'depth' in order to defend Israeli command and control, vital airfields, and mobilization procedures in times of national emergency. In short, the war convinced many in the Israeli government and military that the West Bank and the Golan Heights were even more important to Israeli security than they had been prior to the war.[62] It also convinced many of the strategic importance of Jordan's weak and non-menacing Hashemite kingdom

included disagreement within the coalition on war aims, the narrow 52-47 vote in the Senate authorizing the use of force, the uncertain response of American public opinion to a longer and more ambitious war, and the delicate consensus in the United Nations Security Council which probably would not have survived a continuation of the conflict once Kuwait had been freed.

61 The government knew well in advance that Israel would face some of the toughest diplomatic pressure of its history after the war, a topic apparently discussed in cabinet on 6 January: *Jerusalem Post*, 7 January 1991, 1. As suggested above, this fact may largely account for Shamir's willingness to weather the Scud campaign, in accordance with American wishes, as long as possible.

62 Many Israelis dismiss the prospect of a withdrawal to the 'green line' as particularly suicidal in a missile environment. They note, for example, that from the West Bank, Arab forces could effectively shut down Ben Gurion airport with shoulder-fired Stinger-type surface-to-air missiles.

as a strategic buffer, which effectively shifts Israel's strategic boundary eastward to the Iraqi-Jordanian and Syrian-Jordanian borders — a consideration that was not weighted heavily during the heat of battle. Finally, it drove home the importance of maintaining the IDF's qualitative edge over Arab armies, an edge that the war had weakened somewhat because of American arms transfers to the Arab coalition partners. Maintaining that advantage would require increased United States financial support in the future, an uncertain prospect in view of the looming diplomatic pressure on Israel orchestrated by the Bush administration itself. The postwar environment therefore represented a multidimensional challenge to Israeli security. It is interesting to note the contrasting perception of American officials: namely, that Israel was 'the big winner' or 'the major net beneficiary' of the war. This is a view that Israelis find difficult to fathom.

THEORETICAL IMPLICATIONS

Israeli behaviour during the Gulf War illustrates the poverty of the dominant models of decision-making in international relations theory, whose primary collective failure is to reduce decision-making to a wholly left-brain function. Above all, this event demonstrates the importance of non-cognitive considerations in situations that touch national survival and the vulnerability of populations. It does so in at least three ways:

1 The Israelis' greatest impulse to respond was a function of emotional pressures associated with the preservation instinct and retribution rather than a function of deliberation.

2 The Israelis' deeply rooted association of chemical attack with the Holocaust generated emotional pressures to retaliate that virtually all agree would have been irresistible had that contingency materialized; moreover, the possibility that Israeli leaders might have authorized a nuclear response suggests that they might not have considered calculations of costs and benefits germane under those circumstances.

3 The very high value Israeli leaders placed on taking *some* part in the defence of their country illustrates the independ-

ent force of a basic efficacy need, which can be (and was) satisfied by an active, though not necessarily consequential, role in hunting Scuds. Passivity was simply psychologically impossible.

None of these dynamics is captured well by decision-making models that concentrate on the ways in which leaders assess costs, benefits, and probabilities, handle risk or uncertainty, and set about solving a preference function. Yet they are all fully understandable aspects of normal human psychology. Clearly, international relations theory badly needs to rediscover the human soul.[63]

Nevertheless, the fact that Israel did *not* retaliate illustrates at least a partial triumph of reason over inclination (although it more trenchantly illustrates the triumph of luck over probability). The question is which theoretical model best explains Israeli behaviour.

It is tempting to conclude that Israel's compliance with American wishes may be neatly explained in 'realist' terms, by appealing to the asymmetrical power or the asymmetrical dependence of the two countries. Once the United States decided that it felt strongly on the issue, according to this style of analysis, Israel could not hope to win a contest of wills. Indeed, if by explanation one merely means a decent fit with a parsimonious general theory of international politics, structural realism would seem to have much to commend it – not least the fact that it is completely indifferent to the processes generating observed behaviour and therefore makes no demands upon the analyst to get the process 'right.'[64] But the value of such theories is directly

63 It may well be possible to account for certain emotional effects on decision-making within existing theories of decision; see, eg, note 69, below. Whether that can be done without loss of parsimony and generality – and without impenetrable mathematics – is, in my view, open to doubt. Could Israel's particular sensitivity to the use of chemical weapons be handled, for example, by a weighting coefficient in an expected utility model?

64 See the discussion in Milton Friedman, 'The methodology of positive economics,' in his *Essays in Positive Economics* (Chicago: University of Chicago Press 1953), 3-43.

proportional to their rate of success over a large number of cases; a clock that is accurate only twice a day is of little value to anyone. We may justly wonder how satisfied we should be with a structural realist explanation in this case when the United States has frequently proven unable to influence Israeli behaviour on issues where it has expressed strong preferences – Lebanon, the occupied territories, and the never-ending Middle East peace process, to name but a few. That Israel came so close to retaliating, and probably would have done so had the red lines been crossed, casts further doubt on an essentially deterministic explanation such as this. It is also tempting to conclude that Israeli behaviour may be explained satisfactorily in classical rational-actor terms.[65] After all, Israel appears to have done the 'smart' thing by not retaliating and demonstrated (contrary, for example, to the expectations of an organizational-process model) that it was capable of abandoning its operational codes in an unusual and unforeseen strategic context in such a way as to optimize its security.[66] In short, Israel appears to have behaved in an instrumentally rational fashion.

It may well be, in fact, that Israel's behaviour was instrumentally rational. This does not, however, justify the conclusion that rational-actor analysis provides an adequate or satisfying account of Israeli behaviour. It is often helpful to recall that when we call an actor rational, we may mean one or more of at least three different things:

1 We may mean that the actor was *substantively rational*; that is, her ends were rational. Normally, we consider someone substantively rational if she prefers life over death, prosperity over poverty, pleasure over pain, and so forth. Substantive rationality is an attribute of a value set.

65 In the following discussion, I will be using the term 'rational' in a technical micro-economic sense synonymous with 'utility-maximizing.' While the term normally carries positive connotations, I believe, as will become clear, that those connotations are inappropriate. When I argue, therefore, that Israeli behaviour does not meet the technical standards of rational action, I am implicitly criticizing the technical standards of rational action, not Israeli behaviour.

66 I am indebted to an anonymous reviewer for drawing this point to my attention.

2 We may mean that the actor was *procedurally rational*; that is, she engaged in a decision-making process that might be expected to maximize the likelihood that she will match means to ends. Normally, we consider someone procedurally rational if she considers all available courses of action, searches widely for relevant information, attempts to assess the prospective costs and benefits of her alternatives and to assign probabilities to each, and chooses the alternative with the highest subjective expected utility. Procedural rationality is an attribute of the deliberation phase of decision-making prior to the implementation of one's chosen course of action.

3 We may mean that the actor was *instrumentally rational*; that is, she succeeded in behaving optimally. No other course of action would have been preferable to her on balance. Instrumental rationality is an attribute of the course of action chosen.

Each of these types of rationality is logically independent from the rest. For example, an actor may be substantively rational, but procedurally and instrumentally irrational (she prefers prosperity over poverty but looks to an astrologer for investment advice and consistently loses money). Or an actor may be procedurally rational but substantively and instrumentally irrational (she is suicidal and carefully plots her demise but through sheer bad luck always survives). In fact, an actor will exhibit any one of $2^3 = 8$ possible combinations of these attributes at any one time.

Substantive rationality is an inadequate – indeed inappropriate – requirement for rational-actor analysis. While it is always either true or false that an actor is substantively rational, that in and of itself will not enable the analyst to predict any particular type of behaviour in any particular circumstance, and the ability to make predictions – even if only probabilistic forecasts or statements of tendency – is a minimum requirement for any theory of decision. Israel indeed preferred survival to extinction and more security to less; but for rational-actor analysis to provide a satisfying account of Israeli behaviour, it had to be able to point *in advance* to which of the alternative courses of action Israel would choose under the widely anticipated contingency of an Iraqi missile attack. Moreover, according to the postulates of classical economics, preferences should be treated as exogenous, and discovered; they should not be specified by the theory in advance. The realist tradition in international politics is fortunate indeed that most states are substantively rational, preferring survival to extinction and more welfare to less; but its central maxim that 'all states seek power' is a methodological faux pas.

Requiring that Israel merely be *instrumentally rational* is not enough, either. This would enable us to predict only that, at the end of the day, Israel would succeed in doing whatever it perceived to be in its interest; it would not provide us with any guidance as to which of the available courses of action would result in that outcome. Indeed, because the consequences of rejected alternatives often cannot be known (particularly in complex and fluid situations such as the Gulf War), it is rarely possible to be confident that an actor has indeed succeeded in behaving instrumentally. It is possible to imagine, for example, that if Israel had mounted an impressive retaliatory strike against Iraq without disrupting the coalition, in the process successfully calling the Bush administration's bluff on its veiled threat to withdraw its postwar support, it would have emerged better off than it did in both the short and the long run.

To predict which of several courses of action an actor will take, a rational-actor analyst must discover her preferences and ascertain what the outcome of a rational procedure would be — whether or not the actor does, in fact, follow such a procedure. This clearly requires the analyst to be able to assess the costs, benefits, and probabilities of the available courses of action with some useful degree of accuracy. If the actor indeed follows the same procedure (that is, if she is, in fact, procedurally rational), a high-quality analysis will succeed in predicting which course of action she will follow. But even if she does not follow such a procedure (and is, in fact, procedurally *irrational*), it is still possible to predict her choice *provided that she is instrumentally rational and provided that a rational procedure would also result in instrumentally rational behaviour.* Under these circumstances, we may engage in 'as-if' theorizing and generate reliable predictions.[67] The crucial analytical requirement in either case is that the analyst be able to imagine a rational process and to predict the outcome of that process.

How amenable to rational-actor analysis was Israeli decision-making in the Gulf War? It is plain that the actual Israeli decision-making process did not live up to the standards of procedural rationality. First, Israeli leaders thought primarily in categorical terms (the use of simplifying mechanisms such as 'red lines' being the clearest illustration of this) and made no attempt to map out a decision-tree with assigned values for the estimated costs, benefits, and probabilities of its various possible branches. Given the multi-dimensional uncertainty of the situation they faced, this was of enormous value in economizing resources and preventing paralysis, but it was inconsistent with the procedural expectations of a rational-actor model. Second, Israeli leaders did not handle obvious trade-offs of uncertain value in the way subjective expected utility (SEU) theory would suggest: namely, by attempting to find a basis for assigning each alternative a useful probability and utility so that their expected values could be compared. Instead, they adopted one of two resource-economizing rules of thumb: either they ordered issues according to their apparent urgency, essentially bracketing off or postponing the longer term issue in order to address the more immediate one (as they did by giving the American relationship a higher priority than the potential damage a policy of restraint might wreak on Israeli deterrence), or – for those issues where postponement did

67 Some scholars claim that there is, in fact, a positive correlation between the rationality of a procedure and the instrumentality of its outcome. See, eg, Gregory M. Herek, Irving L. Janis, and Paul Huth, 'Decision making during international crises: is quality of process related to outcome?' *Journal of Conflict Resolution* 31(June 1987), 203-26. It may be, however, that strict adherence to a conception of procedural rationality militates against instrumental rationality in interesting cases – for example, by rendering timely action impossible. See David A. Welch, 'Crisis decision-making reconsidered,' *Journal of Conflict Resolution* 33(September 1989), 430-45.

not seem feasible – they simply ignored one side of the trade-off altogether (as they did by essentially accepting whatever diplomatic, political, or military costs they might have to pay if they chose to implement the military option they considered most effective for defeating the Scuds). A third perplexity from the rational-actor perspective is the fact that the Israeli criteria for taking military action had nothing to do with a cost-benefit 'balance.' The controlling considerations – namely, arbitrary damage thresholds and a chemical 'trip-wire' – did not depend upon an SEU calculation and were closely associated with non-cognitive processes. It is interesting in this regard to note the apparent conditionality of Israeli decision-making at every turn. *Different criteria* were held to be determinative in different contexts in a way that also seems arbitrary from an SEU perspective. Thus, the United States was able to manipulate the Israelis' rough estimates of costs and gains as long as the damage from the Scud attacks remained low. However, once the red lines were crossed (as one American official remarked), 'it would clearly have been a new ball game, and all bets were off.' Principles and emotional needs – not costs and gains – would have governed Israeli behaviour above a certain threshold. A final feature of the Israeli process that defies explication in SEU terms is the change in the Israeli decision horizon as the war approached, and again when the war came to an end. Until January 1991, Israel's primary goal was the destruction of Iraq as a long-term military threat. This was accordingly the predominant subject of American-Israeli diplomacy. During January and February, however, Israel's goal focused and narrowed to the prevention of Scud attacks. By all accounts, this was the sole and consuming topic of American-Israeli discussions during this period. As a result, Israel made no effort to exert leverage to expand American war aims beyond the simple liberation of Kuwait. Given American fears of the consequences of Israeli military action, and the importance placed on preventing it, Israel should have estimated that it had some leverage on this point. But the urgent drove out the important, and the two countries failed to reach an understanding on when the war would end. The priority of the urgent over the important is a normal feature of human experience; but SEU theory fails to capture it because it assumes that preferences are consistent and transitive. An expected utility model would have predicted that Israeli decision-making during the war would continue to reflect the high value attached before and after the war to the destruction of Iraq's military capability, simply because Israel's very tangible interest in that outcome had not changed in the meantime.

Even though Israel's actual decision-making process did not meet the standards of procedural rationality, would an analyst have been able to predict Israeli behaviour by assuming instrumental rationality and examining what the outcome of a rational procedure would have been? It is tempting to answer affirmatively with the benefit of hindsight in view of the undeniable fact that the United States managed to persuade Israel that it stood to suffer serious costs if it undertook military action (primarily because of damage to the American-Israeli relationship), while it faced a negligible prospect of gain (because the United States was already making every effort to find and destroy the Scuds). A cost-benefit calculation, therefore, should have yielded the unambiguous conclusion that Israel should forbear. But to predict Israeli forbearance in advance, an analyst would have had to make a number of controversial interrelated assumptions or inferences about Israeli preferences (since preferences are – or should be – exogenous to rational decision-making models themselves) and about Israeli calculations or beliefs. Two are particularly noteworthy: first, that Israel calculated that its national security would be better served on balance by forbearance than by military action; and, second, that Israel valued its strategic relationship with the United States more highly than either (a) its reputation for swift and decisive retribution, a pillar of its deterrent posture, or (b) its policy of military self-reliance. It is tempting to infer from Israeli behaviour that both of these assertions are correct; but such an inference would involve a circularity. Our natural inclination to assume the necessary conditions for 'rational' behaviour merely reflects the extent to which we have internalized the rational-actor paradigm and cannot be permitted to obscure the fact that neither of these propositions was obviously true to Israeli decision-makers prior to the outbreak of war, let alone to analysts and observers. Indeed, they contradicted the common wisdom.[68] Rational-actor analysis, therefore, provides a poor descriptive fit with actual Israeli behaviour; its predictions *ex ante* would have been indeterminate at best and erroneous at worst; and it cannot provide a satisfying *ex post* account of Israeli behaviour without committing the logical fallacy of inferring preferences from behaviour.

Much of what seems puzzling about Israeli decision-making and behaviour from an SEU perspective may be more satisfactorily explained by prospect theory, although here, too, the fit is imperfect because of prospect theory's imperfect attention to non-cognitive pressures and dynamics.[69] Particularly helpful, however, are prospect theory's hypotheses about the relevance of frames and reference levels – levels of satisfaction, expectation, or aspiration against which leaders measure the status quo and evaluate alternatives – and its emphasis on decision weights rather than probabilities. Also useful is prospect theory's postulate that leaders will edit and simplify complex decision problems in ways that may result in non-utility-maximizing choices or tangled preference orders, an insight closely associated with experimental findings that subjects routinely employ heuristics and cognitive short-cuts that may involve logical inconsistencies.

Reference levels appear to have played a significant role in Israeli decision-making in two respects. First, for Israeli leaders, a world that included a highly militarized Iraq with nuclear, chemical, and biological weapons – and the means to deliver them – was a world in which Israeli national security fell well below an acceptable threshold. As early as the late 1970s, Israeli

68 See, eg, note 3, above.

69 Certain postulates of prospect theory, however, are consistent with our intuitions about how such non-cognitive features might influence decision-making. The willingness to accept poor gambles to avoid serious losses, for example, may be closely associated with panic or desperation.

leaders had little doubt that Iraq, if left unchecked, would eventually obtain a formidable unconventional arsenal. The prospect
of such a serious degradation in Israeli security led Prime Minister Menachem Begin to mount a bold and politically risky attack
on Iraq's Osirak nuclear reactor in 1981 and also led officials in
the government of Prime Minister Shamir to lobby the United
States to take decisive action against Iraq in 1990, threatening to
do so unilaterally if necessary. The expectation once the Gulf
War broke out that the United States would effectively eliminate
Saddam Hussein as a long-term military threat to Israel largely
accounts for Israeli shock and disappointment at the abruptness
with which the war came to an end. American officials could
insist in perfectly good faith that Israel had been the war's major
beneficiary (because the Iraqi armed forces had unquestionably
suffered a major blow). But the difference between the damage
done and the damage Israel *expected* generated disappointment,
much in the way even a 50-per-cent return on an investment
seems disappointing when a 70-per-cent return had been
forecast.

   The second respect in which reference levels appear to have
played an important role is in greatly easing the pressure Israeli
leaders felt to respond to Iraq's attacks. The level of damage
Israeli leaders expected to suffer from Scud attacks, calculated
on the basis of Iranian casualties in the War of the Cities, was
orders of magnitude higher than the level of damage Israel actually suffered. This permitted the inference that Israel was faring
'relatively well' and could afford to give the Americans more time
to deal with the Scuds on their own. An appropriate analogy
would be a shareholders' vote to extend the contract of a chief
executive officer who reported a $100-million loss when a $300-
million loss had been anticipated. However, Iraq proved more
resourceful in sustaining the attacks than had been expected.
The fact that they did not cease somewhat increased Israel's pressure to respond as the war progressed. It may be argued that the
American willingness to give Israel an operational and advisory
role was crucial in alleviating this particular pressure.

It is abundantly clear that Israeli leaders made extensive use
of decision weights and other simplifying mechanisms (such as
red lines) rather than numerical probabilities when considering
contingencies, as prospect theory would suggest. By invoking
heuristics and cognitive short-cuts, it is also possible to provide a
plausible explanation of Israel's remarkably short-sighted
attempt to deter Saddam Hussein prior to the outbreak of war
by threatening certain retaliation if attacked. Because this was
precisely the reaction Saddam Hussein sought to elicit, these
threats played directly into his hands. Apparently, until the very
eve of the war itself, Israel relied fairly uncritically on its stock
deterrent 'script.' One of the most important puzzles from an SEU
perspective – the temporary narrowing of the Israeli decision
horizon during the war itself – may also be explained by prospect
theory's claim that leaders construct their preferences in the light
of changing circumstances. Prospect theory therefore provides a
better fit than does SEU theory with the Israeli decision-making
process itself and renders intelligible aspects of Israeli behaviour
that are inconsistent with the expectations of a classical rational-
actor model.

Finally, the foregoing narrative strongly suggests that, as an
analytical device for understanding Israeli decision-making, relative gains seeking is of limited value. Three aspects of that process seem *prima facie* consistent with the expectation that Israeli
leaders would have concerned themselves with relative gains (or,
more accurately, with avoiding relative losses): (1) Israel assessed
its level of security before and after the war relatively, particularly vis-à-vis Iraq; (2) Israel complained repeatedly that American arms transfers to Syria and Saudi Arabia endangered its
qualitative military advantage over these countries; and (3) Israel
exercised restraint in large part to minimize the danger to American patronage in the postwar environment, so as to maintain a
reasonable margin of security vis-à-vis its regional adversaries.
However, several crucial features of Israeli decision-making and
behaviour are inconsistent with a relative gains analysis. First,
there is no evidence that Israel decided whether or not to take

military action against Iraq on the basis of a putative comparison of the relative positions of Israel and its present and future adversaries. Second, while Israel complained of American arms transfers to its Arab enemies, it did not engage in a concerted effort to obtain an appropriate offset while it had the leverage to do so (namely, during the war itself), consumed as it was by the immediate problem of the Scuds. Third, the primary pressures Israel felt to respond – with perhaps the lone exception of the desire to bolster the credibility of Israeli deterrence – cannot be understood in terms of relative gains or losses at all. Neither SEU theory nor prospect theory fares better on the third point; but prospect theory sheds light on the first and second and provides at least as satisfactory an account as a relative gains analysis of Israel's fears of Iraqi military strength, its concerns about arms transfers to its Arab neighbours, and the future of its relations with the United States. On balance, therefore, it would appear to provide the most satisfying fit.

SOME FINAL THOUGHTS

No discussion of this remarkable case would seem complete without a few practical observations – and a grandiose metaphysical conclusion. I therefore offer the following.

The dynamics of the relationship between Israel and the United States during the Gulf War starkly illustrate how a cooperative outcome may be achieved despite certain fundamental conflicts of interest. If, as officials and observers on both sides insist, the American diplomatic effort made the difference between Israeli action and restraint on several occasions, it did so, first, because the United States was able to manipulate Israel's loss estimates and, second, because of the existence of a robust and effective transgovernmental channel that compensated for weakness and tension in the political relationship – namely, excellent relations between the military establishments of the two countries. These factors are closely interrelated.

The United States deployed every conceivable argument, and pressed them all forcefully, in its attempt to restrain Israel. The argument that proved most effective was one that may or may not have been made explicit: namely, that a failure to co-operate jeopardized future bilateral relations. Under other circumstances, such an argument alone might well have exacerbated tensions between the two countries or precipitated an outright break. But the United States also took enormous pains to accommodate Israel's various requests and demands on technical and operational matters and made every possible effort to demonstrate competence in the campaign against the Scuds. In so doing, it permitted Israel to worry less about what more could be done to stop the Scuds and to dwell at greater length on the potential costs of defection. But Israel made clear that its forbearance depended *principally* on a demonstration of the effectiveness of the American military effort. It was here that the closeness of the relationships between the IDF, on the one hand, and the United States army and air force, on the other, came into play. These relationships had developed and matured over several decades of close collaboration in a wide variety of fields. Here could be found the crucial elements missing in the political relationship: trust and a spirit of genuine co-operation. Several Israelis interviewed for this study insist that without these close relationships, Israel's political leaders could never have been persuaded to set aside – if only temporarily – the country's long-standing and deeply ingrained policy of military self-reliance. The IDF's growing conviction that American soldiers and pilots could get the job done made it much easier for Shamir to give them time to try.

If indeed a style of argument emphasizing the prospect of loss and the availability of a pre-existing transgovernmental channel through which to cultivate a sense of trust were vital components of Washington's diplomatic success in this case, it is possible that they might be useful in other cases, either individually or in concert. If so, the implications for negotiating strategies would be obvious. While one case cannot provide a basis for generalization, it would seem worthwhile to undertake a broader study in order to determine whether such a generalization can be made.

Perhaps it should not be surprising that the United States hit upon a diplomatic formula that worked. After all, it tried everything imaginable. But success, in this case, was never more than tentative, and always uncertain. American officials were never under the misapprehension that they controlled events; indeed, they were aware that, to a great extent, events controlled *them*. It is fortunate indeed that Fate never chose to have a Scud strike a crowded apartment building, killing 100 people, or that Saddam Hussein never launched a chemical attack; for it seems certain that if either of these events had taken place, forces would have been unleashed that American diplomacy could not restrain, and that decision-making theory as we know it simply cannot comprehend.

Six

Avoiding and incurring losses: decision-making in the Suez Crisis

LOUISE RICHARDSON

In the autumn of 1956, Britain, France, and Israel undertook military action against Egypt in an effort to overthrow its president and reverse his nationalization of the Suez Canal. The United States, Britain's closest ally, opposed the operation and ensured its defeat. Unlike other contributions to this volume, therefore, this chapter examines a case of the failure to co-operate. This failure is puzzling when one considers the close diplomatic and personal ties between the two governments and their leaders, the shared perceptions of the canal as a vital artery of Western trade, and similar views of Gamal Abdel Nasser as an unsavoury and obstreperous dictator determined to reduce Western influence in the Middle East. The crucial failure of the United States and Britain to co-operate in response to this crisis led to a humiliating diplomatic defeat for Britain and a serious, albeit temporary, weakening of the Atlantic alliance.[1] I examine the way in which the two most critical decisions were framed by

Assistant Professor of Government, Center for European Studies, Harvard University, Cambridge, Massachusetts.

I am indebted to Janice Gross Stein and David Welch for comments on an earlier draft of this paper.

1 It is worth noting that co-operation, which is usually thought of as desirable, is not necessarily so. Co-operation can lead to bad outcomes just as easily as good ones. Britain and France, France and Israel, and even Britain and Israel co-operated in the invasion of Egypt with results that were little short of disastrous – and not only for the Egyptians. It should certainly not be assumed that the failure of the United States to co-operate with its allies was undesirable or that it led to a poor outcome. In analytical terms, co-operation should be used in a descriptive and value-free sense.

decision-makers in Britain and the United States during this period of crisis in their relationship. The first is the British decision to undo, by force if necessary, Nasser's nationalization of the Suez Canal; the second is the American decision to oppose the British use of force against Egypt.[2]

THE EVENTS

The history of the Suez crisis is well known.[3] In very broad outline the sequence of events was as follows. On 19 July 1956 the American secretary of state, John Foster Dulles, told the Egyptian ambassador that the United States was rescinding its offer to finance the building of a high dam at Aswan. President Nasser retaliated on 26 July by nationalizing the Suez Canal Company. Little or no thought had been given in Washington to Nasser's likely response to the withdrawal of the financing,[4] and the nationalization came as a great surprise. Although London, too, was surprised, the similarity of their reactions ended there. For Washington, Nasser's action was a cause for concern, for London it was a casus belli. Washington resolved to undo Nasser's action,

---

2 There are, of course, a number of complications in this kind of analysis. The major decision-making theories often have data requirements that are close to prohibitive. Because it is impossible to enter the minds of the relevant decision-makers, I have relied on archives, which are not always the most reliable of sources, particularly where governments control the declassification process. Archival materials do, however, provide evidence of private arguments if not private thoughts. They also permit the evaluation of the public rhetoric used by the decision-makers at the time. In addition I have relied heavily on memoirs, although they tend to be self-serving at the best of times and never more so than when written after a policy failure. Nevertheless, the extensive primary sources available on the Suez crisis, particularly after the recent declassification of many of the British papers, do enable us to look inside the decision-making process.

3 For detailed accounts of the crisis, see: Louise M. Richardson, 'Managing Allies and Being Managed by Alliances: Suez and the Falklands,' doctoral dissertation, Harvard University, 1989, from which portions of this paper are drawn; Kenneth Love, *Suez: The Twice-Fought War* (New York: McGraw-Hill 1969); Hugh Thomas, *Suez* (New York: Harper & Row 1966). For the best recent analysis, see William Roger Louis and Roger Owen, eds, *Suez 1956: The Crisis and Its Consequences* (Oxford: At the Clarendon Press 1989).

4 On this point see Love, *Suez: The Twice-Fought War*, 325, and Robert Murphy, *Diplomat among Warriors* (New York: Doubleday 1964), 377.

while London resolved to undo Nasser. Although the reaction of the British public, press, and parliamentary opposition moderated with the passage of time, this difference in the goals of the central decision-makers in London and Washington remained constant.

The Conservative government of Anthony Eden was preoccupied with what its members took as the primary lesson of World War II, namely, that the arbitrary actions of dictators must be opposed. In Washington, however, it was an election year and the peace candidate for president, Dwight D. Eisenhower, and his advisers were seeking to distance the United States from the use of superior force by imperial powers. The extent of these differences was disguised at first by the fact that both governments were at the start anxious to co-operate and confident in their ability to do so. The differences were at times further disguised by the similarity in the language employed by both governments. Both agreed, for example, on the use of force 'as a last resort.' When Eisenhower used the term, he was referring to force as a last resort to maintain the flow of traffic through the canal, a diplomatic goal unlikely to be achieved by force. When Eden spoke of force as a last resort, his aim was to oust Nasser, a political goal unlikely to be achieved other than by force. The British stake in the canal was far higher than that of the United States. Britain, a former colonial power in Egypt, had only recently evacuated a large military base there, and the British government was still the largest single shareholder in the Suez Canal Company. Britain was also by far the greatest user of the canal, with its tonnage accounting for over 28 per cent of all traffic. Significantly, Britain received some two-thirds of its oil imports through the canal, nearly 20.5 million tons on an annual basis; the United States, by comparison, received only 8.6 million tons.[5] For France, too, the stakes were high. A Frenchman had built the canal, and most of the company's individual sharehold-

5 Robert R. Bowie, *International Crises and the Role of Law: Suez 1956* (London: Oxford University Press 1974), 2, and Love, *Suez: The Twice-Fought War*, 366.

ers were French. More importantly, the French government was convinced that Nasser was providing crucial military assistance to the rebels against its rule in Algeria. The British and French governments therefore decided that the nationalization would have to be reversed and Nasser overthrown, and they eventually agreed on a joint military operation to achieve those ends.

In the months immediately following the nationalization, the United States relied on diplomacy in an effort to pre-empt the use of force by ensuring efficient international operation of the canal. Britain, France, and Israel, though determined to undermine Nasser, were worried about the justification of military operations in the absence of any additional provocation from Egypt. They consequently devised a plan to create a pretext for intervention. On 29 October, in accordance with prior arrangements, Israel invaded Egypt across the Sinai desert. Britain and France then issued a joint ultimatum to Israel and Egypt to withdraw ten miles from the canal (which was 100 miles inside Egyptian territory). When Egypt predictably refused, French and British aircraft bombed Egyptian airfields and a combined Anglo-French force set sail from Malta. On 5 November Britain and France dropped paratroopers into Egypt and on the following day a seaborne force landed at Port Said. The ostensible purpose of this operation was to separate the combatants and to safeguard the canal. The United States led the ensuing international opposition to the invasion. Through a combination of diplomatic, economic, and military pressures, the American government ensured a ceasefire by the allied forces shortly after they had landed and before the polls had closed in the presidential election on 6 November. It maintained the pressure until Britain agreed on 3 December to a complete and humiliating withdrawal from Egypt.

Of the many puzzles in this affair, this chapter concentrates on two. First, how could British leaders have miscalculated so badly, jeopardizing Britain's position in the Middle East and the relationship with the United States by allying with France and Israel in a military expedition against Egypt? Second, why did the United States not stand by its closest allies in the interest of preserving the Western alliance, the cornerstone of American foreign policy?

The first puzzle is often cast in terms of the poor personal relationship between Eden and Dulles. Efforts have been made by some, most colourfully by Anthony Nutting, to lay the Suez fiasco entirely at Eden's door.[6] I have argued elsewhere that such an explanation is unfounded and that the crisis was not solely or even primarily of Eden's making.[7] It is nonetheless doubly puzzling that Eden, the consummate diplomat of the age, should have been felled by a diplomatic crisis; that someone who had worked so closely with the United States during the war should have failed to ensure American support for this operation. If one had asked contemporary observers in advance to choose the international leader best equipped to resolve the Suez crisis, most would have chosen Eden. He was, after all, an Oxford-trained Arabist who, over the opposition of the right wing of his party, had successfully negotiated the 1954 Anglo-Egyptian treaty that closed the large British military base at Suez. Eden, moreover, hated war. He had lost his two brothers in the First World War and his son in the Second. Faced with the nationalization of the Suez Canal, one could have reasonably expected the most talented diplomat ever to become prime minister of England to negotiate a clever diplomatic arrangement to resolve the crisis. The appropriate question is why did the British government, replete as it was with men of long diplomatic experience, miscalculate so badly? Indeed, this was the question posed again and again by both Eden's adversaries and his allies. Why would Britain reverse its long-standing pro-Arab policies in the Middle East by allying with Israel and launching a war against Egypt in response to Nasser's nationalization of the Suez Canal Company?

Mohamed Heikal, a close friend and confidante of Nasser, has described Nasser's surprise at learning of the British action:

6 Anthony Nutting, *No End of a Lesson: The Story of Suez* (London: Constable 1967).
7 See Richardson, 'Managing Allies.'

News of the ultimatum was received with astonishment bordering on disbelief. Britain and France's collusion with Israel was now staring us in the face, but this was a possibility which had been discounted, because it was assumed that, however determined on a war Eden might be, he would have had some consideration for his friends in Iraq and other Baghdad Pact countries, and for British prestige and interests in the Middle East, all of which would be irreparably damaged if he committed the one unforgivable sin — combining with Israel to attack an Arab country. Nasser found the whole situation made no sense at all — it was, in fact, quite mad.[8]

In Washington, too, the initial reaction was incredulity. Eisenhower declared to his speech writer, Emmet Hughes: 'I just can't believe it. I can't believe that they would be so stupid as to invite on themselves all the Arab hostility to Israel.'[9] More generally in Washington, it was believed that the Anglo-French operation was ill conceived politically and ill executed militarily.

Eisenhower himself considered, as he had constantly warned Eden in the preceding months, that even if an expeditionary force succeeded in assuming control of the canal, the problem would not be resolved. The canal would be a perennial source of conflict and easily subject to sabotage from a hostile population. Vital oil pipelines from other parts of the Middle East would be put at risk. The action would never receive full domestic support in Britain and could only elicit the hostility of the entire Arab world. Eisenhower was also outraged at the military incompetence that marked the operation. He was infuriated by the apparent indecisiveness of its leaders, and he could not fathom the delay between the expiry of the ultimatum and the landing of the expeditionary force. Nor was he impressed by Eden's scruples in attempting to minimize civilian casualties. As he said to Arthur Burns: 'I cannot understand what they are doing. They

---

8 Mohamed H. Heikal, *Cutting the Lion's Tail: Suez through Egyptian Eyes* (London: Andre Deutsch 1986), 179.

9 Emmet John Hughes, *The Ordeal of Power: A Political Memoir of the Eisenhower Years* (New York: Atheneum 1963), 212.

must have a plan. If so, why don't they move in, hit hard and get it over with quickly? The British and French seem to be operating as if they were confronted by the vast armies of Hitler, rather than by Nasser and the Egyptian armed forces.'[10]

Having resolved to fight, British leaders, for their part, simply discounted all risks attendant on that decision. They casually assumed that the United States would offer, at most, token opposition. They made no effort to marshall international support for their action. Indeed, instead of seeking its support, they determined to keep their closest ally in the dark about their plans. Nor did they observe the niceties of alliance behaviour, once the decision to fight was made. They provided no advance warning of their plans to the United States; Eisenhower first learned about the Anglo-French ultimatum to Israel and Egypt from the press. Furious at this lack of consultation, he made clear in his subsequent radio and television address that 'the United States was not consulted in any way about any phase of these actions, nor were we informed of them in advance.'[11] He was more outspoken in private. He wanted the British to be told that while the United States recognized that the British had a great deal at stake, 'nothing justifies double-crossing us.'[12]

The timing of the operation, moreover, was singularly inconvenient from an American perspective, a fact that does not seem to have entered the calculus of the British decision-makers. The mounting of the Anglo-French action against Egypt at the same time as the Soviet Union took action against the uprising in Hungary contributed greatly to American anger, for it denied the United States an opportunity to exploit Soviet difficulties in East-

---

10 Virgil Pinkley with James Scheer, *Eisenhower Declassified* (Old Tappan NJ: Rivell 1973), 331.
11 Radio and television address by Eisenhower, 31 October 1956, in United States, Department of State, 'U.S. Policy in the Middle East,' September 1956-June 1957, Documents, 149.
12 Memorandum of conference with the president, 7:15 pm, 29 October 1956: Eisenhower Library, Abilene, Kansas, Ann Whitman File (hereafter AWF), Dwight David Eisenhower Diary Series (hereafter DDEDS), Diary-Staff Memos (hereafter DSM), 1956.

ern Europe. As Dulles said at the meeting of the National Security Council on 1 November: 'It is nothing less than tragic that at this very time, when we are on the point of winning an immense and long-hoped-for victory over Soviet colonialism in Eastern Europe, we should be forced to choose between following in the footsteps of Anglo-French colonialism in Asia and Africa, or splitting our course away from their course.'[13] While the events in Eastern Europe could not have been foreseen in London, the elections in the United States were no secret. The British leadership failed to take into account the domestic implications of a military operation by Washington's allies on the eve of a presidential election. In the week before the election, indeed, White House aides were beside themselves with what Hughes described as 'righteous wrath ... as if the real crime of London had been to contrive so thoughtlessly to complicate [the] President's re-election or at least whittle down his majority.'[14] This reaction may have been exaggerated but it should certainly have been predictable, especially for a leadership so skilled in the exercise of diplomacy and so accustomed to close collaboration with the Americans. For most observers of the unrivalled grace and skill with which Britain had divested itself of its colonial possessions, Britain's actions in 1956 remain a enigma.[15]

The second puzzle is why leaders in the United States would abandon their closest allies at a time when they believed their national interests to be in jeopardy. At first glance, the description of the first puzzle may appear to provide an answer to the

13 National Security Council, 302nd meeting, 1 November 1956, AWF, NSC series.
14 Hughes, *Ordeal of Power*, 218.
15 Not everyone would accept this characterization of British behaviour. Certainly participants, in both their political statements at the time and their memoirs, refused to concede responsibility for such gross miscalculation. Others, particularly the right wing of the Tory party argued, both at the time and subsequently, that the mistake was not in going into Egypt but in pulling out. For a particularly unrepentant example of this perspective, see Julian Amery, 'The Suez Group: A Retrospective on Suez,' in Selwyn Ilan Troen and Moshe Shemesh, eds, *The Suez-Sinai Crisis 1956: Retrospective and Reappraisal* (London: Frank Cass 1990), 110-26.

second. Clearly, the American government, and in particular the president, thought the allied operation to be ill conceived both politically and militarily. But that belief is not sufficient to explain why the United States should insist upon ignominious withdrawal. As Hans Morgenthau wrote at the time: 'Regardless of the intrinsic merits of their military operation, once it was started we had a vital interest in its quick and complete success.'[16]

The American decision to oppose its allies actively was by no means a foregone conclusion. Indeed, it came as quite a surprise to contemporaries on all sides of the issue. As Heikal reports: 'There was much discussion in Cairo about what game exactly, the Americans were playing.' The Egyptians concluded that the United States allowed the doomed invasion to proceed knowing that it would weaken both Nasser and its own allies in the belief that 'the United States would then be left dominating the world stage.'[17] This view, incidentally, was shared by many on the right wing of the British Tory party. As Julian Amery expressed it: 'The u.s. wanted British and French dominance ended so that they could replace them.'[18] However satisfactory this explanation may have seemed at the time, it simply does not match the evidence. Analyses of the Middle East done by the National Security Council (NSC) prior to the crisis invariably refer to the service rendered the Atlantic alliance by British and French influence in the region. Even at the time Eisenhower insisted that 'we should give the British every chance to work their way back into a position of influence in the region.'[19]

The vehemence of the American reaction came as a stunning surprise to the British, French, and Israelis. Their operation was based on the assumption that, as Harold Macmillan expressed it

16 *New York Times*, 13 November 1956.
17 Heikal, *Cutting the Lion's Tail*, 188.
18 Interview, Julian Amery, MP, 24 June 1986.
19 See, for example, NSC, Documents on Suez, 1954-1958, 5428, 23 July 1954; Memorandum of conference with the president, 25 November 1956, AWF, DDEDS, DSM, 1956.

in his memorable phrase, 'Ike will lie doggo.'[20] Macmillan subsequently wrote in his memoirs: 'I admit that my judgement was wrong. I felt that the American government, while publicly deploring our action, would be privately sympathetic, and thus content themselves with formal protests.'[21] Faced with the decision in 1956, a realist might well have predicted that, given the centrality of the Western alliance to American foreign policy, the United States would support its allies in their attempt to maintain their influence in the Middle East against the provocations of an authoritarian colonel with close ties to the Soviet Union. Indeed, the American failure to do so elicited harsh criticism from analysts with whom the term realism is most often associated. Shortly after the ceasefire was declared, for example, Morgenthau wrote that the preservation of Britain and France as members of the alliance was a basic assumption of American foreign policy and yet 'we cooperated with the Soviet Union in inflicting probably irreparable damage upon the position of Britain and France in the Middle East and the world at large.'[22] George Kennan made a similar point in a bitter criticism of American actions. Describing himself as more perplexed and unhappy with American policy than at any point in his thirty years' experience, he argued that the foundations of American policy were being swept away, having become 'the victim of an empty legalism, of a fateful inability to maintain intimate communion with our friends, and a style of diplomatic action directed to the grandstand rather than to the realities of our situation.'[23]

THE PROCESS OF DECISION-MAKING IN BRITAIN

News of the nationalization of the canal reached London on the evening of 26 July as Prime Minister Eden was hosting a dinner

20 Cited, amongst other places, in Richard E. Neustadt, *Alliance Politics* (New York: Columbia University Press 1970), 21.
21 Harold Macmillan, *Riding the Storm 1956-1959* (New York: Harper & Row 1971), 149.
22 *New York Times*, 13 November 1956.
23 *Ibid*, 4 November 1956.

for King Faisal of Iraq. The dinner was hastily concluded and an emergency midnight meeting called of the senior cabinet members who were present. The chiefs of staff, the French ambassador, and the American chargé d'affaires were summoned to join the deliberations. The conviction that this was an intolerable action which would have to be effectively countered was evident from the beginning. The consensus of the gathering was that Nasser 'must not be allowed to get away with it.'[24] The chiefs of staff were instructed to produce a study of the military requirements for an operation to seize the canal. They made clear, however, that whatever the prime minister's wishes, the British armed forces could do nothing immediately – an embarrassing admission for a nation which considered itself a global power. With the French and American representatives looking on, the group acknowledged that Nasser's action might in fact be legal, but this in no way tempered their outrage. Because the group recognized that United Nations involvement would likely lead to the issue becoming 'hopelessly bogged down,' the initial emphasis was on the need to join with the United States and France in taking economic, political, and, if necessary, military action to ensure freedom of transit through the canal. Further decisions were deferred to a cabinet meeting the following morning.

The morning press in London bayed for blood. Employing the analogy that was much abused over the next few weeks, the *Daily Mail* declared 'Hitler on the Nile' and the *Herald* 'No more Hitlers,' while the *Daily Mirror* recommended that Nasser study the fate of Mussolini.[25] In the House of Commons, the reaction, even among opposition members, was equally vitriolic. Hugh Gaitskell enthusiastically pledged the Labour party's support for

24 The fullest account of this meeting is contained in a telegram from Foster, the American chargé, who attended the meeting in the absence of the ambassador. See 'Telegram from the embassy in the United Kingdom to the Department of State,' 27 July 1956, in Department of State, Central Files, 974.7301/7-2756.

25 *New York Times*, 28 July 1956. Donald Neff, *Warriors at Suez (Eisenhower Takes America into the Middle East)* (New York: Linder 1981), 277. For a fuller account of the role of the press, see Leon D. Epstein, *British Politics in the Suez Crisis* (Urbana: University of Illinois Press 1964), especially 153-65.

a firm government policy, and he was seconded by the leader of the Liberals. Even Aneurin Bevan, the bête noire among British socialists, said of the nationalization: 'If the sending of one's police and soldiers into the darkness of the night to seize somebody else's property, is nationalization, Ali Baba used the wrong terminology.'[26] There was not a single dissenting voice to be heard in the House of Commons at this time, an accurate reflection of the jingoism evident throughout the country. Winston Churchill characteristically captured the prevailing sentiment: 'We can't have that malicious swine sitting across our communications.'[27]

Amidst this first rush of popular feeling, the full cabinet met on 27 July. The conclusions of this meeting formed the basis of the British position over the ensuing three months.[28] Ministers agreed that as the legal position was weak, opposition must be more broadly based. They decided, therefore, that the canal had to be presented not as Egyptian property but as a critical international asset. Egypt could not be allowed to exploit an international facility for its own advantage — though, of course, there had been no objection to a private company doing so! It was confidently, and quite wrongly, assumed that Egypt lacked the very limited technical ability which would be required to manage the canal and the resources to develop the waterway. Moreover, it was pointed out that in its recent behaviour Egypt had demonstrated that it could not be relied upon to recognize its international obligations.

The discussion moved on to the means available to Britain to redress its grievance. Because economic pressure alone was considered unlikely to produce results, the cabinet agreed that max-

26 Cited in Selwyn Lloyd, *Suez 1956: A Personal Account* (London: Cape 1978), 74.
27 Lord Charles Moran, *Churchill: Taken from the Diaries of Lord Moran – The Struggle for Survival 1940-1965* (Boston: Houghton Mifflin 1966), 747. This unanimity did not last. As time passed with no adverse consequences of the nationalization evident, popular passion on the subject waned, while the Labour party reversed itself. As a result, by the time military action was taken, the country was deeply divided on the issue.
28 Cabinet meeting, 27 June 1956, CAB 128/30, Cabinet Minutes (56), (hereafter CM), 54th Conclusions, Public Record Office (PRO), United Kingdom.

imum political pressure from all interested countries, backed by the threat or use of force, would have to be applied. Military considerations were discussed, and the importance of securing international support was stressed. According to the minutes: 'The Cabinet agreed that our essential interests in this area must, if necessary, be safeguarded by military action and that the necessary preparations to this end must be made. Failure to hold the Suez Canal would lead inevitably to the loss one by one of all our interests and assets in the Middle East and, even if we had to act alone, we could not stop short of using force to protect our position if all other means of protecting it proved unavailing.' The chiefs of staff were instructed to draw up a timetable of military operations, and the responsible ministers were instructed to ensure an adequate supply of shipping for any military action that might be contemplated. The cabinet also agreed to act with France in freezing Egyptian assets in the central banks of the two countries. In addition, arms exports to Egypt were to be stopped and arrangements made for the restriction of oil deliveries. A subcommittee of the cabinet was appointed to deal with the crisis. This group of long-time colleagues, soon to be known as the 'Egypt Committee,' became the locus of decision-making throughout the crisis.

The United States and France were invited to join the general deliberations on the response to the seizure of the canal. Eden later wrote that he and his cabinet expected that France would participate in any expedition against Egypt and that 'the United States would at least be neutral.' Shortly after the meeting Eden sent a personal telegram to Eisenhower in which he relayed the decisions of the cabinet: 'We are all agreed that we cannot afford to allow Nasser to seize control of the canal in this way, in defiance of international agreements. If we take a firm stand over this now we shall have the support of all the maritime powers. If we do not, our influence and yours throughout the Middle East will, we are all convinced, be finally destroyed.'[29]

29 Anthony Eden, *Full Circle: The Memoirs of Anthony Eden* (Boston: Houghton Mifflin 1960), 476-7.

Within this inner circle of decision-makers, preferences remained largely stable throughout the four months of the crisis until, of course, the last minute when the extent of the policy disaster became obvious. The few who did oppose the operation from the beginning remained largely muted. Walter Monckton, the minister of defence, expressed reservations but, instead of resigning, permitted himself to be reassigned to a less demanding cabinet post, ostensibly on the grounds of ill health. Lord Louis Mountbatten, the first sea lord, also opposed the operation but did not resign because he considered that to do so in the midst of a war would constitute dereliction of duty. R.A. Butler, lord privy seal and Eden's heir apparent, while not comfortable with the plans, nevertheless kept his discomfort to himself. In the larger decision-making body of the cabinet, those with reservations were cowed by the stature in international affairs of the lions of the party who were making the critical decisions. And in the months following that first cabinet meeting, those decision-makers remained convinced that the nationalization of the canal posed an intolerable threat to Britain, even after it became obvious that none of the anticipated cataclysmic economic consequences of nationalization had emerged and after much of the popular antipathy to Nasser had waned.

From this brief account of British decision-making in the wake of the nationalization, it is obvious that the process bore little or no relation to rational norms. There was no systematic evaluation of options or calculation of their costs and consequences. Instead, the consequences of acquiescence in Nasser's fait accompli were cast in apocalyptic terms, while the risks attendant on the use of force to reverse it were systematically discounted. No serious effort was made to establish the financial costs of anticipated military operations. The chancellor of the exchequer, Harold Macmillan, cavalierly declared himself willing to pawn the art treasures of the National Gallery; after all, no price was too high to prevent Britain becoming 'another Netherlands.'[30] Moreover, the initial estimates that were made

---

30 Murphy, *Diplomat among Warriors*, 380.

were extraordinarily optimistic. Macmillan told his old friend, Robert Murphy, the number three man in the State Department who had immediately been sent to London by Eisenhower, that military operations requiring a division or two would take place in August, would last no more than ten days, and would be financed by £5 million the government had set aside for the purpose.[31]

Far from calculating the costs and benefits of various options, therefore, as an orthodox utility maximization model of decision-making would suggest, little in the way of rational calculation appears to have impeded the conviction that Nasser must be overthrown. Remarkably, in view of the fact that American economic pressure, more than anything else, was to prove the undoing of the British action, financing the operation does not appear to have been a major concern of the British government during the months of deliberation preceding the actual intervention. The expedition, however, was to cost far more than the £5 million Macmillan had suggested in July. The cabinet later considered the projected cost of the operation and assumed that the Treasury could easily handle the £12 million required by the military precautions, the £2 million-per-month cost of keeping the forces in readiness from mid-September, and even the £100 million for the operation itself.[32] This was far more than the £35- to £50-million estimate that Macmillan would give the House of Commons on 12 November.[33] Nevertheless, there was no effort to reconsider goals or re-evaluate options in light of the ever increasing costs, as might reasonably have been expected. Indeed, Treasury officials were not even included in discussions of the projected costs of the operation or of Britain's ability to meet those costs. No doubt this confidence in their ability to manage the financial costs was at least in part based on the

31 *Ibid.*
32 Eden, *Full Circle*, 622.
33 *Parliamentary Debates*, House of Commons, United Kingdom (hereafter *Hansard*), 5th series, vol. 560, 12 November 1956, col. 684; Macmillan, *Riding the Storm*, 171.

government's assumption that, in the unlikely event of financial difficulties, Britain could always appeal to the International Monetary Fund and the United States for support. At a meeting of the backbench 1922 Committee in September, Sir Alec Spearman had questioned these assumptions, but the chancellor of the exchequer never did.[34] Although Treasury officials warned of the dangers of 'going it alone,' the chancellor and the Egypt Committee remained undeterred.[35]

There were also, of course, political costs to be considered, but here, too, there is no evidence that they were. Eisenhower, in his letters to Eden, constantly warned of the adverse political consequences in the Middle East from military action, of the danger to Europe's oil supply through the vulnerability of the oil pipelines, and of the difficulties of maintaining a military force in the midst of a hostile population.[36] These concerns were blithely ignored by British decision-makers, embarked as they were on a crusade to prevent the reduction of the British standard of living 'to that of the Yugoslavs or Egyptians.'[37]

Most critically, of course, the British leadership greatly underestimated the probability that the United States would oppose the operation. Yet Eisenhower made clear his opposition to the use of force from the beginning. He warned Eden that the American reaction to a military operation would be 'severe.' He also pointed out that if military action were taken, the United States could not become involved without the approval of a special session of Congress.[38] Eisenhower was equally clear in his public statements. At a press conference, for example, he declared that he was 'committed to a peaceful settlement of this

34 Thomas, *Suez*, 146.
35 Alistair Horne, *Harold Macmillan*. 1: *1894-1956* (New York: Viking 1989), 415-16.
36 See, for example, Eisenhower to Eden, 2 September 1956, in D.D. Eisenhower, *The White House Years: Waging Peace 1956-1961* (New York: Doubleday 1965), 667.
37 Evelyn Shuckburgh, *Descent to Suez: Diaries 1951-56* (London: Weidenfeld and Nicolson 1986), 360.
38 Eisenhower to Eden, 31 July 1956, Prime Ministerial Files (hereafter PREM) 11, 1177, 1956, United States (General), PRO.

dispute, nothing else.'[39] Dulles, while never committing the United States to support a use of force, was more ambivalent. In retrospect, it seems clear that he was playing a delicate diplomatic game, in which he endorsed the use of force as a last resort as part of an effort to encourage the exploration of all peaceful means to achieve a solution. The British, however, simply discounted Eisenhower's numerous public and private statements and interpreted Dulles's position in a singularly one-sided manner. As Macmillan wrote: 'I was quite happy to concur in the protracted series of plans and expedients which the maritime nations of the world under Dulles' inspiration were to devise during the next few weeks. I was confident that if and when the moment for action arrived we should have, if not the overt, at least the covert sympathy and support of the Government and people of the United States.'[40] In one particularly striking case, Eisenhower wrote a letter to Eden in which he laid out in the clearest possible terms his view 'as to the unwisdom even of contemplating the use of military force at this moment.' Eden's extraordinary response was that 'the President did not rule out the use of force.'[41] Far from calculating the costs of various potential courses open to them, Britain's decision-makers systematically discounted the costs associated with the option they had decided upon.

It is possible that British leaders may have been motivated by relative gains seeking in the Suez crisis. Certainly, they were preoccupied by the threat Nasser was perceived to pose to Britain's prestige in the region. The documents suggest, however, that these men were far more concerned about their nation's international status, relative to the position it had historically held in the region, than about its current position relative to other regional powers. The British never seem to have considered using the crisis as an opportunity to make gains at the expense of their

---

39 Lloyd, *Suez 1956*, 130.
40 Macmillan, *Riding the Storm*, 104.
41 Eisenhower to Eden, 31 July 1956, PREM 11, 1177, 1956, United States (General); Eden, *Full Circle*, 486.

regional rivals, the United States and France. There is no evidence that they measured the consequences of the use of force in terms of the relative power positions of their regional rivals.

In fact, throughout the months of deliberations before the military operation, British decision-makers did not speak of gains at all but of *losses*. The minutes of the cabinet meeting of 28 August, for example, register estimates of the dire consequences, should Nasser remain unchecked: 'Our whole position in the Middle East would be undermined, our oil supplies would be in jeopardy, and the stability of our national economy would be gravely threatened.'[42] This was a gross overestimation of likely losses, and in his letters to Eden, Eisenhower constantly tried to convince the prime minister that he was overstating the threat from Nasser. The record of the many discussions of the period reveals no consideration of the gains to be achieved from the contemplated action. Indeed, there appears to have been very little planning for future developments once Nasser was toppled; only a casual assumption that he would be replaced by a more compliant leader. The focus was entirely on the avoidance of the threat posed to British prestige and the British economy.

Prospect theory, as outlined in Janice Stein's introduction to this volume, helps to explain the process of British decision-making during the Suez crisis. The availability heuristic explains the strength of the analogy to Hitler and the deeply held conviction that aggressors must not be appeased. Guy Mollet, the French politician, called it his 'Munich complex,' but it was by no means peculiar to him. Discussions throughout the Suez crisis – in government, in parliament, in the press – were suffused with the language of appeasement. In a speech that he was subsequently to regret, Hugh Gaitskell declared on 2 August: 'It is all very familiar. It is exactly the same that we encountered from Mussolini and Hitler in those years before the war.'[43] These

---

42 Cabinet meeting, 28 August 1956, CAB 128/30, CM (56), 62nd Conclusions. As it turned out, it was the bungled military operation which put the British economy, British prestige, and British oil supplies in jeopardy.

43 *Hansard*, 5th ser., vol. 557, 2 August 1956, col. 1613.

images permeated Eden's correspondence with Eisenhower; in one of many such letters, Eden wrote: 'Some say that Nasser is no Hitler or Mussolini. Allowing for a difference in scale, I am not so sure. He has followed Hitler's pattern, even to concentration camps and the propagation of *Mein Kampf* among his officers. He has understood and used the Goebbels pattern of propaganda in all its lying ruthlessness. Egypt's strategic position increases the threat to others from any aggressive militant dictatorship there.'[44] Eisenhower's response to all such statements was to inform his allies that 'you are making of Nasser a much more important figure than he is.'[45]

Britain's leaders were not using these images merely as a useful means to whip up support among the public and the press or to appeal to the sentiments of a wartime ally. They reflected the deeply rooted beliefs of these men and the same views were expressed with the same vehemence in private letters and discussions as in public pronouncements. At a cabinet meeting in August, for example, Lord Salisbury, the lord president of the Privy Council, said to his colleagues: 'The lessons of the 1930s should not be forgotten. Experience with Italy and later with Germany had surely shown that if the encroachments of a dictator were not checked at the outset, when comparatively little strength was needed to check them, the ultimate reckoning involved a far greater convulsion and much greater sacrifice.'[46] Theirs was the generation that had had to live with the consequences of the appeasement of Hitler. Indeed, Eden, Macmillan, and Salisbury were among the minority who had opposed appeasement in the thirties. They had been proven right before, with terrible consequences. The lessons of the thirties were clear: the principal one was that early resistance to aggressors was both more honourable and less costly than waiting. But there were other lessons too. One of these was that one cannot wait for the

44 Eden, *Full Circle*, 481.
45 Eisenhower to Eden, 8 September 1956, PREM 11, 1171, 1956, United States (General).
46 Cabinet meeting, 28 August 1956, CAB 128/30, CM (56), 62nd Conclusions.

United States before acting, that while Washington would eventually join the right side, it would take a painfully long time to do so. Another lesson pertained to a public that had earlier been wrong on appeasement: they must be led and not followed. In consequence, American equivocation and the softening of popular attitudes towards Nasser had little or no impact on the main decision-makers, preoccupied as they were with the 1930s. The many courses of action put forward by the United States and others in the months after the nationalization of the canal made no impact on British decision-makers because they smacked of appeasement.

Britain's leaders, then, used not the status quo but their aspirations as their reference point for decision. They sought the restoration of the status quo prior to the nationalization and the elimination of Nasser. Rejecting arguments by Eisenhower, among others, British leaders treated as certain the losses of accepting the current situation because they reflexively drew an analogy to the disastrous consequences of the appeasement of Hitler. The imperative was to avoid the certain and catastrophic losses of allowing the status quo to stand. British leaders, therefore, dismissed all evidence that acceptance of the status quo might not entail large losses, and they systematically discounted the risks that the use of force to reverse it might entail for both their position in the Middle East and their relationship with the United States. They assumed that the United States would ultimately accept their action; they were motivated to discount the risks of the alternative by their high estimates of the losses of accepting the status quo. British leaders did not, therefore, see themselves as facing a choice between certain losses if they acquiesced in the status quo and the risk of even greater but only probable losses if they used force. Rather, the imperative of avoiding appeasement led them to discount almost completely the risks of using force.

British leaders did not engage in probabilistic thinking. Rather than estimate the likelihood of American support, Soviet intervention, domestic upheaval, or international opposition, they focused almost exclusively on the losses consequent on accepting the status quo. As the secretary of state for the colonies, Alan Lennox-Boyd, wrote in a private letter to Eden: 'I remain firmly convinced that if Nasser wins we might as well as a government (and indeed as a country) go out of business.'[47] As American analysts argued at the time, these losses were by no means certain. But the British decision-makers who engaged in risk-seeking behaviour to avert those losses considered them certain. This case thus offers support for the proposition that people seek to avoid what they believe to be certain losses, but it also suggests that people then minimize the associated risks. Having dismissed the risks of the use of force, the British leaders were not – from their perspective – engaging in risk-seeking behaviour.

In sum, the process of British decision-making and the choice to use force in 1956 bears no resemblance to an orthodox expected utility maximization model or to a relative gains seeking model. The emphasis of prospect theory on loss avoidance, on exaggeration of losses, on reference points, and availability heuristics is more helpful in explaining the many curious and anomalous aspects of British decision-making during this critical postwar crisis.

THE DECISION-MAKING PROCESS IN THE UNITED STATES
American leaders considered Nasser's nationalization of the Suez Canal to be unfortunate but legal and unlikely to have major ramifications for world order. During the ensuing months, the United States tried to resolve the dispute through diplomacy. Dulles led the attempt to arrive at a mutually acceptable arrangement for the international operation or management of the canal. Such an arrangement would ensure that no Egyptian government would have, as Eden graphically phrased it, 'a thumb on our windpipe': that is, Nasser and his successors could not hinder traffic through the canal to further their political

47 Letter from Lennox-Boyd to Eden, 24 August 1956, PREM 11, 1152.

purposes. The other American goal during this period was to persuade Britain and France not to use force in response to Nasser's provocation. The United States promoted this aim both directly in talks and indirectly by, on the one hand, trying to create an acceptable regime for the canal which would undermine any justification for the use of force and, on the other, by playing for time in an effort to allow tempers to cool and domestic opposition to the use of force to grow. Once Britain, France, and Israel launched their operation, however, the American government faced a crisis. It had to respond to its allies.

The subsequent process of American decision-making could hardly have looked more different from the British one. Unlike the unanimity apparent in Britain, there was serious disagreement in Washington about the appropriate response. Although American decision-makers also looked back to World War II, the lesson they stressed was not the iniquities of appeasement but the ability of their allies to drag the United States into war. For them, the reference point was the status quo prior to the invasion rather than before the nationalization of the canal. Drawing on the analogy of entrapment and sensitive to the losses of colluding with renascent colonialism, American leaders rejected the option of acquiescing in the Anglo-French invasion.

The president's view and his sangfroid prevailed throughout the process of decision-making, but the process was careful and considered. At meetings of the National Security Council, differences of opinion were heated and, in contrast to the British process, a variety of opinions was canvassed. Military spokesmen were more sympathetic than the executive towards Britain and in the course of the crisis the Joint Chiefs of Staff (JCS) presented several papers to the NSC which analysed eight possible military courses of action. At the NSC meeting of 30 August, Admiral Radford summarized the general conclusion of the JCS: '[T]he most desirable course of action for the US would be strong public, political and logistical support for Great Britain and France, without direct military intervention by the US in support of these countries against Egypt unless a third party intervened in the hostilities. Such a course of action ... would be likely to prevent a war over Suez from spreading.'[48] Once a ceasefire was declared, Admiral Radford pushed for expediting the clearance of the canal in view of its central importance to Britain and France.[49] He also sought to encourage the other members of the NSC to refrain from blaming Britain and France too much for the current difficulties in the Middle East. Instead, he argued that ultimate responsibility lay with the Soviet Union.[50] At the NSC meeting of 15 November, he complained that 'he failed to see why so much emphasis was placed on the misdeeds of Britain, France and Israel and not on Nasser's long record of provocations.'[51]

These views found some support among the legislative leaders consulted by Eisenhower. On 30 July, Dulles spoke to the Democratic senator, Mike Mansfield, who complained that Nasser possessed all the attributes of an unstable dictator and recommended that the United States, Britain, and France 'take determined action.'[52] On 12 August, at a bipartisan meeting between the president and the congressional leadership, the overriding sentiment was sympathy for Britain and France. Lyndon Johnson, the majority leader in the Senate, captured the mood when he inquired whether: 'we had not had enough experience with this type of situation to realize that we can't deal with this Colonel, and shouldn't we face up to it and say so to our allies. He went on to the effect that they expect us to help and we seem to be sympathetic to their case hence should we not face up to it.'[53] This perspective was also represented in the inner circle of American decision-makers by Harold Stassen, the special assis-

48 National Security Council, 295th meeting, 30 August 1956; Eisenhower Papers, 1953-1961, AWF, Minutes of NSC Meetings with Special Advisory Reports.
49 National Security Council, 305th meeting, 30 November 1956, AWF, NSC series.
50 National Security Council, 303rd meeting, 8 November 1956, *ibid.*
51 National Security Council, 304th meeting, 15 November 1956, *ibid.*
52 Memorandum of telephone conversation, 30 July 1956, General, Telephone Calls Series, John Foster Dulles Papers, Princeton University Library, Princeton, NJ.
53 'Notes on Presidential-Bi-partisan Congressional Leadership Meeting,' 12 August 1956, AWF, Legislative Meetings Series, Legislative Leaders Meetings 1956, July-November.

tant to the president on disarmament problems, who persistently pressed for moderation of the American position. As he wrote to Eisenhower in late November: 'I continue to feel that from the standpoint of the US national interest we are being too tough on the UK and France, and the result can be very serious to us as well as them if long continued.'[54] Earlier in the crisis, arguing that the Suez Canal was a vital lifeline for the British, Stassen had recommended that the United States confine its activities at the United Nations to a demand for a ceasefire. The minutes of the NSC meeting of 1 November illustrate the varying estimates of United States interests:

With great warmth, Secretary Dulles said that he was compelled to point out to Governor Stassen that it was the British and French who had just vetoed the cease-fire. Governor Stassen asked that even so, wasn't this kind of acceptance of a cease-fire to our immediate advantage? Secretary Dulles replied with an emphatic negative, and added that what the British and French had done was nothing but the straight old fashioned variety of colonialism of the most obvious sort. Even so, replied Governor Stassen, it seemed to him that the future of Great Britain and of France was still the most important consideration for the United States, and that all our efforts should now be directed towards a cease-fire.

Stassen went on to argue that the American public could be divided if the government were to 'split away from Britain and France.' To this the president replied: 'How could we possibly support Britain and France if in doing so we lose the whole Arab world?'[55]

Far from the unanimity that prevailed in Britain, therefore, there was real dissent among American leaders. This ensured that various options were considered and their consequences debated. The first option considered was to support Egypt. There was considerable discussion of American responsibilities under the 1950 Tripartite Declaration in which the United States

54 Stassen to Eisenhower, 26 November 1956, White House Confidential File, Subject Series, Suez Canal Crisis, Eisenhower Library, Abilene, Kansas.
55 National Security Council, 302nd meeting, 1 November 1956, AWF, NSC series.

had pledged, along with Britain and France, to aid the victim of aggression in the Middle East.[56] Egypt was clearly the victim of aggression, but to support Egypt with more than words would have forced Washington actively to oppose its closest allies; this the United States was not prepared to do. When Nasser requested American help, he was told that the United States would not fight Britain and France but would help at the United Nations.[57] Eisenhower was furious with Britain and France both for their military action and for their failure to inform the United States in advance, but as he constantly reminded his more zealous subordinates, they were still the country's allies and he was anxious to preserve the relationship. Eisenhower, moreover, was no fan of Nasser. On receiving estimates from the Central Intelligence Agency that Nasser might fall as a result of the invasion, he said: 'Tell Nasser we'll be glad to put him on St Helena and give him a million dollars.'[58] Although Eisenhower would not have been unhappy to see Nasser removed, he considered the method chosen by his allies to be particularly inappropriate and inopportune. American support for Egypt, therefore, was limited to the diplomatic arena.

Another option – simply to do nothing – was not actively considered. Because both sides were appealing to the United States for support, it was never really a practicable choice. It would have smacked of a lack of leadership and moral fibre in an administration that prided itself on both. If Washington had ignored the crisis, the United States would have appeared to condone the invasion of Egypt. American officials quickly rejected this option, largely on the grounds that the United States would be tarred with the same colonialist brush as its allies while the Soviet Union would be given an enormous victory in the Middle East and could then pose as the friend of the oppressed.

Nor did the United States ever seriously consider active sup-

---

56 See, for example, Memorandum of conversation with the president, 29 October 1956, 7:15 pm, AWF, DDEDS.
57 Love, *Suez: The Twice-Fought War*, 557.
58 Hughes, *Ordeal of Power*, 224.

port for its allies. Certainly, American military support was not directly needed to defeat Egypt. The United States might, nonetheless, have been more accommodating to British requests for economic assistance and more supportive at the United Nations, but Washington was determined not to become implicated in an operation it had opposed from the beginning. The response of American leaders to the allied invasion was nuanced and multifaceted. They led the diplomatic opposition but nevertheless ensured that resolutions of condemnation passed at the United Nations were relatively moderate. They refused to help Britain economically and increased the economic pressure by facilitating, if not actually orchestrating, a run on the pound. Finally, they decided to station the Sixth Fleet in the Mediterranean, clearly in the way of the allied armada, as a precautionary measure, but also, no doubt, to demonstrate the seriousness of their opposition.[59]

The American decision-making process conforms broadly to the expectations of a model of rational choice. Decision-makers did not engage in the exhaustive calculation of options, costs, and benefits that orthodox expected utility maximization implies, but the process did approximate rational norms. Not all options were considered and not all consequences were anticipated, but decision-makers did consider and compare alternatives and their consequences before choosing their response to the invasion.

Relative gains seeking does not seem to have been a serious factor. There is very little evidence that American officials saw opportunities to make gains, at the expense of either their allies or their primary adversary, the Soviet Union. British and Egyptian suspicions notwithstanding, there was no serious discussion of using the opportunity created by the crisis to replace Britain and France in the Middle East. Nor was there any effort to make gains at the expense of the Soviet Union by demonstrating the

59 For a more detailed account of the American reaction, see Richardson, 'Managing Allies,' chapter 6.cm

solidarity of the Western alliance at a time when the Warsaw pact appeared to be disintegrating.

While American decision-makers were not attempting to make relative gains, they were nevertheless certainly thinking in relative terms. Specifically, they were concerned about avoiding relative losses, particularly to their primary protagonist in the Cold War, the Soviet Union. In particular, American officials wanted to avoid alienating what Eisenhower referred to as the 'Afro-Asian bloc' that would then give its support to the Soviet Union. The speed with which the United States took the issue to the United Nations and then took the lead in condemning the invasion can be understood only in this context. Eisenhower told the British chargé on the evening of 29 October that he would go to the Security Council 'the first thing in the morning – when the doors open – before the USSR gets there.'[60] When an Anglo-French veto blocked resort to the Security Council, Eisenhower insisted that the United States go to the General Assembly 'to keep ahead of the Soviets on this matter.' As he explained to Dulles: '[A]t all costs the Soviets must be prevented from seizing a mantle of world leadership through a false but convincing exhibition of concern for smaller nations. Since Africa and Asia almost unanimously hate one of the three nations, Britain, France and Israel, the Soviets need only to propose severe and immediate punishment of these three to have the whole of two continents on their side.'[61]

American leaders thus found themselves in the domain of losses, not gains. In retrospect, it is very hard to say whether the Americans exaggerated the potential losses from the Anglo-French action; one can only speculate about the counterfactual. But if the universal opposition to the invasion was an accurate reflection of the stakes, the emphasis on loss does appear to have been reasonable. At the time, American decision-makers could

---

60 Memorandum of conversation with the president, 8:15 pm, 29 October 1956, AWF, DDEDS, DSM, 1956.
61 Knowland to Eisenhower, 31 October 1956, AWF, DDEDS, Phone Calls, October 1956; Memorandum from Eisenhower to Dulles, 1 November 1956, AWF, DHS, November 1956.

identify no 'good' option, but only absolute and relative losses from the available alternatives. Their critical task was to choose the option involving the fewest losses. Although loss avoidance rather than gains seeking appears to have been uppermost in their minds, there is no evidence that American decision-makers were prepared to accept the risk entailed in losses of moderate or high probability or that they engaged in risk-seeking behaviour. Again, leaders' calculations of probabilities are difficult to reconstruct, but the evidence is that the American decision-makers believed that the losses they feared were highly likely. In a reasonable approximation of rational norms, they searched for options, calculated the costs and likely consequences of those options, and chose accordingly. This process was not systematic, as orthodox utility maximization requires, but it conformed implicitly to rational norms. The extensive debates among American officials provide evidence of careful consideration of the consequences of alternative options.

From the beginning of the Suez crisis, the American government was sensitive to the adverse political consequences in the Afro-Asian bloc of the Anglo-French reaction to Nasser's nationalization of the canal. They accordingly tried to distance themselves from a 'colonialist' action. When the bluff and avowedly pro-British Australian prime minister presented the recommendations of the London Conference to Nasser in threatening terms, Loy Henderson, the American representative, made clear that his country would not be a party to any imposed agreement on Egypt. He told Nasser: 'I want to explain that the United States is not a colonial power. Our policy has been against colonization since independence. We could never agree to join any colonialist arrangement, and if the American government had thought that the purpose of this committee was to impose a solution on Egypt we would not have taken part in it. Our only wish is to reach a solution that is compatible with Egypt's full exercise of its sovereignty.'[62] The United States, moreover, did not confine its objections to the colonialist overtones of its allies' policies to

62 Cited in Heikal, *Cutting the Lion's Tail*, 152.

the privacy of diplomatic gatherings. In his celebrated press conference of 2 October, Dulles caused consternation in Britain when he declared: 'The United States cannot be expected to identify itself 100 per cent. ... with the colonial powers ... For while we stand together ... in treaty relations covering the North Atlantic, any areas encroaching in some form or manner on the problem of so-called colonialism, find the United States playing a somewhat independent role.'[63] Later Vice-President Richard Nixon added fuel to the fire. Referring to the American vote against its allies at the United Nations, he said in a campaign speech: 'For the first time in history we have shown independence of Anglo-French policies toward Asia and Africa which seemed to us to reflect the colonial tradition. That declaration of independence has had an electrifying effect throughout the world.'[64]

The expression of these views was more than grandstanding or electioneering. It reflected a genuine opposition to colonialism among the American leaders. As soon as they learned of British intentions to respond forcibly to Nasser's nationalization, the president and his advisers had argued that this was an outmoded response, inappropriate to the 1950s. In Eisenhower's words: 'The British were out-of-date in thinking of this as a mode of action.'[65] He insisted that, however undesirable the action was, Nasser was legally entitled to nationalize the Suez Canal Company and derided British claims that the Egyptians did not have the technical competence to run the canal. The reaction of the secretary of the treasury, George Humphrey, was similar; the British, he said, 'were simply trying to reverse the trend away from colonialism, and turn the clock back fifty years.'[66]

The belief that the British were acting in an inappropriately

63 Cited in Eden, *Full Circle*, 556. For the complete transcript of the press conference, see *Department of State Bulletin* 35(15 October 1956), 574-80.
64 Cited in Herman Finer, *Dulles over Suez: The Theory and Practice of His Diplomacy* (Chicago: Quadrangle 1964), 397.
65 Memorandum of conference with the president, 31 July 1956, AWF, DDEDS, DSM, 1956.
66 *Ibid.*

'colonialist' fashion remained Eisenhower's constant theme throughout the crisis. In October he 'wondered if the hand of Churchill might not be behind this inasmuch as this action is in the mid-Victorian style.' In November he wrote to a friend: 'I believe that Eden and his associates have become convinced that this is the last straw and Britain simply *had* to react in the manner of the Victorian period.'[67] The style of the operation, entailing as it did the dispatch of an enormous flotilla against a country which could not possibly hope to defend itself, and the bombing of Cairo, the capital of a country with which Britain was not at war, strengthened the American view that this was an abuse of power characteristic of an earlier period. The United States could not associate itself with such actions.

While a principled commitment to anti-colonialism was an important element in American thinking, it was reinforced by a strong perception of the loss that would ensue from the support of colonialist action. Dulles spelled out these estimates of relative loss to the National Security Council:

If we were not now prepared to assert our leadership in this cause, leadership would certainly be seized by the Soviet Union ... Unless we now assert and maintain this leadership, all of these newly independent countries will turn from us to the USSR. We will be looked upon as forever tied to British and French colonialist policies. In short, the United States would survive or go down on the basis of the fate of colonialism if the United States supports the French and the British on the colonial issue. Win or lose, we will share the fate of Britain and France.[68]

This combination of anti-colonialism and anti-communism helps to explain the apparent puzzle of American policy in the Suez crisis. American officials saw only losses from an attempt to use force to reverse the nationalization of the canal. In consequence, the only viable option for the United States was to oppose its

---

67 Memorandum of conference with the president, 30 October 1956, AWF, DDEDS, DSM, 1956; Eisenhower, *Waging Peace*, 85.
68 National Security Council, 302nd meeting, 1 November 1956, AWF, NSC series.

allies. In so doing, Washington could take a stand on principle while denying to the Soviet Union additional prestige in the former colonies of Africa and Asia.

The American decision can be explained in terms of loss avoidance, framed by a status quo that was anti-colonialist. Although American leaders approximated rational choice, they did so within a frame they constructed for the problem they faced. The intriguing question is why American decision-makers appraised the losses from supporting their allies to be so great. Why did they not focus, as Morgenthau and Kennan did, on the damage to the Western alliance if the United States did not support its allies? Why was anti-colonialism more important than alliance solidarity? Prospect theory points to the importance of framing, but it does not provide a theory of framing which enables us to predict the manner in which a problem will be framed in any given set of circumstances.

In the absence of a theory of framing, we must seek particular explanations in particular cases. In 1956, British and American leaders framed the problem very differently. Why did Britain choose as its reference point its aspirations to restore the status quo ante and the elimination of Nasser, while the United States chose another reference point, a functioning canal? One persuasive answer points to their relative power positions in the region. Britain, like France, wanted a reversion to the status quo ante because its position in the region was declining. The United States, whose influence in the region was on the increase, was quite happy with the new state of affairs, once it was clear that Egypt could operate the canal. It would appear that decision-makers from different states are particularly likely to choose different reference points at a time when the power structure in a region is perceived to be changing, as was true of the Middle East in the mid-1950s. Nasser succinctly captured this change in his description of the United States and Britain as, respectively, 'el gayin wa el rayin,' the 'coming' and the 'going.'[69]

69 Heikal, *Cutting the Lion's Tail*, 41.

CONCLUSION

British and American leaders both sought to avoid loss when they made their critical choices in 1956, but they did so in different ways. British decisions in the Suez crisis fit well with the expectations of prospect theory. Decision-makers chose as their reference point their aspiration to restore the status quo ante and to overthrow Nasser, focused on the – to them – certain losses of a nationalized canal, greatly exaggerated both the scale and the likelihood of the losses they feared, and, as a result, made a risky choice while denying the risks of that choice. The British miscalculated so badly in large part because of the power of the appeasement analogy. American decisions correspond more closely to an orthodox utility maximization model. Options were identified and their costs and consequences calculated and compared. The decisions of the American administration were consistent with both anti-colonialism and anti-communism, while the option favoured by some of its critics – to support the allies – would only have met the needs of alliance solidarity in the face of the Soviet threat. American leaders chose rationally to avoid the highest expected losses.

The evidence from this case suggests that the process of decision-making, so dramatically different in London and Washington, is significant once the problem has been framed. It also suggests that the framing of the problem itself was important in both Washington and London. British and American leaders both paid attention to losses highlighted by the decision frames they chose. The evidence suggests as well that frames are not given, but chosen. In the United States, military leaders and realist critics framed the problem very differently than Eisenhower and Dulles did and therefore urged a very different choice. Framing does matter. If we are to improve our explanations of decision-making, we need to learn a great deal more about why leaders frame problems the way they do.

Seven

Decision processes and co-operation in foreign policy

TIMOTHY J. MCKEOWN

> Foreign policy can be characterized as a goal directed activity only if governments have a capability for such activity. Whether governments have this capability can only be determined by a theory of the foreign policy process. Thus the study of foreign policy must be based on a theory of the policy making process.[1]

> Descriptive accuracy at the micro-level and theoretical power at the macro-level go together.[2]

> [T]o fully flesh out a rational choice model, a theory of preference formation is required.[3]

The case-studies in this volume have tried to understand foreign policy decisions to co-operate with other governments by exploring how decision-makers frame specific problems. We have examined how decision-makers gather information about the situations they face, how they evaluate what they have learned, and how these evaluations affect their policy choices. The five cases provide descriptively accurate accounts of policy-making processes across a range of international economic and security issues. In the analysis of these cases, we focused on a specific set

Associate Professor of Political Science, University of North Carolina, Chapel Hill, North Carolina; co-author of *Organizing Business: Trade Associations in America and Japan*.

1 Paul Anderson, 'Foreign policy as a goal-directed activity,' *Philosophy of the Social Sciences* 14(June 1984), 159-81, 172.
2 Christopher Achen, 'A state with bureaucratic politics is representable as a unitary rational actor,' paper presented at the annual meeting of the American Political Science Association, 1988.
3 Frank C. Zagare, 'Rationality and deterrence,' *World Politics* 42(January 1990), 238-60, 247.

of questions about the decision process. The results of these analyses provide a basis for a qualitative comparative assessment of the ability of the principal theories of decision-making to explain both the processes leaders used and the choices they made. This chapter attempts to assess the theoretical and policy implications of these case-studies for a broader theory of political choice.

CONTRASTING FRAMEWORKS FOR THE ANALYSIS OF FOREIGN POLICY DECISIONS

Not everyone agrees that theories of decision-making apply to processes of decision rather than simply to the choices that are made. Some analysts argue that currently dominant models of rational choice, based on a concept of 'instrumental' rather than 'procedural' rationality, make claims only about the consistency of choices with one another and with the underlying preferences of decision-makers; they make no claim to explain decision processes.[4] Such an approach has been common among advocates of rational choice models at least since the time of Milton Friedman's well-known essay on positive economics.[5] We do not adopt this approach.

The general difficulties created by 'as if' theorizing have been extensively discussed.[6] Beyond these difficulties, the assumption of instrumental rationality unnecessarily precludes the use of a powerful theory of decision-making that, for all of its well-known weaknesses as a theory of decision processes, nonetheless does make distinctive and testable claims about behaviour. Obviously human beings are capable of thinking about political choices as quasi-micro-economic problems – if they could not, a voluminous and growing academic literature would be hard to justify. Moreover, decision-makers do sometimes appear to behave in accor-

4 *Ibid*, 238-60.
5 Milton Friedman, *Essays in Positive Economics* (Chicago IL: University of Chicago Press 1953).
6 Timothy J. McKeown, 'The limitations of "structural" theories of commercial policy,' *International Organization* 40(winter 1986), 43-64.

dance with relatively strict definitions of utility maximization.[7]
It therefore seems reasonable to ask just how closely actual decision processes approximate rational choice, and whether rational
choice is approximated more closely in certain kinds of environments than in others. A decision process that approached the
rational choice ideal could then be seen as a special case of decision-making in general. Analysis would then seek to identify the
domain where this approximation occurs and to explain why it
occurs there and not elsewhere. Prospect theory, behavioural
decision theory, and other cognitive approaches to decision-making are, as Janice Gross Stein notes in the introduction to this
volume, also most appropriately viewed as context-dependent
theories.[8]

The argument that foreign policy decision-makers seek relative rather than absolute gains originates not from a theory of
decision but from a 'realist' theory of international politics. As
Stein observed, relative gains seeking can often be treated as
maximization of some higher order goal; for example, the oli-
gopolist's struggle for market share in a world of increasing
returns to scale can translate into long-run profit maximization.
Disposing of relative gains on the conceptual level does not, however, dispose of it on the behavioural level. The link between
intermediate and higher goals may be imperfectly understood,
or understood differently by different decision-makers, and leaders may devote scarce attention to consideration of relative
advantage at the expense of a search for integrative solutions.
Finally, because arguments about relative gains seeking are

---

7 Historical accounts presented by Maoz and Berman seem to conform well to
even fairly demanding standards of what constitutes utility maximization
behaviour. See Zeev Maoz, 'The decision to raid Entebbe,' *Journal of Conflict
Resolution* 25(December 1981), 677-708, and Larry Berman, *Planning a
Tragedy: The Americanization of the War in Vietnam* (New York: Norton
1982), 138-41.

8 Since prospect theory has been developed and tested largely in controlled
experimental settings, however, the question of how well prospect theory fares
when applied to decision-making in naturalistic settings is largely unanswered.

derived from the properties of the international system in which decision-makers find themselves, in principle they are compatible with either orthodox utility maximization or cognitive approaches. Not surprisingly, therefore, we find evidence of all three kinds of behaviour in the case-studies in this volume.

Several of the choices examined in these cases are consistent with utility maximization. In Debora Spar's study of the FSX decision, the initial Japanese and American definitions of the situation can be reconstructed from a rational choice perspective. Based on what we know about the information available to both sets of decision-makers and about their overall preferences, the Japanese government's initial view of the situation as one where co-operation was not an issue as well as the American government's view that co-operation was vital are readily comprehended by such a perspective. The search by American officials for new options when the immediate options all appeared unpalatable is broadly consistent with the micro-economics of optimal search.[9] The evolution of the Japanese position may be understood in terms of the new information Japanese decision-makers received: the United States government communicated implied and sometimes explicit threats of significant loss if the Japanese persisted in their original course.

Similarly, in Michael Mastanduno's discussion of the Structural Impediments Initiative (SII) enough evidence is offered about the preferences of Congress and of important executive branch agencies to enable us to see the bilateral negotiation as a straightforward calculation of interests. The lack of search and evaluation of the SII proposal noted by Mastanduno can make sense from a utility maximization standpoint if decision-makers saw themselves as so highly constrained that more detailed information about the costs and benefits of pursuing the SII would have been irrelevant. If pleasing Congress was the dominant motivation of the American decision to participate in the SII,

9 It also provides a classic example of search triggered by failure to satisfice.

then the failure to attempt to make trade-offs among negotiating objectives can also be understood. American officials may have considered that such trade-offs would yield no incremental benefits in Congress but could entail the additional costs of bureaucratic infighting and conflict within the administration. From this perspective, it is not surprising that the American negotiating strategy seemed a collusive solution among the component parts of President Bush's governing coalition.

The Israeli response to Scud missile attacks during the Gulf War of 1991 can likewise be at least partly explained as a demonstration of resolve not to be coerced – in this case, coerced into going to war. Israel's decision-makers also considered the questionable efficacy of the proposed attacks on Scud launchers, given the effort already being mounted by the anti-Iraq coalition and, probably most importantly, the pressure from the United States not to respond. Building on these considerations, it is possible to construct an orthodox if informal 'realist' explanation of Israel's choice. As David Welch notes, however, such an orthodox interpretation provides a thin and unsatisfying account which leaves many important puzzles unresolved.

Even in the case where evidence that is consistent with orthodox maximization behaviour is the most difficult to find – the Suez crisis in 1956 – at least American decision-making bore a substantial resemblance to a conventional rational choice interpretation. In comparison with the deliberations of the British government, the decision-making process in the United States was marked by a substantial search for information and alternatives, an extensive and spirited discussion of options, and a capacity to revise estimates as new information was received. American choices can be seen as a reasonable attempt to satisfy conflicting demands: to deprive the Soviet Union of an opportunity for increased influence in the Middle East, to avoid rewarding Nasser for his actions, and to restrain the British and French in ways that would not permanently damage their alliance with the United States. We find only sporadic evidence of relative gains seeking in these cases. Although neo-realist explanations stress its importance for judgments about the security consequences of policy choices, it is noteworthy that relative gains considerations were most visible in the two cases involving gains from economic interaction between two allies.[10] In the FSX and Structural Impediments Initiative cases, the arguments of some American officials were cast in terms of relative gains, and some Japanese officials appear to have made similar calculations in the FSX case as well. In other cases, however, there is little evidence of explicit relative gains thinking. Surprisingly, Israeli officials who faced an acute security crisis did not consider relative gains as the crisis intensified but focused overwhelmingly on loss in their relationship with the United States. Even in the cases where concern about relative gains was present, they were considered only by a minority of participants, and the definition of the situation that prevailed in these cases was one which emphasized the avoidance of loss rather than the achievement of relative gain.

One hypothesis suggested by these cases is that relative gains concerns will be voiced under fairly narrow circumstances – specifically, when decision-makers are highly attentive to economic gains in a situation where advantages from sales tend to cumulate either because of economies of scale or because of learning-by-doing effects. Other decision-makers, who adopt wider (or at least different) conceptions of the stakes, do not seem to find relative gains considerations persuasive in shaping their policy choices, or do not consider them at all. It is noteworthy that the prior empirical substantiation for relative gains calculations encompasses cases of economic bargaining involving either allies or countries that had historically experienced little overt conflict: the bargaining between the United States and Europe over rules on non-tariff barriers under the General Agreement on Tariffs

10 Joseph Grieco, 'Anarchy and the limits of cooperation: a realist critique of the newest liberal institutionalism,' *International Organization* 42(summer 1988), 485-507.

and Trade, bargaining among members of regional customs unions, and bargaining between the United States and Japan over joint development efforts in high-technology industries.[11]

PROSPECT THEORY AND THE EVIDENCE

Many aspects of our cases that are not readily understood from the standpoint of orthodox utility maximization are more easily interpreted through the lens of some form of behavioural decision theory, such as prospect theory. A concern with loss avoidance rather than with either absolute or relative gains, as Stein noted in the introduction, is consistent with prospect theory to the extent that the status quo is defined as acceptable and thereby provides a reference point for the assessment of alternative choices and potential outcomes. A decision to avoid loss may be inferior in an expected utility sense to riskier choices with higher expected values. Thus, the argument of prospect theory about the importance of loss avoidance offers predictions of choice which are different from those under expected utility theory under some conditions. It also differs from many versions of expected utility theory by treating the decision-maker's response to risk as arising from characteristics of the decision situation rather than from the personality of the decision-maker.

Evidence of loss avoidance can be found in all the cases that we examined. In Suez, the initial British reaction was framed largely in terms of restoring the status quo, although removing Nasser quickly became one of the British objectives. One could argue, however, that the British had never adjusted their reference level to include Nasser and that restoration of the status quo ante was still the goal. American decision-makers also framed the problem during the Suez crisis in terms of avoiding twin losses – to the cohesion of the North Atlantic Treaty Organization and

11 Joseph Grieco, 'Realist theory and the problem of international cooperation: analysis with an amended prisoner's dilemma,' *Journal of Politics* 50(August 1988), 600-24, and *Cooperation among Nations: Europe, America, and Non-Tariff Barriers to Trade* (Ithaca NY: Cornell University Press 1990), and Michael Mastanduno, 'Do relative gains matter? America's response to Japanese industrial policy,' *International Security* 16(summer 1991), 73-113.

to Western influence in the Middle East. Israel's decision not to retaliate against Iraqi missile attacks in 1991 was also framed in terms of loss avoidance. Its leaders focused on the losses Israel would suffer in its relationship with the United States if it retaliated directly against Iraq.

In the case of the Structural Impediments Initiative, the American decision to initiate talks seems to have been motivated by a desire to avoid domestic political losses. As well, the way in which the Bush administration conducted the negotiations was motivated largely by a desire to avoid conflict within the administration rather than by the positive goals of achieving absolute or relative gains in negotiations with Japan. In the FSX case, those in both Japan and the United States who were concerned about the political losses from a failed agreement dominated those who were concerned about the relative gains associated with such an agreement. In the negotiations over surveillance by the International Monetary Fund (IMF), one of the most frequently invoked arguments to garner American support for multilateral oversight mechanisms was the spectre of the welfare losses of the 1930s, with the clear implication that lapses from multilateralism raised the risk that such losses would occur again. The final decisions appear at first to conform neatly to the logic of egoistic states trading off autonomy for the stability brought about by mutual restraint. But the pervasive concerns about avoiding losses arising from 'anarchy' coupled with significant differences between international conditions in the 1930s and in the post-1945 years and the questionable accuracy of the basic contention that currency instability in itself was harmful are all troublesome from the standpoint of orthodox decision theory.

The ubiquity of concern for loss avoidance can be reconciled to some extent with orthodox utility maximization. This is in part because our evidence about the location or even the existence of meaningful reference levels for decision-makers in a naturalistic setting is weak. If the status quo were viewed by decision-makers as unsatisfactory — that is, if they had not yet adjusted for past losses — then prospect theory would not provide a firm basis for the conclusion that they will act to avoid certain losses. A second reason for caution lies in the nature of the decision situations themselves. If the decision situations were such that no gains could be had, then it would not be surprising to observe all outcomes being evaluated as losses and the decision-making task defined as one of avoiding the highest expected loss. Even if there were some gains to be achieved through negotiation, the situation facing decision-makers might be one in which potential losses were (rightly) judged to exceed potential gains in a substantial way. Dwelling on the avoidance of losses in such a situation would be sensible from the standpoint of either prospect theory or expected utility theory. The SII, IMF surveillance, and FSX cases could plausibly be interpreted in this light. Finally, the simple assumption of declining marginal utility implies greater efforts to avoid a given loss than to achieve the same amount of gain.

A closer consideration of loss avoidance behaviour in these cases, however, suggests that accommodating it within an orthodox utility maximization framework is not easily done. Herbert Simon suggested that organizational decision-making can be treated as a linear programming problem in which each politically significant organizational sub-unit imposes its own independent constraint on decisions.[12] Each sub-unit participating in the decision thus attempts to ensure that the constraints that it imposes are not violated by any proposed solution. There may be many such constraints, many alternative courses of action, and the attention of decision-makers is often limited to the issues immediately before them. In the kind of process suggested by Simon, goals (or constraints) can be evoked by the generation of new alternatives and the mention of one goal evokes consideration of others. Nor would it be surprising that alternatives are discussed and evaluated in terms of whether they would lead to outcomes that would violate one or more goals that various decision-makers are attempting to impose upon the decision. If

12 Herbert A. Simon, 'On the concept of organizational goal,' in Amitai Etzioni, ed, *A Sociological Reader on Complex Organizations* (New York: Holt, Rinehart and Winston 1969), 158-74.

'good' alternatives (those that promise a high probability of success and a low probability of failure) are not available or cannot be identified, it is likely that 'bland' alternatives (those promising neither large successes nor great losses) will be chosen.[13] From this perspective, decision-makers try to choose policies that do not have a high probability of making things worse, with 'worse' usually defined in terms of the status quo.[14] Such decisions may in some cases coincide with those following from orthodox utility maximization behaviour, but they may also depart substantially from such behaviour.

American decision-making during the Cuban missile crisis has been convincingly interpreted from this perspective, and the results from some of our cases are generally consistent with this 'decision-making by objection' process as well.[15] Prospect theory contends that decisions at the individual level depart in systematic ways from decisions made on the basis of utility maximization behaviour. It needs, however, to be combined with some theory of social choice, such as 'decision-making by objection,' if we are to explain the behaviour of a collectivity, such as a government, as a chronic loss avoider.

The distinctive view of the search and evaluation process offered by behavioural decision theory makes a solid contribution to solving puzzles left unresolved by utility maximization approaches. One of the clearest examples of this is the Suez case. Even the Americans, who by comparison with the British seem to have behaved in a reasonably sensible fashion, had earlier failed to consider how Nasser might react to the withdrawal of financing for the Aswan dam. This pales in comparison, however, with a process of search and evaluation by the British that is simply bizarre: no alternative to the use of force seems to have been considered, the estimates of the costs and benefits of the proposed course were limited and highly inaccurate, and – per-

13 James G. March and Herbert A. Simon, *Organizations* (New York: Wiley 1958), 113-16.
14 Paul A. Anderson, 'Decision-making by objection and the Cuban missile crisis,' *Administrative Science Quarterly* 28(June 1983), 201-22.
15 *Ibid.*

haps most devastating to an orthodox optimizing interpretation – there seems to have been no revision of estimates within the British government as new information became available. Indeed, the British government's avoidance of contact with the Americans seems consistent with a 'don't confuse me with the facts' approach to the value of obtaining additional information. Many of the pathologies that have long been identified by students of foreign policy crisis decision-making – rigid attachment to a single option, wishful thinking about the responses of others, avoidance of search and inability to assimilate new information, a stereotyped view of the adversary – are highly visible in this case.[16] Behavioural decision theory begins to offer an explanation for both the rigidity of the attachment to a single option and the lack of serious search by its invocation of various decision heuristics – in this case, an availability heuristic founded on the generational experience of Eden and other senior British officials between 1933 and 1945. In so far as prospect theory is a theory of individual rather than social decision-making, however, it is of less help in explaining why the government as a whole remained attached to a faulty view of the situation for so long.

The Structural Impediments Initiative negotiations also displayed evidence of a search process that can be reconciled with conventional utility maximization perspectives only if one assumes that the negotiations were entirely an exercise in symbolic politics, with no serious intention to achieve any substantive results. This is a questionable assumption. On the American side there were no attempts to calculate the costs and benefits of various policy proposals, no attempts to rank order negotiating priorities, no attempts to identify jointly optimal policies or to pursue integrative bargaining strategies, and no explicit attempts to link Japanese concessions to American concessions.

16 Ole R. Holsti and Alexander L. George, 'The effects of stress on the performance of foreign policy makers,' in C.P. Cotter, ed, *Political Science Annual*, vol. 6 (Indianapolis: Bobbs-Merrill 1975), 255-319, and Alexander L. George, 'Towards a more soundly based foreign policy: making better use of information,' in *Commission on the Organization of the Government for the Conduct of Foreign Policy*, vol 2 (Washington: United States Government Printing Office 1975), appendix D.

As Mastanduno notes, this apparently odd behaviour is explained more persuasively by reference to the external political constraints under which the Bush administration was working than by the particular characteristics of the American foreign policy-making apparatus or the information-processing methods of American decision-makers. However, if one believes that there were substantive gains to be reaped in the negotiations, the lack of American interest in either absolute or relative gains constitutes a policy failure. To the extent that the Bush administration did want to reduce the United States trade deficit and was strongly interested in changing Japan's domestic arrangements, its approach to the negotiations must appear irrational from the standpoint of orthodox utility maximization. It is more readily comprehended as 'decision-making by objection,' because any attempt to obtain a 'good' outcome would probably have caused some sub-units to raise loud objections and would likely have created a substantial amount of intra-administration conflict. The choice of a 'bland' negotiating strategy, which sought above all to avoid domestic political losses, is therefore understandable, if perhaps regrettable.

Other cases exhibit only somewhat less anomalous search processes. In the Israeli decision not to retaliate against Scud attacks, it first appears that the government sought to obtain from the American-led coalition exactly the kind of information an external observer would expect it to seek: on Iraqi military capabilities, on efforts being made to destroy those capabilities, and on the success of those efforts. However, the search was narrowly confined to the single issue of Iraq's capability to launch missile attacks against Israel; surprisingly, all other issues directly related to the longer term threat posed by Iraq received no attention.

In the FSX case, the Japanese at least gave the appearance of examining a variety of foreign sources for aircraft. Circumstantial evidence suggests, however, that their evaluation was *pro forma*: the strong interest of important elements of the Japanese government in purely indigenous production is no secret while their surprise at the American reaction indicates that their earlier analysis was deficient. On the American side, the response of Gregg Rubinstein to the unpalatability of the existing options was to develop the new option of co-development. This is consistent with either an orthodox maximization perspective or behavioural theories which treat search as stimulated by failures to achieve performance targets.

In the IMF surveillance case, it is interesting that invocation of the spectre of the 1930s to justify continuing American support for the role of the IMF was both commonplace and apparently effective, even long after objective economic conditions had changed. Louis Pauly notes the obvious difficulty: in that troubled decade, it was not the countries that maintained their commitment to a fixed exchange rate that fared well but those that acted unilaterally by going off gold. Since this relationship has been revealed by relatively simple statistical analysis, one might ask why policy was so successfully promoted on the basis of such a flawed understanding of historical events. In so far as behavioural decision theory directs our attention to the vividness and availability of cognitions, it provides a plausible explanation for the power of the 1930s analogy. Those who had the most sophisticated knowledge of the 1930s, however, were also those who had the greatest commitment to Fund surveillance and were therefore unlikely to present a view of the past that would permit the drawing of contrary conclusions. Yet there is no evidence to suggest that they did not sincerely believe a reversion to 1930s-style 'anarchy' was possible.

Examination of the processes of search in all these cases identified significant anomalies that are not easily reconciled with orthodox utility maximization. Our analysis demonstrates the importance of the process of choosing, not only at the individual level, but also in the broader social and political context in which choice is embedded. We turn now to the examination of the requirements of a broader theory of social choice.

RESEARCH DIRECTIONS

Analysis of our cases highlights two features of decision-making that are not generally addressed by the theories of individual choice we have examined. In both the FSX and SII negotiations, the role of sub-national interests in shaping the ways in which governments make foreign policy choices is apparent. In the British decision on Suez and in Israel's decision-making during the Gulf War, the role of emotion was an important factor. On a formal level, existing theories of national decision-making can be extended without a great deal of difficulty to accommodate sub-national interests.[17] Modifying 'cold' theories of decision-making to take emotion into account is more demanding. The role of emotion in foreign policy decision-making has been systematically studied through assessments of the relevance and prevalence of motivated biases in perception or the role of stress in affecting crisis decision-making.[18] Recent psychological research suggests a rich set of connections between motivational and cognitive factors.[19] Taking these connections seriously will probably mean abandoning the orthodox utility maximization position that preferences are logically distinct from and exist prior to information about events.

The findings from these case-studies suggest that there is much that we need to learn about decision-making processes in real world settings. Is the phenomenon of loss avoidance deci-

17 Bruce Bueno de Mesquita and David Lalman, 'Domestic opposition and foreign war,' *American Political Science Review* 84(September 1990), 747-66; Stephen P. Magee, William A. Brock, and Leslie Young, *Black Hole Tariffs and Endogenous Policy Theory* (Cambridge: Cambridge University Press 1989); and Arye L. Hillman, *The Political Economy of Protection* (New York: Harwood Academic 1989).

18 Robert Jervis, *Perception and Misperception in International Politics* (Princeton NJ: Princeton University Press 1976), 356-81; Richard Ned Lebow, *Between Peace and War* (Baltimore MD: Johns Hopkins University Press 1981); Robert Jervis, Richard Ned Lebow, and Janice Gross Stein, *Psychology and Deterrence* (Baltimore MD: Johns Hopkins University Press 1985); and Holsti and George, 'The effects of stress on the performance of foreign policy makers,' 255-319.

19 R.B. Zajonc, 'Feeling and thinking: preferences need no inferences,' *American Psychologist* 35(February 1980), 151-75; Henry Zukier, 'The paradigmatic and narrative modes in goal-guided inference,' in Richard M. Sorrentino and E. Tory Higgins, *Handbook of Motivation and Cognition* (New York: Guilford Press 1986), 465-502; A. Tesser, 'Self-generated attitude change,' in L. Berkowitz, ed, *Advances in Experimental Social Psychology*, vol 11 (New York: Academic Press 1978), 289-338; and S.L. Nielson and I.G. Sarason, 'Emotion, personality, and selective attention,' *Journal of Personality and Social Psychology* 41(November 1981), 945-60.

sion-making as pervasive as the results from the analysis of these cases suggest? Is loss avoidance sensitive to organizational structure and the distribution of political assets among sub-units? Is it sensitive to peculiarities in the preference orderings or reference levels of decision-makers in the way suggested by prospect theory? Is it sensitive to the level of knowledge or sophistication that decision-makers possess? How do domestic political calculations by high-level officials affect the evaluation of foreign policy choices?

We also need to develop a much better understanding of the ways in which foreign policy bureaucracies generate and evaluate alternative courses of action. While both processes may well be based in organizational sub-unit interests and competencies, and while the avoidance of explicit trade-offs has been noticed for some time, there is still much that we do not know.[20] One analysis of the decision-making process in the Cuban missile crisis suggests that the discovery of goals, the generation of alternatives, and the evaluation of alternatives all stimulated each other.[21] Is this a generally accurate description of decision-making? Governmental search processes in almost all the cases in this volume were less than optimal. In the cases of Suez and the FSX aircraft, processes of search were insufficient to identify likely sources of difficulty; in the SII case and Israel's choices during the Gulf War, opportunities for gains were not identified; and in the IMF surveillance case, questionable premises underlying earlier policy choices were not exposed. Do foreign policy bureaucracies chronically execute searches for information that are less than optimal? At present we lack both the theory and the empirical evidence to answer this question with confidence.

Despite the limits to our theory and evidence, it is still possi-

---

20 Graham T. Allison, *Essence of Decision: Explaining the Cuban Missile Crisis* (Boston: Little, Brown 1971); Graham T. Allison and Morton Halperin, 'Bureaucratic politics,' in Raymond Tanter and Richard Ullman, eds, *Theory and Policy in International Relations* (Princeton NJ: Princeton University Press 1974), 40-79; and John Steinbruner, *The Cybernetic Theory of Decision* (Princeton NJ: Princeton University Press 1974).

21 Anderson, 'Decision-making by objection and the Cuban missile crisis.'

ble to suggest some implications for policy-making of a shift in the theoretical focus of foreign policy decision-making studies from orthodox utility maximization (of either a 'realist' or a 'liberal institutionalist' variety) to more behaviourally oriented theories.

First, if the conclusions we have drawn about loss avoidance are correct, then in the absence of clearly 'good' alternatives, we should normally expect governments to select 'bland' foreign policies. Loss avoidance is important in so far as it leads political decision-makers to make bland choices. This generalization is of course subject to the qualifications that one can identify the state of affairs that a government chooses to regard as the status quo and that there do indeed exist 'bland' choices that might be made in light of that status quo. In the absence of either 'good' or 'bland' choices, governments may select 'mixed' (high risk) choices rather than settle for a 'poor' choice that has a high probability of failing to achieve, and little probability of surpassing, its target. If, as Stein noted, two opposing governments both perceive an absence of 'bland' choices, both may resort to risky policies, with potentially disastrous consequences. However, if co-operation, while risky, is perceived as the only alternative to certain losses, then co-operative solutions will emerge because of the joint interest of decision-makers in avoiding worse outcomes.

A second implication follows directly. The choice of risk-acceptant or risk-averse policies can be understood as a response to the decision situation facing a government rather than to personality variables which impart a certain risk-taking style to a given set of government officials. While these factors may indeed be at work, they should not distract the analyst from the important insight of behavioural decision theories that situations may vary in ways that provide drastically different incentives to governments to engage in risk-taking. Conclusions about the risk-taking propensity of a government that do not take into account the specific features of the situations could be highly misleading.

Behavioural decision theories also have direct policy implications for the design of strategies of influence. They suggest that the way one government influences another is considerably more complicated than the making of threats or promises that are not anticipated by the recipient. If the attention of decision-makers is a scarce resource, then the timing of communications could have a critical effect on their reaction. Recipients have to be listening; they have to have an available response that they can choose and make, and those who might object need to be occupied elsewhere. As a result, the success of a given strategy could be heavily dependent on the context within which it is attempted.

When one government attempts to influence another, it must also take into account (and perhaps exploit) the vividness or psychological prominence of the possible outcomes of choices. Credibility in the simple sense of having a reputation for accurate claims may in some instances be much less important than the use of messages that evoke vivid and powerful examples. In the negotiations on IMF surveillance, for example, the vividness and prominence of the evoked image of a return to the anarchy of the 1930s was an important component in the calculations of leaders. The impact of vividness and prominence are neglected in theories of rational choice.

Finally, messages can be designed to alter a recipient's view of what constitutes a normal state of affairs. If these messages can affect another government's definition of an acceptable status quo, they can alter aspiration or reference levels and hence have large effects on the recipient's policy choices.

Behavioural decision theories also suggest a different and more optimistic view of the constraining power of international institutions and international law than that implied by orthodox utility maximization and the 'new institutional economics.' Because existing rules become salient simply because they exist, they likely constrain behaviour more than would be considered likely in a world where all possible courses of action were equally 'available' for the consideration of decision-makers. As Robert Keohane has noted, as long as outcomes under a given set of rules meet or exceed aspiration levels, behavioural decision theory suggests that there is little reason to expect a search for a new course of action.[22] Most of the insights from behavioural theories of decision-making have not yet been incorporated into the formal theories of decision-making. The five case-studies in this volume, for example, have described a focus by leaders across a wide variety of contexts and issues on avoiding loss as they considered whether or not to choose to co-operate. They also demonstrated that the process of choosing does matter. The results are relevant not only to the analysis of international co-operation but to the larger problem of the explanation of government decisions.

If we are to enhance our understanding of governmental decision-making and improve the design of policy, we must learn a great deal more about how political decision-makers structure problems in real world situations, why they frame problems the way they do, and how they manage the risk and uncertainty that are so endemic in international politics. We need both better theory and better evidence. We must also consider not only how individuals but also how collectivities choose. Decisions to co-operate, like all foreign policy decision-making, are embedded in a broader social and political context. We must move beyond the explanation of individual decisions towards a behavioural theory of social choice.

22 Robert O. Keohane, *After Hegemony: Cooperation and Discord in the World Political Economy* (Princeton NJ: Princeton University Press 1984), 112-14.

INDEX

Absolute gains: explanation for FSX decisions, 74, 75; framing decisions in terms of, 11-12; neo-liberal institutionalism, 6-8, 13; not a factor in support for IMF surveillance, 104, 125-6; re-specification to relative gains as time horizon lengthens, 10-11; the state as 'egoist,' 6-7; U.S. approach to SII lacks calculations for, 40, 50-1, 59, 62

Absolute losses. See Loss avoidance

Anchoring, with reference points, 16, 26

Arens, Moishe, and Gulf War, 136, 141, 143, 147, 151, 153

Armitage, Richard L., and FSX, 77, 78-9

Aspiration levels: British decision-making on Suez, 189, 201; Japanese decisions on FSX, 73, 76, 88; as reference point, 15, 26, 218

Auer, James E., and FSX, 74, 76

Availability, 16, 26; British decision-making on Suez, 187-9, 190, 201, 212

Baker, James, 31, 139n23

Baucus, Max, and SII, 42, 46, 48

Bazerman, Max, on bargaining, 31n67

Behavioural decision theory, 5, 13, 217-19; decision-making by objection, 211, 213; treatment of choice, 13, 26-7. See also Prospect theory; Reference points

Bretton Woods Conference (1944), 93, 99-100, 101-2; ratification of agreement, 102-4

Bureaucratic politics, and FSX decisions, 86, 89-90, 91

Bush, George: and SII, 43, 44, 57, 61; and Gulf War, 141, 148, 151n52, 153

Certainty effect, 18-19; impact on a strategy of deterrence, 21-2; influence on decisions to co-operate, 22, 23, 25, 31

Choice process: case-studies, 27; evaluating alternative courses, 216; guidelines for investigating, 32-4; prospect theory on, 26; psychological models of, 4; rational models of, 25-6

Cognitive psychology: explanations for co-operation, 4, 5. See also Behavioural decision theory; Prospect theory

Commerce Department (U.S.): objections to FSX deal, 80-1, 84, 85, 90

Congress (U.S.): factor in SII decisions, 41-8, 53, 55, 56, 60, 61, 63, 205-6; objections to FSX deal, 40, 81-4, 86-7; views on economic surveillance, 102-3, 117-18, 119

Co-operation, international: conditions inhibiting, 7, 8; endowment effect impedes, 22, 31; explanations for, 2-6; importance of framing, 29-31; not necessarily desirable, 170n1

Cuban missile crisis: generation of alternative courses of action, 216; Soviet behaviour as evidence of loss avoidance, 21n50, 23n54; U.S. actions as evidence of loss avoidance,

Waltz, Kenneth, 9
War, as consequence of loss aversion,
   21
Weinberger, Caspar, on FSX, 77, 78
Welch, David A. (Israel and Gulf War
   case-study): 6, 24, 25, 28, 31, 128-
   69, 206
White, Harry Dexter, and Bretton
   Woods, 101-2, 103, 105

Whyte, Glen, on Cuban missile crisis,
   16n31, 20n47

Yeo, Edwin H., III, and multilateral
   economic surveillance, 113, 117-
   18, 119n44